IN THE
TWINKLE
OF AN
"I"

Lisa

Thank you so m—
for all your love.
you has been a real.
love, Daniel

IN THE
TWINKLE
OF AN
"I"

There Is Something New Under the Son

Transforming Purpose into Character

Daniel L. Tocchini

www.inthetwinkleofani.com
dan@inthetwinkleofani.com

ACKNOWLEDGMENTS

Aileen, your love has covered a multitude of my sins. You are the inspiration of my life.

Very special thanks to Eileen Chambers my dear friend and editor for the hours of love and commitment you invested in me. Your guidance and friendship have awakened my passion for story. I am forever grateful.

To JR Young, thank you for your wise counsel through the years and for your commitment to integrity and excellence in this project.

My thanks to Dallas Willard for encouraging me to publish this book because my work was not meant to gather dust on the shelves. Your presence in my life is an inspiration to walk the talk.

To Keith Matthews, I am grateful for the provision of your loyal friendship, wisdom and guidance.

To Daniel Z. Tocchini, my son, who has inspired me to look beyond the horizon and for his outstanding work on the cover design.

To Elizabeth Tocchini, my daughter who helped me think more about others than myself and who has lifted my head in the most difficult times of my life.

To Roya J. Tocchini, my loving and dedicated daughter-in-law who contributed so much with the diligent editing work that was so vitally needed in the end!!

To Jean Marie Jobs for teaching me what a true friend is and for racking your brain on the quotes.

To Dr. Scott Larson, thank you for your trust with the at risk youth as they have forever transformed what it means for me to be alive!

To my loyal friend Greg for all your diligence and research. Without you I would never had made it!

To all my fellow laborers at the Association for Christian Character Development whom I have had the privilege of working with. I am forever grateful for your love and commitment.

TABLE OF CONTENTS

FOREWORD

Welcome to a journey of sorts! Dan Tocchini invites us on a ride that at times sounds too good to be true, yet is so desirable one can't let go. No, this isn't warmed over Tony Robbins, or a positive thinking Robert Schuller book of "how to get the life I want" but an honest, gritty, straight forward account of Dan's real life interactions, teachings and stories, that combined, give a portrait of HOPE . . . I mean a kind of hope that life can *really* be new, that transformation is not a distant dream, but as close as your next decision.

I have known Dan as a friend and watched him in the "training room," dealing with the depths and complexities of human dynamics, and the same magic that fills those "trainings," fills these pages. *In the Twinkle of an "I"* is a story about life, life that comes at us at an alarming speed, filled with many unknowns, great pains, joys and sorrows, and yet constantly surrounding us in God's grace and infinite opportunities.

Let's face it though; life has a way of undermining hope, even for people of faith. As a Pastor for over 20 years and now as a professor, teaching students for pastoral ministry, I believe that the gospel of Jesus Christ really is good news! That at its core the gospel is a promise of a new kind of life, one filled with purpose and new possibilities. Dan knows this experientially, and with great candor he lets us in on his own life and journey. No big issues are evaded. Topics such as forgiveness, reconciliation, redemption, possibilities, change, and on and on are treated with humor, honesty, and insight. Connecting Dan's story with scripture, movies, literature, and pop culture, you vicariously live on the edge of your seat, laughing one moment and crying the next. Yet, with all of the emotive energy created, one never feels manipulated or indulged. In the end, the portrait is clear . . . life can be new, no matter where you are, what you've done or what's been done to you . . . *There Is Something New Under the Son!*

Each chapter will challenge you, each story will touch you, and Dan's relentless passion for personal transformation will encourage you! I pray that you will read this book with whatever hope you have flickering in your soul, and just maybe, you'll be set ablaze.

Keith J. Matthews, D. Min.
Graduate School of Theology
Azusa Pacific University

December 2008

INTRODUCTION

✡ ✡ ✡

Uniquely the Same

✡ ✡ ✡

His eyes looked right through me.

By the hard, cold stare on his face, the young man in prison blues was speaking volumes to me.

"You don't know *nothin'*, man," he was thinking but not saying. "You come in here from the outside. And, what? You think *you* know *my* life. That *I* should listen to *you*? What the hell do you know 'bout what I've been through? I've looked at the scoreboard, man. I know what it is saying. Don't you *get it*? My game is up, finished, done. There ain't nothing that's gonna change that."

In some ways, I knew he was absolutely right.

The young man staring me down was a murderer, convicted when he was just fourteen years old. Now three years later, Raul had seventeen long years left to serve on his sentence. What could have been the best years of his life would probably amount to little behind these Rhode Island prison bars.

If he saw it that way, I was certain they would.

"Even when I get out," Raul said, glancing at the window, "I'm told that I've got an eighty percent chance of ending up right back here after being paroled. Get that? *Shit.* Tell me, Mr. Dan, why, just why, should I set myself up to be disappointed by imagining I have a future?"

I responded to Raul straight. No platitudes, no false hopes, no dodging the pain in his life. Just challenged him straight-on with something he had never considered before.

"How would you experience life here," I said, "if every day you could walk down to the front gate and pull a ticket from a special box. If the number on your ticket matched the winning number for that day, then the gate would open, you would be free and, upon leaving, be given one million dollars start a new life, whatever you wanted it to be? The only catch is that the odds of pulling a winning number are two out of ten. If this scenario was a possibility, how would you see every day you had left here in prison?"

"Worth getting out of the joint, man," Raul said with a snort. "Walk out these gates with a million bucks to do anything I wanted? Hey, if that was goin' down, I would be working now to set myself up good for being gone. I'd be getting it goin' right. Look to get married, kids, some bling job on the fourteenth floor."

"Why?" I asked in all seriousness. "Why would you get ready for a life out there?"

"Look at them odds," he answered clear as a bell. "Two out of ten, ain't bad odds at all. I'd have a good shot. It could happen."

"What if you could increase the odds of drawing the winning ticket? Would you be interested?"

"Hell yeah. I'd do anything to increase the odds."

With Raul's answer, it was my turn to look him straight in the eyes. "Tell me, Raul. How is my life any different than yours?"

My question surprised him. "I don't get what you are saying, Mr. Dan."

"I understand, Raul, what you are saying about being in prison and returning back here. You're right. Statistically, about eighty percent of incarcerated youth just like you will return to adult penitentiaries where they will spend most of their lives behind bars. But I know of people who are turning that around, doing things that increase their odds of success after being paroled."

"So?"

"What I am saying is that how you're relating to being incarcerated is a bigger prison than these cement walls and razor wire fences."

"What do you mean?"

"When I opened up something different than what your history has told you, this fictional lottery ticket, what happened? You started telling me about the future you wanted, a future worth having. You were seeing something. Right?"

"Yeah. Some fantasy."

"Raul. You want to know what I really think."

"Sure, Mr. Dan. Hit me."

"I think you want to be *free from* prison instead of being *free to go* forward on what you want most in life. Whether you are here behind bars or high up in some corporate ladder, friend, there is something uniquely the same with all of us. The future worth having isn't out there somewhere. It's now. You could be free right now, Raul, to start living that future worth having, if you were willing. All you have to give up is your complaint about how life *should be* instead of *how it is showing up.* You'd have to throw out some illusions and even what you make up about dying. And, instead, choose a new conversation."

"Tell me about this new conversation, Mr. Dan."

Somewhere in Raul's dark brown eyes, I had hit pay dirt. I was not blowing smoke at my young friend. I knew what I was talking about. I had built my life on this one sure thing: *the transformational life offered to us in Jesus.*

"What does that have to do with me?" you might be asking.

You might be thinking, *I am doing okay in life. Is this another self-improvement book or some religious thing that makes a lot of promises but doesn't deliver? Will it solve all my relationship problems? Crack the millionaire code? Help me lose weight? Unleash the power within? Teach me how to succeed at business, politics or getting what I want in bed? Will I become a better Christian, Jew, Muslim, Buddhist or atheist?*

"Tell me, Dan," you ask, "Are there free cash and prizes at the end? Not a chance, on that last one. That's for sure."

Although I would not be surprised if some of those other things did happen in your life, I am no snake charmer nor is this book about all the lessons I have learned in life.

Rather, *In the Twinkle of an "I": There Is Something New Under the Son* is ultimately about you and how you choose to live the life you have been given. It is about you taking a stand for a future worth having now.

A stand is when you choose to live out your deepest longings regardless of your history, present circumstances or human nature. If you are willing to investigate and challenge who you think you are, what you think is possible and how you think about.

God, I believe you will find a level of freedom in your life that you never imagined possible. Just like my friend, Raul, you will get out of jail free. *In the Twinkle of an "I": There Is Something New Under the Son will* challenge how you view your future and therefore how you are living right now. In these pages, you will discover ideas you might not have considered before. Some may sound great. Others might kill a few sacred cows, like those romantic sensations that go something like, "Fulfillment is the result of accomplishment" or "I am self made!"

This book is an invitation for you to access the greatest possibility in your life through transforming your most passionate purpose into reality in the twinkle of an eye. Like Raul, who discovered what he didn't know he didn't know, the impossible suddenly became possible through one conversation.

In the Twinkle of an "I": There Is Something New Under the Son is designed to provoke new possibility for your life. It will equip you to see, discover and act on choices available to you in any circumstance so that you can experience the liberating transformation of being true to what matters most to you.

Isn't there more to life than turning mud into bricks? Is there something new under the sun? Can heaven come to earth? Can we be made new instantaneously?

Yes.

JAIL BIRDS

"And I'm free, free falling…"
Tom Petty (and Jeff Lynne)

The call went something like this.

Hi honey. It's me. Yep. Danny and I got to Tahoe a few hours ago. Great. The weather? Oh, the weather is great. Snow? Oh, the snow's perfect, just perfect. Ah, then why am I calling?

No, Aileen. I didn't lose my wallet. Wrong? What makes you think anything is wrong? Voices? You hear a lot of voices? What's going on? Honey, I am trying to tell you sweetheart if you would… Now, Aileen. Give me a chance. No. Danny's fine. No. I didn't wreck the car.

What's that siren noise? Well, honey, it's the ambulance. What ambulance? Ah, the one that just arrived outside the emergency room here at the hospital I am in. Aileen. Aileen. You see, I was skiing down the mountain kind of fast. I looked really good, honey. Even Danny said that I looked great even when I took the "gnarly fall." I know I'm not twenty-five years old anymore.

Well, that depends. How would you exactly define a little hurt?

Ever been arrested? I have.

Call it a life arrest.

I got busted on the slopes of Alpine Meadows in Northern California. Without much warning I found myself taken out of action when I least expected it. The day had started out *so* right and the future looked even better, then boom, an interruption the size of an elephant.

One minute I was at the top of the ski lift completely ignoring some persistent thoughts about shooting a line down a very steep run. Then, I was going about forty mph down the slope, picking up speed and thinking I looked pretty good. Suddenly, my ski caught an edge and all my weight landed on my left leg. I felt my knee pop and intense pain told me in no uncertain terms that something in my leg was not right. Like a train off the tracks, I crashed out of control rolling and sliding hundreds of feet down the hill.

"Dad!" I heard my son, Danny, shouting to me. "Dad! You okay?"

Sorry, son. This was not how I had planned our weekend together.

Just that morning, Danny and I had plotted our way to the ski slopes to catch the season's best snow and simply be together. Few things in life are as rewarding to me than hanging out with my son or daughter, and today had been planned to be something special. But right now my body looked like something out of the movie *Alien*.

Face deep in snow, shock and humiliation hit me. Talking to myself, God and anyone else who would listen, I fought the reality of what had just happened. "No. Please. No."

I refused to admit the obvious. "Everything is on track right now; all the pistons are firing. The business is taking off; the ministry is in major growth period. This cannot be happening. We were working a plan. I'll be okay. Won't I?" As much as I argued, moaned and rationalized, the truth would not budge an inch. There was nothing I could do to rewind the tape. I had skied myself into one monster interruption.

Fear, anger and excruciating pain bombarded me.

Now what? All my utilitarian thoughts automatically kicked in. What was this going to cost me in time, money and future opportunities? How was my life about to change? What if something was seriously wrong with my body? What if there was permanent damage? What would this mean for my family's future? How long would it be before I could stand, drive or fly on a plane? Why this? Why now? Then I remembered something. Like a break in the clouds, something opened up in my thinking.

Surrender, Dan. Surrender.

You see, I have worked for years as a police chaplain in my hometown. There, I had learned that if we surrender to the crisis *as it is* without striving to sugarcoat or placate its harsh reality, then we can *be with it* without being *ruled by it.* If we surrender and view everything that shows up as a resource for the unprecedented future, then our reactions to the unforeseen can be steadied and we can open up a space for the presence of God and others.

In my own crisis, the thoughts, fears and adrenaline rush that I was experiencing were a part of my natural desire to survive. Although they wanted to relieve my fears and assuage my anger, I could see that what was happening was just my automatic defense mechanism kicking into gear.

I could be in this problem without being ruled by it.

This interruption did not have to determine my actions or define my character. Although I could not imagine how, this accident could be a possible resource for something unprecedented. It could actually open something remarkable. At the very least I would set out to discover what possibilities could emerge from it.

So face deep in snow, I became my own police chaplain. In the freezing cold, I smiled and surrendered. I quieted my complaining and reminded myself that Dan Tocchini was not the Master and Commander of the Universe, just the master of his own ship. I chose to believe that I am a son who is intimately and infinitely loved by an immensely powerful God, who has given me the freedom to chose who I can from moment to moment. This was a chance to walk that talk.

God didn't break my leg; I broke my leg. However, He now had a new space to be in relationship with me, if I would surrender to life as it was showing up. Would this setback be a good thing in disguise? If it was, I hadn't seen what that good thing looked like yet.

"Wow, Dad! Took that last hill a little fast, didn't ya?" My son's smirk told me he was trying very hard not to laugh out loud. "So, Dad, is this the 'agony of defeat' part?"

"Pretty cool, huh?" I laughed instead of screaming.

"Hang on, sir." said the ski patrol officer as he put his hand reassuringly on my shoulder. "We'll have you down the mountain in no time. Hope you have nothing important planned for next few months. Looks like you are going to be a jailbird for quite awhile."

"Great. Thanks!" I joked, refusing to think of the important things that were now stuck on the shelf.

Everything is not *stuck on the shelf,* responded a thought inside of me.

I quibbled back to that thought, "Ha. Like what?"

Your book, for starters, the thought answered back.

"*The* book. That's right." I laughed.

Suddenly I felt like the Monopoly player whose final opponent just landed on his hotel-filled Boardwalk.

✡ ✡ ✡

Doing Time

✡ ✡ ✡

"We are disturbed not by events,
but by the views that we take of them."[1]
Epictetus

The prison guards were getting restless.

I caught them out of the corner of my eye, shuffling and joking with each other. They were thinking that this training gig was history, finished, a nice experiment. The guards had smelled defeat before; this thing was going down. Today would be a score for those who had bet that our bags would be packed before the end of first day.

Win, lose or draw, I knew something the prison guards did not.

I had learned that living the transformational life is like throwing a pitch at the World Series when it is the bottom of the ninth with two outs and bases loaded. There you are standing on the pitcher's mound, one out away from everything for which you have dreamed and trained. If you can strike out the next batter, the Series will be yours.

Then, you see who the opposing team puts up to bat. It's their clean-up hitter with the .850 slugging average!

What do you do? Bow out? Call it day? Hope that the odds get better next season? You could but who is guaranteed a second season?

The other option?

View the situation as perfect. Remember the reason why you are standing on the mound in the first place and that the only thing you can control right now is how you throw the baseball. Once that ball leaves your hand, everything else—the roaring crowds, the catcher, the umpire, the batter and all the other players—is out of your sphere of influence. All you can do then is to trust the wind and react to what shows up.

Being at ease in a training room with whatever is showing up is something that I have practiced for years. Whether the training is in a five-star hotel or behind prison walls, I have taught myself how to sink into my pitch. I knew that the guards were calling the game way too early.

This training was far from over. In fact, what was happening in the room *was* perfect. I looked at my good friend, Scott Larson, and smiled.

Almost a year ago, Scott had invited me to the prison to do this three-day training. Scott runs a cutting edge organization known as Straight Ahead Ministries. Their goal is to incrementally transform America's justice system from a pain-based process to a choice-based process. The results of their new paradigm and approach have been phenomenal.

Over the last thirteen years, the recidivism rate (the percentage of inmates returning to prison after finishing their sentences) among the graduates of Scott's programs is about six percent compared to a national average of seventy-eight percent. Even though Scott is the last person to seek any limelight, Straight Ahead has received substantial recognition from their local community all the way to the White House for their effectiveness in helping youth offenders to transform their lives.

Through another friend, Scott had heard about my work in the arena of personal and organizational transformation. After participating in a few of our trainings, Scott said that what I was doing powerfully expressed what he was seeking to provide to his kids. We soon found ourselves developing a transformational training specifically designed for incarcerated youth offenders, and we made the decision to launch it at this correctional facility in Rhode Island.

During the months leading up to the launch, Scott had talked to me several times about the inmates. "Dan, I don't know why the prison systems call it 'rehabilitation,'" Scott said. "Rehabilitation assumes that you are restoring these youth offenders to something good. The truth is that my kids never had *something good* in the first place. Just about everyone has given up hope on them. No one knows what to do except, in essence, warehouse them in prison. Our whole aim is to empower them to the *unprecedented future in their lives*. Our objective is to first train them to use their imaginations and dream what they have never known, let alone imagined possible for them."

"These kids have committed all the big crimes," Scott went on to alert me. "Murder. Rape. Theft. Drugs. Prostitution. All of them are gang affiliated, Bloods, Crips. You name it. These boys have done it. Where we are going is a high security, locked-down facility called 'a training school.' Gates of security. Twenty-foot high cyclone fencing topped with razor wire. Like something out of World War II."

"Got it," I assured Scott. Undaunted, I landed in Rhode Island believing that I was prepared for anything. Then I saw the inmates' faces and discovered that I was completely wrong.

They were *kids*, the notorious hard-core criminals. *Just kids.*

When I saw them face-to-face, everything shifted inside of me. The faces starring at me were someone's children. The youngest were thirteen years; the oldest, maybe twenty. These teens locked down in prison blues had their entire lives ahead of them. They were jailbirds, living inside a very big interruption. Immediately my heart was captured, bound to them like a pair of handcuffs. Before I spoke one word, I was ruined inside.

The only difference between you and them, Dan, I said to myself, *was that you never got caught.*

How many countless times had I sold cocaine on the streets, narrowly escaping a bust? How many lies had I told to make myself right about what I was doing? What life would I have had if just one cop had caught me? I wonder would I even be married, or have had a family? Would I have ever traveled the globe or experienced the phenomenal choices afforded by my freedom?

I could never know for sure, but I think it is safe to say that I would probably have had a very different life than I am experiencing today.

For the next three days, these boys would get everything I could give them. God hadn't sent me here for nothing. I was all in—the good, the bad and the ugly!

✡ ✡ ✡

Crabs in the Basket

✡ ✡ ✡

"How much happier would you be,
how much more of you would there be if the hammer
of the high God would smash your small cosmos."[2]
G.K. Chesterton

Right from the start of the training, things got pretty wild. Small wonder that the guards were convinced that we would bail out. Tensions around the training room were running hot because there was a strong possibility of violence breaking out. By bringing together whole units of offenders—such as opposing gangs of the Bloods and the Crips—we were doing something that had never been done before. There was a huge likelihood of problems because these were tough, proud members of their gangs who were always looking for a chance to fight for control of whatever was going on.

On top of that, I did something else that made everyone else nervous. As the trainer, I gave the offenders complete choice to say and do whatever they wanted within the confines of the training room. It was the first time anyone had given them this freedom since the first day of their incarceration.

And, chaos was their response. They started giving me a lot of flack. Interrupting me. Cussing me. Refusing to listen. Swearing. Farting. Laughing at what I was doing.

It was absolutely perfect.

It was like that pitcher sinking into his pitch. I continued with my presentation about the unprecedented future, not letting what was happening in the room phase me in the least. Calm as a cucumber, I was studying the batter intensely. Was he in the front of the box or the back? Was he leaning on his back or front foot, crowding the plate or away? Open in his stance, or closed up?

As the chaos went to the next level, the chaplain who had been instrumental in getting Scott and me into the prison finally had

had enough. "Knock it off, man," Pastor Mike shouted out to the kids. "This is disrespectful." Hearing Pastor Mike, I saw the prison guards move towards taking over the room.

"No. No. No!" I shouted back, surprising everyone. "Hey, don't. That's all right. This is the way it is. This is their life!"

The juvenile offenders looked at me, stunned.

"This training is about discovery," I said. "I told these guys that whatever they do here in the training is perfect. It is like a snapshot into their life. If this is the future they want to choose now, that is up to them. If dishonor, disrespect, and chaos are the future they want, then you can't stop them, Pastor Mike. Sure, they outwardly appear to acquiesce to you guys, but the reality is that this prison hasn't changed what they think inside."

Immediately, calm settled like rain all over the room, and I heard a strong voice bark at me from the back of the room.

"What are you talking about, white boy?" asked Jason, a gang leader in the prison.

I turned to look. The batter was at the plate, ready for the ball, and so I reached back and threw it. Walking towards Jason, I started talking about the unprecedented future from the context of what was happening right at that moment.

"You are just doing what you normally automatically do," I answered him, "which produces more of what you already have. It appears to me that this type of behavior and the results it produces is familiar and it is predictable, giving you a sense of control over your life. If you continue to do *that*, then *this* is what you are always going to get!"

"What do you mean?" Jason responded.

"I think you are just an unconscious animal living through your instincts," I gave it to him straight. "This is what you choose. This is what you do. *But* you could be free."

"Free? What are you saying, man?" he demanded.

"You *could* live, even in here, according to an unprecedented future. A future that you want but probably don't believe is possible. But what you do is settle for what little you can get; what is predictable."

You could have heard a pin drop. Out of perfect chaos, a real dialogue and this training had truly begun.

What happened next was even more perfect, although you needed eyes to recognize its perfection at the time. At lunch, one of the offenders, Peter, started a fight with a younger teen. Immediately the guards pulled both of them out of the training and threw them into lockdown. Once again tensions flared.

Some of the guards and members of our team were looking a little concerned, which I could understand given their history with these kids, but I thought, "Perfect. This is beautiful." What made the situation perfect was that Peter had made a great leap forward in the training room just moments before lunch.

As we assembled back into the training room, one of the kids asked, "So what do you think, Mr. Dan?"

"Think about what?" I answered.

"About what just happened?"

"Well, I think that was just more of the past," I said evenly. "I say, Peter experienced a breakthrough and was starting to see possibilities he had never seen before. However, the fight was his way of sabotaging himself. He pulled himself back into the box or basket of familiarity!"

"Basket?" the teen asked.

"You know about Mexican crabs, right?"

"That's some kind of gang?"

"No, man," I said with a smile. "In Mexico, when you go to the open air markets, there are these baskets filled with live crabs."

"Oh."

"Now the merchants never have to worry about any of the crabs escaping out of the baskets."

"Why?"

"Because when one crab tries to climb out of the basket, some other crab pulls him back into the basket. See, by taunting that kid into a fight, Peter was choosing something that was familiar, known and predictable."

"The bottom of the basket."

"Right. He let himself be yanked back down. Right now, that is the path he has chosen. However, as long as he is breathing, Peter could choose the unprecedented future. Peter is doing what I used to do to myself when I was a cocaine addict. I was just like him, a dog returning to its own vomit, a fool repeating his folly."

The teen stared back at me like a calf in a new gate.

"So the only real question is this," I stared back. "What are *you* going to choose for this weekend?"

✡ ✡ ✡

The Vultures and the Dove

✡ ✡ ✡

Crabs. Baskets. Claws. Slopping around at the bottom.
I wasn't talking theologically with these young men. I had firsthand experience of what I was saying. In the early 1990s, I was accused of being some kind of cult leader. I even made national headlines for all of about thirty seconds. Even *Oprah* investigated.

At that time, my life was like a ship hunting for safe harbor. My wife, Aileen, and I had been together for over fifteen years and had weathered some very rough storms including the death of three family members, my being hooked on cocaine, a life-threatening car accident without our ship going down.

In the early years of our relationship, I had worked as a professional trainer for a San Francisco-based organization called Lifespring, developed originally as a personal effectiveness program. Although I had philosophical differences with some of Lifespring's core tenets, Lifespring helped me recognize I did not have to relate to unfortunate or even tragic events as a victim even if I were truly victimized. There was one thing I could control. It was how I related to what life threw my way or how I stood in life.

Working at Lifespring developed me as a trainer. Working with all sorts of people in multifaceted situations allowed a learning curve that opened up opportunities I had never anticipated before in my life. What I learned at Lifespring was not only transferable professionally but also greatly supported my vision for communicating with my wife and children in meaningful ways. Finally, the more I worked as a trainer, the more I developed my natural listening abilities and talents for leading teams through challenging circumstances.

After eight years, I decided to leave Lifespring and try my hand at entrepreneurship. I bought into a ship-brokering business and was able to settle down from my hectic travel schedule as a trainer at Lifespring and raise my young family. Now, I was drug free and rebuilding what I had almost destroyed with Aileen through numerous betrayals. By the grace of God, our relationship was transforming from all the suspicion caused by the flagrant broken promises of my past to one of love, trust and mutual respect. I was grateful to experience what God could do in the life of a willing disciple. Although I was passionate about God, people and life, I was still living in the crab basket. I was down at the bottom of the familiar, clueless to what was possible.

Until, a series of events occurred causing me to rethink my life and calling.

Aileen and I were a part of an Episcopal church near our home in California. At that time, we were co-leading a small home fellowship group. To everyone's surprise, our little fellowship group exploded like a three-for-the-price-of-one sale at Macy's. Some nights the only space we had left was a tiny corner on the floor by the kitchen door.

When the priest of the church found out, he wanted to know what I was "doing." I simply told him that I was applying my experience from working with so many people as a trainer at Lifespring in the fellowship group. I said that I wanted to give what I could to those who wanted more in life than survival. What I was "doing" in the Bible study was what I did as trainer: I was standing with others to intentionally begin to experience the longings of their hearts rather than just performing for others' approval, personal comfort or some sense of control. In the face of what seemed impossible, we were calling each other out to trust that Jesus would reveal His purpose and blessing even in the most difficult life circumstance and that our partnership with Him and each other would yield fulfillment.

"Wow. Great. Do you think you could develop something that would assist the leaders of the church to do the same?" the priest asked.

"Sure," I said.

By summer's end 1990, my declaration was a reality. I had implemented three trainings for the church. Each one produced a deeper level of breakthrough for the participants, and the results were tremendously exciting. Before my eyes, our little church was getting passionate about life and what we were discovering about God's rule or kingdom in our lives. Leaders and regular folks alike were transforming their way of being with each other and especially with those they had felt alienated by or for whom they carried offense. Those who were once reserved and in the shadows stepped out of their shells and begin to stand for what mattered most in their lives. Many sought out others to ask for forgiveness for things that had been broken between them. It was beautiful. Joyous. Unprecedented.

And, completely disruptive to the status quo!

After six months, we reached a turning point. One of our training participants had sought out the priest who had commissioned me to develop the leadership training to ask him for forgiveness for unspoken differences that had piled up for her in their relationship. She confessed that she had stopped being authentic with him and had begun to withhold judgments she had developed. By not giving him a chance to respond to what she was making up about him and his actions, their relationship had been dying a long, slow death.

After asking for and receiving his forgiveness, the participant asked the priest if he would be interested in exploring her concerns so that he might better understand her. When he responded affirmatively, the participant cited specific examples of his behavior, which made her believe that he had sexist attitudes towards women and that he abused his position of authority over others.

Hearing her examples, the priest completely shut down. After their meeting, accusations of insubordination started flying in the church community like a hail of arrows. Some came right at me.

When I sought the priest out to investigate rumors that he was angry with me about her conversation, I discovered he wouldn't talk to me. No matter what I tried he wouldn't talk, and finally it all came to a head.

A few months later, he did accept a meeting with me and asked me to take my family somewhere else to worship because I was "a distraction to the church growth agenda." I was confused. I was torn between the good fruit I saw in the lives of the training participants and his reactions to them. I knew of nothing in the training that was either anti-God or even against the church. I was completely baffled. I loved these good people and was grieved over how this barrage of accusation had hurt everyone.

We left sadly, and I settled back into the bottom of the crab basket, wounded and confused.

A good six months passed. After thinking about what had happened, I decided that I was done with this whole training business. The last thing I wanted was to stir up another heap of trouble; I had seen enough turmoil in my own life to last several lifetimes. I didn't need this grief or difficulty.

Sure, I had seen the good that the trainings accomplished. I remembered all the breakthroughs that people had experienced in their lives. But it was much safer at the bottom of the basket. Down there, everything is familiar. I know what people expect of me and can deliver on their expectations and be accepted and liked.

Then I discovered that *God* isn't found in the familiar and acceptable. Dane, a friend of mine who had been part of the leadership meetings, taught me that God is found beyond familiar and well into the uncomfortable extremes of life.

One day, Dane probed me like a master surgeon. "Hey, what are you doing with the training?"

I found myself expounding on ideas I had been privately entertaining. What I really wanted to do was help others radically pursue unprecedented possibilities in their lives in a sustainable, life-changing way. And, yes the vehicle I wanted to use were those trainings that I had developed.

The more I spoke to Dane, the more I saw that I was not happy at the bottom of the crab basket. I wanted out.

Less than a year later, we launched The Breakthrough Training in March 1992. The results of this first full-scale transformational training far exceeded anyone's expectations and Breakthrough took off like wildfire. Within a few short months people from across the United States were calling me requesting The Breakthrough Training along with any additional materials that could help them.

Feeling like Alice in Wonderland, I found myself on the edge of the impossible being possible.

I had approached Breakthrough as a part-time experiment. The last thing I had anticipated was the nature of the response I was getting. I never expected to participate so fully that I disappeared into action.

Up until this time in my life, I had known such full participation only a couple of times. The first time was playing linebacker on my high school football team. Near the end of a very important game, I passed out while walking off the field. I woke up on a table in the locker room looking up into the face of our team doctor.

"What? What happened?" I asked him.

"Sheer exhaustion, Dan," he replied.

"But I don't remember anything, Doc!" I said. My mind was completely blank.

With a smile, the team doctor proceeded to tell me that we had won the game. Moreover, I had made fifteen unassisted tackles and in the final seconds of the game had run fifty yards a touchdown.

Seeing the anxious look on my face, the doctor reassured me saying that he had seen this kind of thing before when a player so fully engages with the game that they become *one* with it. It is as though they *disappear into the action,* like a piece of sheet music bearing the notes of a symphony.

Well, actually it wasn't like I disappeared, it was more like I was *transparent* in action. I was there, but my focus wasn't on how I was doing, how I looked and if I was comfortable or in control. Years later while reading *The Sickness Unto Death* by Søren Kierkegaard I was astounded to read what Kierkegaard describes as the ideal state for human being. He stated that it is when the self is "resting transparent in the presence of the One who established it." I realized that this was the experience I had when I played ball and when I worked with people in the training room to be able to rest in the presence of God in such a way that my energy could be liberated for others. Kierkegaard's words gave me a very concrete experience of how faith could express itself in action.

I never forgot that experience on the football field and, with Breakthrough, it was happening again. The hours I spent developing the training and working with the team of people who had come together passed by like minutes. As we developed the trainings, personal needs and comforts were part of the process, but not the focus or purpose of our work together.

Then, once again, the unexpected happened. A firestorm of controversy exploded around the training.

The training participants were everyday people active in their local churches. After taking the training, they began to walk out their freedom in new ways, and some church leaders were not quite sure what to do with what they were encountering. Within a year of the 1992 launch, I was getting pressure to stop the trainings.

Like a crab at the rim, I felt a tug on my back. Inside my head, a war raged between the safety of the familiar and what might lie outside the basket.

One voice shouted, "Drop the training, man. You don't need this heat. Do what you need to do to survive. Think of Aileen and the kids. Let go of the rim, man. Stay at the bottom of the basket with us. It's nice and warm down here. A little crowded, but you'll get use to it."

I was tempted by the broad, familiar road—the road that would have me take a job offer with a company in Japan or a position as general manager at my father's cinema business. Both jobs would guarantee a good income, and I would be done with the stress involved with Breakthrough. I could create a life for my family that was predictable, comfortable and a lot less complicated.

Another option was more compelling but in a different, peaceful way. "Get out of the basket, Dan. No one belongs down there. Climb out. Declare who you are and the future you long for. Stand and let the chips fall where they may and rest in Me. Think, Dan, even if you fail, what is more fulfilling? Failing at the unprecedented or succeeding at the predictable?"

This calm voice made no money-back guarantees nor did it detail for me what I would face in being free. It required me being *all in* and not looking back. The voice invited me to a new and uncharted horizon, an unprecedented future.

One night, I laid everything out before Aileen telling her what was going on inside of me. I went through the directions we could take and the risks in either direction. After listening intently, Aileen said, "Let's sell the house and put the funds into developing the training."

My jaw hit the floor. I could not believe my ears. What? Sell the house? This house meant everything to Aileen. It was the expression of her heart, creativity and generosity. However, Aileen was ready to climb out of the basket. Already, life was showing up very different than I had anticipated!

Only one questioned remained; was I ready to climb out of the basket?

A couple of days later we put our house on the market.

One of the things I began to learn in the process was that all commitments get tested and this was no exception. Before long, a leader from my church who consulted with several churches around the country including my own called a meeting and accused me of not honoring the authority of the church. Although he had never participated in a training himself, he demanded that I stop doing Breakthrough indefinitely.

I told him, "No. I will not do that."

Somewhere inside, I thought that if he experienced the training he would change his views. He was not my enemy. He was a highly intelligent man, a natural leader who loved God and had given his life over to serving Him. I had asked him time and time again to come and watch a training, but he refused.

Before this meeting, I had met with him again and again and had sought to respond to every complaint brought against me and Breakthrough. I had revised certain aspects of it based upon his concerns and had even let him read through the entire trainer's manual for his evaluation and discussion.

Instead of clearing up, the situation had gotten even more convoluted.

Other churches across the country had gotten upset. Newspaper articles were written and a so-called cult research institute had started to pursue us. Friends and loved ones found themselves caught in the middle of the brew and an ugly air of suspicion permeated the atmosphere. Fiction became fact, and I even caught someone going through my trash one evening. Just after a newspaper article was published came the call from *Oprah* asking us to appear on a show about cults.

Had I stolen anyone's money? No. Had I seduced young women or men? No. Was I hoarding a stockpile of guns? No. Was I doing anything illegal, illicit or immoral? No. Was I manipulating anyone? No. Was I doing anything that I could not do with a clean conscience before the face of God? Absolutely not.

To me, it was as though some of my fellow crabs were not crazy about what I was doing. Yet when I said, "No. I will not do that," I meant it. I was climbing out of that stinking basket.

In the midst of the controversy, I fluctuated between hatred, despair, sorrow and complete frustration. Some days I did not know if I was going to make it. I had put everything I had on the line and the end result had been tough and disappointing. I was exhausted in every way.

Finally one afternoon, I drove to the top of my favorite mountain outside my hometown. It was a clear, magnificent California day, and I could see for miles and miles.

Getting out of the car, I let God have it with both barrels.

"God, what the hell are you doing to me?" I opened with everything I had. "Haven't I been faithful here? I did what I believed You would have me do. I extended an open hand to my enemies.

I did *everything* I knew to do to be reconciled with them. For what? Nothing. Now Aileen and I are about to lose everything."

"What are you trying to tell me?" I demanded. "Do you want me to quit? Fine. Just tell me. What do You want? God, I don't know what to do. Do You even care? Give me some kind of sign! Please, God. Please."

In those moments, I was tempted to curse God and run. Yet, I could not and would not forget all the mercy shown by God to me. If He hadn't shown up in my life, I would have been still hooked on cocaine, homeless and most likely dead. Even though everything was a big mess, I still loved Jesus too much to turn my back on Him.

Talked out, I stopped and leaned against a fence rail. Just then, something in the valley below me caught my eye. There I saw a group of vultures circling around something lying on the ground.

"I feel like that dead thing they are about to pick apart," I murmured.

Suddenly I spied a tiny white speck flying out of that black, ugly circle of vultures. I strained forward to see. The white speck was a dove and it was flying right towards me! Closer and closer, the delicate bird flew until, unbelievably, the dove landed on a fence post no more than ten feet away from me.

The sight took my breath away.

Its soft pink eyes looked at me from one side, then from the other. As we exchanged glances, my heart began to rest. Then, as decisively as it had landed, the dove flew into the air and straight for me. I ducked, feeling the beating of its wings as it passed over my head.

What? What had just happened?

In an instant, tears filled my eyes. It did not take a genius to put this one together. It was an answer to my prayer just moments before.

He had silenced my complaint with awe, telling me that I was not that dead thing waiting for the vultures' claws. I was the object of His great, immeasurable love, and I would never have to face anything without Him. I could rest in His presence and paradoxically experience joy in my journey, no matter how unbearable the circumstances of that journey might become. They might be ugly or the best. None of that really mattered. What did matter was that He and I were in it together and that each person connected could enter into this rest as well.

If I stood on my commitment to love others as I wanted to be loved, I would be a free man. I was out of the crab basket. The vision wasn't about accomplishing anything; it was about how we could be together regardless of circumstance. Nobody could take that away from us!

✡ ✡ ✡

The Right Question

✡ ✡ ✡

"When you make a sacrifice, you don't just give something up, you acknowledge a realm greater than yourself. Sacrifice means 'to make sacred.' You go beyond self. You make room for a greater mystery. You may experience this larger sense of sacrifice in ordinary deprivations, as you give up many freedoms and soften your willfulness. You listen to your partner's opinions and plans. Your whole life may take a different direction because you're willing to share your vision."[3]
Thomas Moore, *Dark Nights of the Soul*

"Yo, Mr. Dan."
It was Sunday afternoon behind bars with only a few hours left of the training. Over the previous two days, the boys and I had experienced significant breakthroughs together. All the previous bravado had fallen away, and they were working with each other. The Spirit of God was all over the place, and even the prison guards had softened from their hardened, cynical posture of the first day.

I turned to see who was calling out my name. It was Andrew, and I was surprised. For the last three days, Andrew had not said one word. Up until now.

"Yo, Mr. Dan. I have a question, and I want you to answer it."

"What is it?" I replied.

"If God is so loving or so good," Andrew asked, "why did He let all these things happen to us?"

I was stunned *and* impressed.

Andrew had the guts to ask one of life's most authentic questions, a question that everyone wrestles with in one way or another, especially Christians. Hearing his question, I realized that Andrew had been contributing throughout the training by how deeply he had been thinking. I started to acknowledge him for it, but he quickly interrupted me.

"Well, yeah, I hear you. What I want to know is what *you* think, Mr. Dan."

"Why do you want to know what I think?" I asked.

"Because, I have heard all this *religious bullshit* before—from everybody who comes in here preaching *Christianity*. Telling me this and that about what God will do for me. Telling me that God is good. Well, I am looking around me, and I say to them that God *ain't* good. Look at the crap I have lived in since the day I was born. Look at where I am now. Their only answer is like, 'God loves you.' Shit. Their answers don't make no sense. When I listen to what these folks are saying, they sound as lost as I am."

I got it. What Andrew was really saying to me was, "Don't wreck it now, Mr. Dan. You've been really honest with us these last three days. Don't shine us on with a bunch of religious platitudes. We aren't interested in what you think is the *right answer* I just want to know what *you really think*."

I asked Andrew, "Who do you love?"

"I love my mother and my sister," Andrew replied.

"How much do you love them?"

"Well, I love them a whole lot."

I continued. "Did your dad love them?"

"No. My dad beat 'em."

"So, then beating them was not loving them."

"Yeah."

"Why did your dad beat them?"

"He wanted to control us."

"Right," I said. "So basically your dad was not willing to let you guys be free."

Andrew took a moment and answered, "Yeah."

"Would you say that if you love somebody," I kept going deeper with him, "that you would want them to be free, to be who they are?"

Andrew pondered my question and then replied in a clear and certain tone, "Yeah, that's right!"

"So when you expect God to keep other people from freely choosing evil, destructive choices, what you are saying is that you want God to be like your dad," I answered.

Andrew bristled. "No way, Mr. Dan."

"You are. You want freedom so long it doesn't involve the free choice to hurt someone else. But you see, God is love. He has set *everyone* free. You. Me. Your dad. *But you want your freedom without being hurt by someone else's freedom!*"

Andrew looked at me, silently.

"That's impossible." I continued, "Freedom necessitates suffering because freedom includes the possibility of choosing to do to others what we would not want done to us. Freedom means that God has set us free in deed, which means I can choose to disobey Him; that's how much He loves us. He wants us to freely choose to love Him."

Andrew took in every word. Then I asked him another question, "Do you have a girlfriend, Andrew?"

With a sheepish smile, Andrew nodded his head and took some razzing from the other guys in the room.

I asked, "How would you feel if she went out with you because she was afraid of what you would do to her or her family if she didn't? What do you imagine your relationship with your girlfriend would look like?"

Without a moment of hesitation, he answered, "I know *exactly* what it would be like because that is what my father did to us!"

"How do you think it feels from your father's perspective?" I asked him to consider. "Knowing that his family only does what he asks because they are afraid of him, not because they love or respect him?"

Light bulbs started going off all over the place. Andrew was beginning to see other possibilities that up until that point were hidden behind his suspicion of God.

"Here is what I think," I continued. "Authentic love, as opposed to the romantic sensation our culture identifies as love, necessitates freedom of choice. The only kind of relationship that lasts is one where both people are completely free to choose each other. This is why God has set us free—so we can freely choose Him. Love is not something that can be forced or coerced. Love is a choice."

Andrew kept on standing, thinking through what I had said.

"That's what I think." I said to him, "What do *you* think?"

Long silence.

Then, Andrew answered. "Wow. I never thought about it like that, Mr. Dan. I have always felt like God has been with me but somehow I have confused God being with me with what God was going to do about my situation. Now I am seeing God has set me free to determine how I am going stand in or relate to my situation!"

"What if life was just about choosing to love regardless of the circumstances, Andrew?" I answered. "What if when we choose to love in any situation, we are actually connecting with God Himself?"

I let the thought rest in the air. "Here is what it looks like. Do you remember the first day? You all chose to 'dis' me for hours. I kept choosing to respect your choices and love you by thinking the best of you. I showed my respect for you by the way I wanted you to respect me. I was honest with you."

The boys were quiet as my words sank in.

Then I asked. "Can I ask you guys a question?"

They unanimously replied, "Yeah."

"You guys confuse the hell out of me because you have this double-message happening. Why do you try to get it from both sides?"

"What do you mean?" they asked me, as if I were speaking Italian.

"Can you see that you being here in prison tells me that, at some level, you are saying to yourself that you *want* to be here?" I felt their resistance to that possibility but didn't stop. "Your result is telling me your true intention and true vision. You being behind bars, tells me that you want to be here—even though you are telling yourself that you don't want to be here. Remember during the first day when I asked you what you were committed to? All of you said, 'Getting out of here.' When you answered that way, I knew you would be coming back here because you were using 'here,' being in prison, as the basis of your commitment instead a future you imagined would be worth having."

"Now when you are in here, you bitch about living behind bars. Yet in the same breath, you talk about how worried you are about getting caught up again with your crew, those guys from your gang who don't even bother to visit while you are here. That confuses me. Tell me, why do you do that? What if your result were telling you your true intentions?"

It was not long before the boys came up with some great answers. "When I think about it like that," one said, "I guess it means that I think it is probably safer here than out there, in my own life." Another added, "While we are here, we keep bitching about it instead of using this time to build ourselves up so that we don't get hooked again into what we were doing."

I smiled. The jail birds were starting to fly.

"What if prison was an opening," I said, "to develop your character so that when you leave here you are not stuck in the same old game? What if you started living from an unprecedented future now and for the rest of your lives no matter what the circumstances? What if wherever you are is the *perfect* place to be at that time and from there you can go anywhere?"

✧ ✧ ✧

Dying to Live

✧ ✧ ✧

"No misunderstandings are ever healed, no brokenness made whole, no deadlocks broken unless someone is willing to resolve all the tensions within his own soul and become the one in whom the solution is brought into being. That always costs something, and it is the human act most closely related to the Divine. In it there are the traces of Gethsemane and Calvary."
The Journal of Reuben Nelson

"You're the closest thing to a father that I have ever had," Fernando wrote in a letter, which brought me to tears. Despite my best efforts, word leaked out swiftly about my skiing fiasco.

Even my boys back in Rhode Island had heard about my skiing accident. One night when pain was keeping me awake, I thought about the great time we had together. The boys had been so hungry and empty that they were willing to give up what they had filled themselves with for the possibility of an unprecedented future.

Like them, when I broke my leg, it had forced me to cast off how I had filled my life. Once again, I realized that what we think we know is not enough in this life.

We are finite beings who will someday die. Here under the sun, there is never enough time, knowledge or money to resolve the upcoming reality of our deaths. The only significant issue at hand is how are we going to choose to lose our lives? What will be the legacy of our existence here on earth? What will others know as our character?

As Mel Gibson's William Wallace said so aptly in the movie, Braveheart (Paramount Pictures, 1995), "Every man dies, not every man really lives." Mark Twain drove the point home when he said, "Men die at 27, we just bury them at 72!"

Lying awake that night, I wondered how much of my life had been an unconscious attempt to prevent my own death. How many dreams had I scuttled because I could not guarantee my way through the inevitable failures that are part of any great accomplishment? How many times have I not said something out of fear of being wrong, judged or considered foolish? How much has our unspoken, and often unconscious, need to survive kept us from the longing of our futures?

When Jesus walked this earth knowing not only that He would die but also the horrific suffering He would experience, what went on inside for Him? What were His meditations?

How much of His courage, character and passion for life was a result of completely surrendering to the fact that He was already dead?

Could it be that He had to give up any shred of hope that He could avoid death before He could choose to walk the road to Calvary and forgive us all for how we have crucified Him?

Was it through His obedient surrender to "rest in the presence of the One who established Him, that He was resurrected?

That night, remembering my Rhode Island boys, I wanted to know.

I was dying to live.

✡ ✡ ✡

Notes:

[1] The Enchiridion (or "Handbook").

[2] G. K. Chesterton, *Orthodoxy: The Romance of Faith* (Doubleday, 1990), p. 4.

[3] *Dark Nights of the Soul: A Guide To Finding Your Way Through Life's Ordeals* (Gotham Books, 2005).

THE COMPLAINT

"You know quite well, deep within you, that there is only a single magic, a single power, a single salvation… and that is called loving. Well, then, love your suffering. Do not resist it, do not flee from it. It is your aversion that hurts, nothing else." [1]

Herman Hesse

✧ ✧ ✧

Dispatched

✧ ✧ ✧

The first thing I saw was a pair of boy's tennis shoes lying empty in the middle of the road. A few yards further sat another pair, vacant and silent as death in the fading sunset.

Instantly my foot jerked off the gas pedal and my stomach turned over as my heart pounded like a freight train. My breathing turned into hyperventilation. As I sat in my car staring, waves of dizziness and nausea overcame me. I was about to buckle over and unless I did something quickly, I was going to be in trouble.

Today was my first day soloing as a police chaplain. My first call. Nothing in my nine months of training could have prepared me for this horror.

I had joined the police chaplaincy because I wanted to give something back to my community. For three-quarters of a year, I had been mentored by other volunteer police chaplains in an intensive training program. Our job was to be among the first responders to accidents, violent crimes, natural disasters and other life-or-death emergencies for the purpose of providing comfort to victims and supporting law enforcement officers in every way we could.

My pastor, J.R. Young, had told me about his involvement in the Sonoma County Law Enforcement Chaplaincy Program and the great group of people he had met there. I will never forget one of my first ride-along appointments with a local sheriff who patrolled sections of the county. As we drove through the rural neighborhoods, I was amazed at how much he knew about the people who lived there.

He knew their names, what they did for a living, their children and even about some of their problems. I saw that the sheriff was not just going through the motions. Rather, he was a real professional who was authentically concerned with the health and wellbeing of his community.

Near the end of the ride-along, we had dinner at a small restaurant on the border of a tough neighborhood. As we were eating dinner, we got a call from dispatch. Someone was in the process of breaking into a woman's house. The assailant was still on the front porch of the home.

We immediately took off and arrived at the home just as another sheriff arrived. Both of the police cars converged with their headlights on the front door. There I saw a man staggering on the porch and screaming in Spanish, "Let me in! I want to go to bed!" He had a huge pipe in his hand and looked as though he would use it either on the door or on anyone who got close.

With lightning speed, the four police officers got out of their patrol cars, drew their weapons and told the man to drop the pipe. Still swaying, the man started walking toward the police officers as if he were deaf.

The police yelled again, "Stop where you are. Drop your weapon and get on the ground," but the man kept walking toward them. I froze, not knowing what was about to happen. From the chaplaincy training, I knew that if anyone moved closer than twenty-eight feet—the distance between a suspect and an officer then a police officer would fire his weapon.

Fortunately, the man hit the ground before it was too late.

As officers frisked and cuffed him, I saw two young men running towards us from behind the officers. Seeing them, the officers commanded the kids to stop. Once again, the officers drew their weapons and demanded that the teens stop.

Instead of stopping, the kids kept running. The officers shouted again, "Stop where you are! Stop now! Stop or we will shoot!" My own heart pounded as I realized that these kids were about to be seriously hurt.

To my relief, the boys stopped just outside of thirty feet. They explained quickly that they were the sons of the man on the ground, adding that their father had recently arrived from Mexico and didn't know his way around the neighborhood.

Their story sounded believable to me. Not to the sheriff.

He started asking some questions and, within minutes, the boys told him a completely different story. The truth was that there were arrest-warrants out on their dad for jumping bail. This particular night, he had been drinking, and, after getting drunk, tried to break back into his own home.

As the officers arrested the husband, I sat with his wife. She had been the one who called the police on her husband, and, showing me a baseball bat, told me that she had intended to hit her husband with it once the officers had subdued him.

From that experience that night, I learned quickly that *out there* anything can happen. As my nine months of chaplaincy training drew to a close, I was prepared in every way I knew. All that remained was for dispatch to call.

One picture-perfect summer afternoon, they did.

The preliminary report was bad, very bad. Two young boys had been playing a game of chicken with trucks going across a bridge, and the boys had lost to a plumbing truck. The dispatcher asked me, "How fast can you get there, Dan?" By the tone in her voice, I knew that the situation was urgent.

"I will be there in fifteen minutes," I answered.

What I saw was beyond any parent's worst nightmare.

One of the boys was lying alongside the road; the other child was still caught in the truck's wheel-well, his feet dangling down from the top of the wheel. Obviously shaken, the highway patrol officer was on the radio with his head in his hands leaning against his car. Near the bridge, the father of one of the boys sat on the ground in shock.

As I saw an emergency helicopter land, the words "This should not be!" screamed inside of my soul. In the face of this brutal reality, all my theoretical concepts and lofty thoughts about the despair of this life looked like nothing. I felt helpless, weak, insufficient and unprepared.

"You have to make this better," my survival instinct demanded, "You *must* intervene. You *have* to do something." I did not like all this blood, tragedy, injustice and death. I hated it with every fiber of my being.

Hearing my thoughts, I grabbed around my throat.

I had to make a choice: Hide in the illusion that I could somehow make this horror any better, or come out from behind my idea about how life should be, rest in His presence, and engage the reality of what was happening there at that moment showing up for the people there.

✧ ✧ ✧

Delivering the News

✧ ✧ ✧

"We cannot live for ourselves alone. Our lives are connected by a thousand invisible threads, and along these sympathetic fibers, our actions run as causes and return to us as results."
Herman Melville

The radio blasted the news.

A bridge worker had accidentally fallen off the Golden Gate Bridge and had died in the arms of his co-workers at the base of the South Tower.

At 12:10 p.m., my cell phone rang. It was dispatch calling. "Dan, would you do a death notification for the bridge worker? His family lived in the nearby town of Cotati."

He was a single father, I learned, who had moved back to his mom's house with his young son. A single dad working a dangerous job supporting his family the best way he knew how that was this guy.

Now he was gone.

Although I had been a police chaplain for couple of years, I had no clue how I was going to do what had been asked of me. How do you tell a mother that her son is dead? How do you tell a child that all the memories he has right now of his dad are all the memories he will *ever* have?

As I drove into his neighborhood, I could tell it was a nice, working-class block filled with freshly cut lawns and tons of kids playing on them. As I went up and down the streets hunting for his house, the weight of what lie ahead grew heavier.

Finding the home, my heart sank. The driveway was empty.

I went to the front door and knocked. No answer. I went around to the back door and knocked. Again, no answer.

"She went to pick up the boy," barked an older man working out in his yard next door. "Picks him up from school right about now." Seeing my uniform and badge, his face filled with shock and disbelief.

"You're with the police. Oh, no. The accident at the bridge? Was it -"

"I am afraid so. It would be best if I could tell Mrs. Henderson first," I answered.

He responded sadly. "Look, can I get you some ice tea while you wait? Come on inside."

"Sure, that'd be great," I answered.

As the San Francisco Giants baseball game played on his television, I felt as though I was waiting in some kind of Twilight Zone. I had one foot in the middle of this horrible tragedy and the other one wanted to be at the baseball game, oblivious to the suffering happening around me.

"Can I help somehow?" the neighbor asked. "I could ask Jeremy to come over while you talk with his grandmother."

"Sure, that would be very helpful. Thank you."

"Here she comes now."

Going outside, I watched as her car pulled into the driveway. A little boy bounded out like a bird set free from a cage with only his grandmother's voice keeping him in tow. As much as my thoughts wanted to shout, "This should not be!" I silenced them. This awful moment had come and now wasn't about me.

"Jeremy," the neighbor called out, "Could you help me here for a minute?"

As the little boy ran past me, he gave me a friendly look of curiosity. Little could he imagine that I was a messenger bearing the worst news of his life.

Pulling groceries out of the trunk, Mrs. Henderson didn't see me approaching her. "Mrs. Henderson," I said as gently as I could.

Startled, she turned around quickly, her arms overflowing with grocery bags. Time stood still as her eyes went immediately to my chaplaincy badge. Without a word, Mrs. Henderson screamed in utter despair.

"No, God. No. No!" she cried out.

Like a rag doll, she collapsed to the pavement with her groceries tumbling down the street like so many marbles. I caught her and carried her into the house.

✧ ✧ ✧

Lasting the Night

✧ ✧ ✧

"If you can't feed a hundred people, then feed just one."
Mother Teresa

"Where?" I asked the dispatcher a second time just to make sure. "On the bed? She did it on his bed?"

It had been a lover's dispute turned ugly. A boyfriend had returned home late at night only to discover that his girlfriend had committed suicide on his bed.

The clock in my car read 2:00 a.m. as I reached the small, rural ranch house. Red lights from the sheriff's car cast an intermittent red mist over the oak trees, illuminating the long hanging Spanish moss.

As I reached the front door, it opened and there stood the county sheriff and the coroner.

Be prepared, their looks warned me.

How does anyone prepare for death?

What can you say to that vulgar Resident Alien? It is cruel, heartless and unswerving; an ugly bastard who has claimed earth as *his* home. Our only consolation is that some day, on some horizon moment, Death itself will die.

As a wall of police officers parted for me, I entered the house only to be hit by the smell of death hanging over the atmosphere like a shroud. I asked how long the body had been there. More than ten hours, was the response. Waving me on, an officer led me to the boyfriend who was sitting in a disheveled bedroom down the stairs.

"I…I simply told her it was over," the dazed boyfriend looked up at me. "I…I was breaking up with her. I never thought. She…I… How could she? It just wasn't working out. I…I… I had no idea she would do this! All I wanted to do was untangle what wasn't working for any of us. How do I live with this? How will I ever forget this night?"

I did not know. I didn't have the answers. I had no nice, neat package of four spiritual laws in my pocket that would make this terrible tragedy better. All I had to give him was my companionship in his suffering.

He was right; the memory of this night would be his forever. The boyfriend would never forget his girlfriend now; her sad and irretrievable act of revenge guaranteed it. In her anguish and disappointment, the girlfriend had voiced her complaint to the Universe. Life had not turned out the way she had thought it should.

Nor as he could have ever imagined.

✡ ✡ ✡

Bitching

✡ ✡ ✡

"To be grateful for the good things that happen in our lives is easy, but to be grateful for all our lives the good as well as the bad, the moments of joy as well as the moments of sorrow, the successes as well as the

failures, the rewards as well as the rejections that requires hard spiritual work…. As long as we keep dividing our lives between events and people we would like to remember and those we would rather forget, we cannot claim the fullness of our beings as a gift from God to be grateful for."[2]

Henri Nouwen

Blah. Blah. Blah. Blah.	*I feel sick.*
Blah. Blah. Blah. Blah.	*Why did I ever agree to do this training?*
Blah. Blah. Blah. Blah.	*I am sick and I probably got it from someone in*
here.	
Blah. Blah. Blah. Blah.	*How much longer? I want out.*
Blah. Blah. Blah. Blah.	*I wish all these people would get off it.*
Blah. Blah. Blah. Blah.	*I bet if I run away no one would even notice.*
Blah. Blah. Blah. Blah.	*Hey. Look. Somebody! I'm sick up in here.*

"**D**an!" A direct hit by Sarah's elbow into my ribcage interrupted my internal complaining.

"Still with us? Tune in, big guy. Your smile looks pasted on. Dan?" Sarah pressed her face next to mine, "Dan!"

I was caught red-handed with my own thoughts. "I am listening, Sarah." I said, lying so cordially that it impressed her immensely.

"Right, liar."

We were in the middle of Day Two of a Discovery Seminar and I was sick as a dog. The truth was that despite all my overt professional caring for those participating in this training, I was complaining where no one but me and God could hear and I was pretty sure He had checked out on me a few hours ago.

The participant who had been speaking was talking about how his wife didn't understand him, saying that he was certain that if she would have attended this Discovery Seminar, then there might have been some possibility to revive the passion in their relationship.

As much as I intended to focus on what he and others were saying, I found myself becoming more and more impatient with all of them. "Get to the bottom line," I murmured inside my feverish head *with* a smile, "Before I help you get to the bottom line."

With that lovely gesture, a thought smacked me right across the head. *So, Dan. You want the bottom line, huh?*

Pleeease.

All right, the thought responded. *Listen to what is being said.*

Ah. I was.

Not.

Okay. The participants are sharing *about important things in their lives.*

Try again. With some authenticity.

Hum. He's complaining about his wife. I'm complaining about being here. Ugh. Everyone is just complaining.

What do you think would happen, Dan, if you actively gave up your complaint? What if you stopped hiding behind how you think life should be and started participating fully in it as it is showing up?

Great question. Well, I would lose the payoff I get out of complaining. Being right. Being in control. Holding onto the offenses I have towards other people. I would lose my license to do to others what I would not want done to me.

And then?

I would be responsible for myself. And, I'd be free. Probably scared at the ambiguity of what I can't control. Even grateful because I would see possibility instead of what's not working. Wow. Now, that is something, the more I think about it. I was like a blind man seeing for the first time.

We are complaining machines. We even complain about the complaining, "I am sorry for complaining about this, but…" As human beings we have a complaint, a big one with God and life in general. We are angry because the only truly predictable thing is that we are going to die, which isn't how we believe life "should" ultimately turn out.

Grumble. Murmur. Self-Ambition. Bitch. Moan. Gripe. Maneuvering. Scorn. Lament. Self-Preservation. Interpretation. Isolation. Rudeness. Pissed Off. Dissed. Whine. Impatience. Self-martyrdom. Hatred. Compromise. Disdain. Extortion. Criticism. Threat. Withdrawal. All uniquely the same version of the same fundamental underlying complaint.

Death.

Although we often dress up our complaint in pretty, socially acceptable language, I have found that it goes something like this:

I am going to die.
Because I am going to die everything about life is futile, scarce and inevitable.
Life should not be this way!
God has not provided for me ultimately because He knows that I am going to die.
This means that God doesn't mean what He promises and does not really love me and I am on my own down here. So I am going to do whatever I need to do for myself in order to survive.

Don't believe me? Test it for yourself.

In the next twenty-four hours, observe your thoughts and your conversations when something does not go your way—i.e. the way you think it *should go*. What are you thinking when someone cuts in front of you in line? Or your stock price falls? Are you saying the drive-thru window line is moving slowly? How do you react when the dentist makes you wait for thirty minutes? The bank account is overdrawn?

Do you disguise your complaint in something like this: "When my wife tells me that I am XYZ, it is clear that she just does not understand me. She's not getting who I am." Or are you blatantly out there saying, "My boss is the worst manager. Why did they ever decide to hire him?"

Be honest.

Are you grateful for how your life is showing up? Or how many different ways are you saying to yourself, "Life *(my life)* should not be this way?" How are you commiserating with others about *the state of affairs* in your lives and then calling that *friendship*?

For example, I was raging on our local city council with a friend, telling what I did not like about what the council was deciding. After my friend left, my wife mentioned that there was a city council meeting that evening dealing with a new street in our neighborhood that we did not want. When she asked me to go and even call my friend to go with me, I told her I had better things to do with my time.

"You know, Dan," Aileen answered with some feedback, "I think you and your friend are more accomplices than friends!"

I retorted sharply, "What are you talking about?"

Aileen smiled, "It seems to me that you two seem to have a relationship that is established on complaining. However, your actions tell me that you don't really mean what you say and your friendship is simply a way to make you feel good about not doing any-thing. You get to be right about government not working well and you don't have to do anything about what it is you see as possible."

Wow. I got her point. There was a long silence between us until finally she said, "Did you hear what I said, Dan?"

As I walked to my closet to get dressed for the city council meet-ing, I replied, "Only too well."

You and I exist in an equation that includes death, and there is nothing that we can do about it. No matter what winning ways we concoct to keep ourselves protected from loss, suffering and being nonexistent, we know deep down that we will lose in the end at some point.

We hear Peter Pan's alligator, the one who swallowed the clock, always coming for us. Although we don't see that monster, the ever-present sound of his ticking clock tells us that he won't stop trying to swallow us alive. No matter how hard we work to get away, we hear his clock ticking.

It shows up every day in our pain, indifference, anxieties and despair.

Whether this pain is physical, emotional, mental or spiritual, our complaint is never fully satisfied. Whether it is the wrinkle creams we buy, the business deals that run amok or even our immaculate attendance at work, we can still feel the hangman's noose hovering above our heads.

Each bit of pain reminds us that someday we will lose everything including our own lives, and all we worked for, saved and cultivated will go to somebody else to do with as they please.

Like an ever-present, always continuing hunger, the complaint going on inside us is like a rogue computer virus. Every day we listen to it as we play the game of survival with ourselves and each other, acting as though we can grab that brass ring that this life, God or whatever seems so unwilling or unable to give us. Through it, we voice our refusal to let go of our uniquely-the-same version of how life *should be* instead of surrendering to the way that *it is*.

"Life should not be this way, but it is," we murmur. "Where is God and why the hell isn't He doing something about it? Why did God do this to us? And, if He didn't do this to us, why did He allow it to happen?"

Our complaint is something that we hide behind. I say, it is an expression of *contempt* that we use as a mechanism to make life about us and to justify our selfish actions or lack of action in our relationships with others. It is the gasoline in the tank of our winning ways and those survival strategies that we employ to get what we believe we deserve and are afraid we will never receive.

Go back to Adam in the Garden and you will see that the complaint existed even in Paradise. Listen to Adam's response to God after Adam did what God had told him not to do.

"It was the woman You gave me." (Translation: "The fact that I am now going to die is all your fault, God because of what you did to me.")

Now I am a man and I *know* that Adam was thinking a lot more than what was coming out of his mouth.

"I couldn't do anything when Eve was talking to the Serpent or she would have left me. There was nothing I could say that would have made a difference. Of course, I ate the fruit because I don't want her to leave me by dying. Or did You give her to me only to have her leave me now?" Where were You when I was about to screw everything up? You did not provide for me. Now my days are numbered. Time is short. All that I do is ultimately futile."

Despite his intimate relationship with God, Adam made an incredible choice.

He aligned himself with *a conversation* based on a lie one that I assert existed before he did. Consider for a second the possibility that lie-based conversations the Serpent's lie, the accusation of God and the complaint all pre-existed Adam. What if the complaint was waiting for Adam when he was yet dust in the earth?

Take a look at Genesis 3:2-5 (NIV):

The woman (Eve) said to the serpent, "We may eat fruit from the trees in the garden, but God did say, 'You must not eat fruit from the tree that is in the middle of the garden, and you must not touch it, or you will die.'"
"You will not surely die," the serpent said to the woman. "For God knows that when you eat of it your eyes will be opened, and you will be like God, knowing good and evil."

We know *now* that "You will not surely die" was the lie which caused Adam and Eve to be suspicious of God. However, does the possibility that this lie-based conversation existed before Adam and Eve get them off the hook?

I don't think so.

God was no stranger to these first humans. They talked face-to-face every day. They had no walls between them, no secret agendas, no mistrust. However before Adam took the forbidden fruit into his hands, something occurred that transformed his relationship with God.

Adam chose to *agree with thoughts* that cast doubt on the goodness of God.

By taking those thoughts as his own, Adam began to suspect the One who had never once restrained His love, affection and attention towards him. In doing so, Adam shifted his internal conversation about God so radically that it showed up in his actions.

And, for the first time in his life, Adam hid from God because "as a man thinketh, so is he." (Proverbs 23:7)

In *The Brothers Karamazov*[3] by Fyodor Dostoevsky, there are some powerful insights into our complaint. In the story, Father Zossima is a priest who mentors the youngest Karamazov brother. One day, when the priest is visiting a nearby village, townsfolk race out of their homes to ask him for prayer and help, including a mother who begs the priest for help with her ill daughter.

In the face of her dire suffering, this is what the priest has to say to the woman with the ill daughter.

*If you do **not** attain happiness, always remember that you are on a good path and try not to leave it. Above all, **avoid lies**, all lies, **especially the lie to yourself**.*

*Keep watch on your own lie **and examine it** every hour, every minute. And avoid **contempt**, both of others and of yourself: **what seems bad to you** in yourself is purified by the very fact that you have **noticed it in yourself**.*

*And avoid fear, though **fear is simply the consequence of every lie**. Never be frightened at your own faintheartedness in attaining love, and meanwhile do not even be very frightened by your own bad acts. I am sorry that I cannot say anything more comforting, for **active love is a harsh and fearful thing compared with love in dreams**. Love in dreams thirsts for immediate action, quickly performed, and with everyone watching. Indeed, it will go as far as the giving even of one's life, provided it does not take long but is soon over, as on stage, and everyone is looking on and praising.*

*Whereas **active love is labor and perseverance**, and for some people, perhaps, a whole science.*

*But I predict that even in that very moment when you see with horror that despite all your efforts, you **not** only have **not** come nearer your goal but seem to have gotten farther from it, at that very moment I predict this to you, you will suddenly reach your goal and will clearly behold over you **the wonder-working power of the Lord, who all the while has been loving you,** and all the while has been mysteriously guiding you."*

✧ ✧ ✧

Too Expensive

✧ ✧ ✧

"With certainty of death, and little chance for success; what are we waiting for?"
Dwarf King: *The Return of the King* (New Line Cinema, 2003)

The actor's line caught my attention:
"This is the only thing in my life I feel good about."
I thought, "Hum. That was said with such subtle contempt. This isn't a boxing movie. This film is about our complaint."
The movie I was watching was Clint Eastwood's *Million Dollar Baby* (Warner Bros. Pictures, 2005). Some audiences loved it, describing the film as an inspirational love story with heart and courage. Others were much less enthusiastic, calling the film a total set-up for a lecture on euthanasia.

Critics aside, if you take the time to watch *Million Dollar Baby*, you will see the complaint staring you in the face.

Shot in despairing gray-green colors, *Million Dollar Baby* is a story about Frankie Dunn, a broken-down L.A. boxing trainer who reluctantly takes on an unlikely boxer in the form of Maggie Fitzgerald, a thirty-one-year-old, ex-trailer trash turned champion-in-the-making woman.

Estranged from his own daughter, Frankie is an Irish Catholic who goes to mass daily sometimes, it appears, to simply irritate the living daylights out of the priest. "So the Holy Trinity is something like Snap, Crackle and Pop?" Frankie quips.

Underneath that cynicism, however, Frankie appears to be on a *continual and unresolved search* to come to terms with the past (things that *should not* have happened) and the future (where things that *should not* happen *could* occur). The world that Frankie creates with his gym which looks like some relic of a by-gone era is one of never-ending, unsatisfied penance.

In his complaint, Frank's winning way is something like this: *Above all else, protect yourself.* Through this life-mantra (or scam), Frankie displays his contempt for what has happened to him in the past.

Sound familiar? *Just take care of #1. If you don't take care of yourself, who will?* Basically the bottom line is: "*It's a cruel world out there and to get by you need to look out for yourself because nobody else will!*"

Stop for a second.

How many different versions of this winning way might you be using yourself? How many times have you thought these thoughts in your relationships with other people?

Certainly this scam will keep you surviving but forget about developing relationships that are anything more than utilitarian. Once people have lost their purpose, the only thing left to do is suspect them because they might be playing the same game with you!

Into the middle of Frankie's failed attempts at self-redemption comes Maggie Fitzgerald. Sure. All of us want to root for Maggie. She is a dreamer who. despite having all the odds being stacked against her (age, economic status, past experience or training), is going for the gold.

At times, we feel just like her. We want the impossible to be possible. We want to feel like champions when it comes to our winning ways down here on Planet Earth. Maggie is going for her dream just like we wish *we* were. In the game of boxing, Maggie has found purpose.

As she tells Frankie, "This is the only thing in my life I feel good about." Her winning way goes something like this: *Be willing to do whatever it takes to get what you want and life will turn out the way it should.*

How many motivational, get-ahead programs tell us the same thing?

As Frankie tells Maggie, "Girlie, tough ain't enough." How often are we just performing to get what we want or to feel good about ourselves? How many lies will we tell? How many relationships will we trash? How many game plans will we concoct? How many 12-step dances will we trip through trying to win the title belt?

As the film boxes on and Maggie under Frankie's training starts to climb the success ladder, you start to get this feeling that somehow this is *all too easy*. Your intuitive "oh no" feelings are confirmed like a flashing neon sign during a scene at a gas station when Maggie tells Frankie about her father killing their crippled dog with a shovel.

Like hearing that unforgettable music in *Jaws*, you sense that a deadly Great White shark is swimming in these seas.

Sure enough.

The minute Maggie captures the title fight and has proven all her critics wrong, her evil opponent *breaks the rules of the game*. Her opponent plays Maggie's own winning strategy against her by *doing whatever it takes to get what* she *wants*.

Her opponent hits Maggie from behind. and Maggie breaks her neck on a chair because Frankie is unable to move it in time. Frankie fails in his winning way to protect his now surrogate daughter, simultaneously reinforcing his complaint and stoking his contempt for the way that life is turning out. Boxer turned paraplegic; Maggie has lost "the only good thing in her life."

At that moment, the whole movie, which is based on a true story, turns on the question: *What is the value of living when you have lost your dream?* And, we understand. In Maggie's loss, we see our own paraplegic life. We are staring in the face of the divorce we are going through, the career that we never had, the death of a child or loved one, or the business we loved that had gone bankrupt.

In final scenes of the movie, Maggie asks Frankie to end her life and we universally understand why he pulls the plug. If I can't have what I want the way I want it, then life is not worth living; life is meaningless. Maggie is acting out our contempt of being deprived of what we have set our hearts on and not getting what we want. When all possibility of having what we think we should have is dead, what else is there to live for?

To me, the misfortune of *Million Dollar Baby* is not that they decided as filmmakers to end the film this way. That's their perspective. Rather it is that the film ignores the proverbial elephant in the room.

In *Million Dollar Baby,* no one is talking possibility, only complaint.

The film does not consider the value that exists in suffering. Maybe that is because there is no understanding of the value of being met in our suffering by something beyond our expectations; Someone beyond us. Instead of dealing with or even considering the tougher choice of living a life when all hope for that one good thing is gone when life is not turning out as it should they opt out, certain that all there is, is what we can see and what we know. They pursue the logical result of the complaint. Because life is scarce, futile and inevitable, then life is ultimately not worth living. Suicide then becomes the ultimate expression of contempt for life not turning out the way one thinks it should.

The film bypasses the countless people who have risen out of the ashes of ruin and disappointment to live rewarding and world-changing lives. Take, for example, Christopher Reeve, Joni Eriksson Tada, Franklin D. Roosevelt, Helen Keller and Lance Armstrong to name just a few. Their character in the midst of suffering and their creative expression of the indomitable human spirit will speak well of them beyond their deaths to generations of people. Their character was defined by something bigger than themselves. I doubt that these people didn't complain, but there must have been something about how they related to their complaints that opened up possibility for them to "presence" the character to persevere. I believe there was some way of relating or standing in the circumstances that transformed the purpose that was being served in their life by doing what they were so good at into the very core of their character.

Even as a paraplegic, Maggie could have been a champion to the world. It just would have been in a different form and with different possibilities.

Maggie and Frankie could have come out of hiding and stood, engaging reality as a provision for a future worth having with others. They could have lived through their complaint, showing up from a perspective of being met in the midst of their suffering by a possibility bigger than their lost expectations.

I have actually witnessed this kind of character firsthand in my own life. When I was in high school my dear friend Rob was one of the best athletes I knew. We played together on a football team and he was an all star half-back. Rob was always a sports enthusiast who was extremely close to his family. During a high school football practice he was tackled and broke his neck, paralyzing him from the neck down, leaving him with only limited movement in his arms. Initially, his tragic circumstances were devastating to all of us.

But, through the years Rob's stand became a powerful inspiration for me and all of his teammates, as well as the rest of the school and faculty. He stood for something bigger than being a great athlete. His commitment to contributing to others through sports transformed into new expressions of life. While I know he struggled with many difficult questions and tough situations and he had very real complaints on his journey, he managed to stand in such a way that the treacherous traps of despair didn't take him out, but actually formed his character in a way that opened possibility for our community.

Today Rob is married and has a beautiful family. He has managed an athletic center for well over twenty years. When I see Rob, I am always moved by his authenticity, love and commitment to others. He is one of my heroes, and his life has demonstrated what is possible when a person chooses to stand for what they long for in the face of what looks like impossible circumstances. Rob has literally transformed his purpose into his own character, and in doing so has left a mark on my life as well as the character of our community.

So, complaining in and of itself doesn't have to destroy a life, in fact, complaining is a cathartic way to lament misfortune. The Psalms are great examples of the power of complaint in this context, which is a whole other book. The question is: What am I using the complaint for?

Is my complaint a story to justify my resignation from life, or is it a way of passing through great suffering to new possibility, a way of passing through death expecting to be resurrected?

Really the vision behind the complaint, will determine our intent in the complaint. For example:

If I have a vision of a God who is with me and will emerge in the midst of the suffering with new possibility, then my intention in my complaint is to give myself to the catharsis in the process of waiting on God to meet me.

If my vision is that there is no God or that He doesn't provide and I must provide for myself, then the intent in my complaint will be to resign from life using the complaint as my justification for being self absorbed.

Ultimately, I say we long for what our complaint can't give us.

✧ ✧ ✧

The Man in the Mirror

✧ ✧ ✧

"It is Doubt (so often experienced initially as weakness) that changes things. When a man feels unsteady, when he falters, when hard-won knowledge evaporates before his eyes, he's on the verge of growth. The subtle or violent reconciliation of the outer person and the inner core often seems at first like a mistake; like you've gone the wrong way and you're lost. But this is just emotion longing for the familiar. Life happens when the tectonic power of your speechless soul breaks through the dead habits of the mind. Doubt is nothing less than an opportunity to reenter the Present."[4]
John Patrick Shanley

"You are always interrupting me, Dan."

I had known Joe for over ten years now. Over the last few months, our friendship had hit a huge ditch over a business situation that had gone south. After too much avoidance and too many bruised feelings, we bit the bullet and sat down together at his house.

Up until this time, Joe and I had been close. He is a creative man who had always been a generous supporter of our ministry work. We were so close that a few years ago he even asked me and another friend to help him restore his marriage. Yet at this moment we were swimming in breakdown, hoping that the sharks would get the other guy first.

"Shut up, Dan!" he said again, "You always interrupt me."

Okay. Got it. For two hours straight, I said nothing.

As I fumed under my collar, I was sure beyond any shadow of a doubt that I was completely legitimate in my complaint against Joe. The fact that he had not asked me once about where I was in our relationship further proved to me that I was on the mark. I knew *I was right*. All Joe wanted was to be right about his point of view.

As much as I sought to listen, what I was really thinking inside was, *It is crystal clear to me that you don't understand me, Joe. If you did, it would certainly help you a lot.*

Then, for a split second, I caught myself and what I was saying inside my head. *Hum. It's getting awful loud inside here*, I realized. I began to see that my complaint and contempt for Joe was so distracting that I was having difficulty hearing *anything* he was trying to tell me.

My complaint that I was misunderstood had me snookered, hooked like a bass on a line; it was such a great justification to resign from the conversation by not listening to what my friend had to say.

Taking a deep breath, I took the hook out of my mouth. I rigorously refused to engage my complaint against him and instead chose to consider him, my good friend. Remembering who we were for each other, I started to actually hear what he was saying. I realized that he thought (just like me) that he was legitimate in his complaint, and I began to see *why* he thought the way he did. I got his assertions about me even though they were not what I meant or even intended.

As I listened, I saw that I could appreciate his point of view without having to defend mine. Even though I didn't agree with most of his judgments concerning me, I did get the impact my actions and lack of actions had on his life and hearing them gave me a powerful experience of how he was feeling and the source of his pain and frustration.

Because I had taken the log of my complaint out of my own eye, I saw how Joe got to where he was in our relationship. I saw how my complaint perverted everything, like mud on a camera lens. I realized that I could love Joe instead of making him the object of my anger.

When *it* (relationships, work, desires, personal ambition) does not show up the way we think *it should*, we tend to get offended. Instead of giving up the complaint in order to see what possibilities might exist, we get more and more offended at what we view as our loss.

We blame our spouse, partner, God, friends, employer and our past. We use everything to justify our complaint against life not turning out as it should. Every additional experience makes us completely blind and oblivious to the innumerable routes of reconciliation that are possible when we are willing to show up. In other words, willing to come out from behind the way we think life should be and engage the reality of how it is.

When we engage our complaint to avoid life and justify resigning, we build a case for the pittance we have produced through our winning ways. We fill our lives with endless rows of body bags; little deaths, failed expectations and endless reminders that tell us that our winning approaches to life are not sufficient. Each one sits there as ever-present deadly evidence telling us that life is scarce, inevitable and futile.

As we hide behind what *should be,* we fill our life with sacred cows.

"Now that I have Jesus, Mohammed, Buddha *(you can fill in the blanks),* I'm saved and going to heaven, Nirvana, Valhalla, the Happy Hunting Grounds."

Instead of faith being about a relationship with God through others, our winning ways end up being another version of Survival 101, where we reduce the Divine down to insipid self-help formulas or some street philosophy that does more to justify my playing not to lose the little I have settled for instead of playing to win my heart's desire.

We choose the lie that we can protect ourselves from the truth that our lives will end and there is nothing we can do about it. We ignore our latent contempt for God's seemingly lack of action in what we want the most namely, to beat death and as a result, we reduce God down to what can be defined or figured out on our terms. We strip the Infinite One down to a formula, a tradition or a nice feeling and make a complete mockery of the glorious, wild and uncontrollable being that He is and we are in Him.

As a result, instead of getting out of the boat and walking on that water despite our fears and doubts, we ignore the fact that playing not to lose has its own inheritance of resignation, ambivalence and cordial hypocrisy.

All the while we go to church, synagogue, mosque, or the movies thanking God for the little we do have instead of receiving all of the blessings that are possible if we would just drop the complaint.

And, come out of our shadows into the light.

✡ ✡ ✡

Playing to Win

✡ ✡ ✡

It came on suddenly. Aileen's mother had cancer. Hearing the news, my complaint became very obvious and trivial.

Great. There goes Aileen for the next few years. Call it just another version of: *God isn't taking care of me.*

As I looked at my complaint, I saw a root in my childhood. During my early childhood years, my mother was manic-depressive and my parents eventually got divorced. Despite having four children, Mom and Dad were most often wrapped up with the problems in their own lives, and even into my early twenties I felt alone and unable to handle the pressures that I was experiencing.

Now, flash forward.

I am in my late thirties and Aileen tells me that my mother-in-law, Eva, has been diagnosed with a severe form of cancer. Automatically my mind goes to my complaint: no one is going to be around to take care of me.

As I catch myself thinking these thoughts, I realize that if I indulge this complaint right now, I am going to destroy everything I value my relationship with Aileen and my children and the future worth having together. My horrid, God-forsaken complaint would eventually cause me to resent my mother-in-law Eva for dying and alienate me from my family.

Like a lightning bolt, I saw that my inheritance in this life was coming to me in a way that I did not expect. In fact, how life was showing up looked like a threat, and if I treated it as such, then I would lose everything.

Seeing, I started to have waves of guilt for how I was feeling. Then I saw that these feelings were simply another back door into my complaint.

I was *still scamming* myself for the purpose of avoiding the reality and getting what I thought I deserved.

If I felt guilty, then I could feel sorry for myself and ask for forgiveness. Once again, I could become the center of attention and turn everyone towards *taking care of me*—full of myself.

The truth of that fact hit me full-force.

If I wanted an intimate, loving family, then I was being called to a much bigger game. I had to take on my complaint by coming out of hiding and confront the way I wanted life to show up and purposefully and intentionally engage life as it really was.

Although I could not stop the voice of the complaint inside, I could ignore and forsake it. I could choose to love Eva 1000%.

So I did. I jumped with both feet into this crisis. I chose to act against satisfying my own needs first. Instead, I took care of Eva, my wife and our family in every way I could.

And as all of us stood together in how life was showing up *in death*, I found that Someone else was standing with us.

✧ ✧ ✧

The Rest of the Story

✧ ✧ ✧

"There's something deep and enduring within all of us that is so strong that unless we have been challenged we'd never have known we have it."

Marty Head, Businesswoman

I still have their cards tucked away. Their stories have turned out differently than anyone would have predicted.

For years after the truck accident, the father of the two boys faithfully sent me a card on the day of its anniversary. Although the boys were pronounced brain-dead at the scene, they had survived miraculously. The last I heard, they were going to school and being kids once again. To this day, when I see the highway patrol officer from the tragedy, he goes out of his way to greet me.

Many months after her son's death, I heard from Mrs. Henderson. She thanked me for helping her on that day and the days that followed. She told me that despite their suffering, their lives were moving forward.

On the night of his girlfriend's suicide, the boyfriend had nowhere to go. So I invited him home and we talked into the early morning about his feelings and loss. We read the suicide note together and wept over the choice his girlfriend had made. In the morning, Aileen cooked us both breakfast. About five months later, he wrote us a letter to thank us. In the letter, he said he had thought of us many times since the suicide, saying that words could not describe how our presence that night helped him in his mourning and then eventually into the next phase of his life.

I wish I could take some credit here but I can't.

With each crisis, all I did was manage the complaint going on inside my head and come out from behind it. I listened, wept with those who were suffering and let myself be with what *was* instead of running away or trying to fix it. In a very real and tangible way, I surrendered to reality and began to *rest in the presence of the one who established me.* In the calm of that surrender, I looked, listened and waited for God's presence He who is that "peace which surpasses all understanding."

In our helplessness, God showed up and dwelt among us.

In the face of death, He provided His presence and, as my friend Dostoevsky has said, we saw and "clearly beheld over us the wonder-working power of the Lord, who all the while was loving us, and all the while had been mysteriously guiding us."

Notes:

[1] Herman Hesse, "My Belief: Essays on Life and Art"; *Diary* (1918).
[2] Henri Nouwen, *Bread for the Journey* (HarperCollins Publishers, 1997).
[3] Fyodor Dostoevsky, *The Brothers Karamazov*, Chapter 4: "A Lady of Little Faith" (1880).
[4] Foreword to the play "Doubt: A Parable" by John Patrick Shanley (2004).

DOWN IN THE FOX HOLE

✧ ✧ ✧

Being "With It"

✧ ✧ ✧

"May the words of my mouth and the meditation of my heart
be pleasing in your sight,
O LORD, my Rock and my Redeemer."
Psalm 19:14 (NIV)

My beard is scruffy; my hair's even worse.
I feel like grizzly bear wakened too soon from his hibernation. Yesterday's sweats are today, tomorrow and the next day's clothes of choice and, with a leg harnessed in a torture device left over from the polio era, I am hobbling around like an old gold miner who has been underground in the dark for way too many years.

A friend has even nicknamed me, "Mountain Man Dan."

Although the near demise of my knee on the ski slopes happened only three weeks ago, it feels like centuries and, despite the great news from our surgeon that I would walk without crutches and would someday be able to run and bike again, cabin fever has set in like cement. I am beginning to suspect that Aileen and the kids are thinking that a vacation *alone* in Tahiti would be a nice idea right now.

Truth be told, what occupies my thoughts, heart and meditations with God the most right now is not my leg but engaging
life fully as it is showing up. What attitude will open up the greatest possibility for my family and me during this time of recovery?
What ways of relating will open resources where there seem to be
none?

Where can I find conversations that will bring character, courage
and love?

I found some, in the last place you might expect. The movies.

✡ ✡ ✡

Band of Brothers
Episode Three: Caretan

✡ ✡ ✡

*"Courage is almost a contradiction in terms. It means a strong desire to
live taking the form of a readiness to die. 'He that will lose his life, the
same shall save it,' is not a piece of mysticism for saints and heroes…a
soldier surrounded by enemies, if he is to cut his way out, needs to
combine a strong desire for living with a strange carelessness about
dying. He must not merely cling to life, for then he will be a coward,
and will not escape. He must not merely wait for death, for then he
will be a suicide, and will not escape. He must seek his life in a spirit of
furious indifference to it; he must desire life like water and yet
drink death like wine."[1]*

G.K. Chesterton

The night was thick with lightning, thunder and fear.

On D-Day (June 4, 1944), the men from Easy Company, part of
America's 106th Parachute Infantry Regiment, had parachuted into
hell at Normandy. Some of the men survived the jump; others did
not. The remainder were scattered across occupied France like burning embers in the wind.

This night, the soldiers of Easy Company were slammed
down along a ridge. Within earshot were the Germans, who were

well-armed and positioned on a nearby ridge. At dawn's first light, the fighting will begin and men will die.

Hunkered down in a mud-filled foxhole, a young American private, Albert Blithe, waits in terror at what the morning will inevitably bring. Then out of the night's darkness walks Lieutenant Spears, a man of few words, who has a reputation for insane acts of courage and merciless killing of the enemy. Unlike the rest of the soldiers hiding in their foxholes, the lieutenant is upright, walking the ridgeline.

Seeing Blithe, he stops.

LIEUTENANT SPEARS: Have some nervous privates in your company?

PRIVATE BLITHE: Do, sir. Can vouch for that.

LIEUTENANT SPEARS: They just don't see how simple it is.

PRIVATE BLITHE: Simple. What is, sir?

LIEUTENANT SPEARS: Just do what you have to do.

PRIVATE BLITHE: Like you did on D-Day, sir?

Lieutenant Spears looks at Blithe silently.

PRIVATE BLITHE: Sir, when I landed on D-Day I found myself in a ditch all by myself. I fell asleep. I think it was those air sickness pills they gave us. When I woke up, I didn't try to find my unit to fight. I just kind of stayed put.

LIEUTENANT SPEARS: What's your name, trooper?

PRIVATE BLITHE: Albert Blithe, sir.

LIEUTENANT SPEARS: You know why you hid in that ditch, Blithe?

PRIVATE BLITHE: I was scared.

LIEUTENANT SPEARS: We are all scared. You hid in that ditch because you think there is still hope. But Blithe, the only hope you have is to accept the fact that you are already dead. As soon as you accept that, the sooner you will be able to function as a soldier is supposed to function. All war depends upon it.

Watching this scene from *Band of Brothers* (HBO 2001)[2], I was stunned.

Lieutenant Spears told Blithe the last words he wanted to hear. The first enemy Blithe had to kill was the hope that he was going to make it out alive. In other words, Blithe needed to let go of the way he thought life *should be* and engage it as it was.

If he was ever going to live *now* and answer the call to fight for his fellow soldiers and his country, Blithe had to accept the fact that he was a dead man walking.

The only thing Blithe *could* choose was *how* he was going to live life until that final moment arrived.

Would he die as a coward or as a man who had transcended his fears? Would he choose ignominy or would the life of Albert Blithe be a statement of honor, glory and transcendent love? Was there a vision Blithe could make his own? A vision so significant that he would get out of the foxhole and die for its possibility?

I wondered.

What keeps us hunkered down in our foxholes? Why are we so convinced that life is somehow safer down there?

As I said before, I believe we create foxholes because we don't think that God has our back.

Instead of having our heels down on the necks of our fears, we squat down in the mud, sweat and blood of this life. Although we know that the enemy is out there in the dark, we don't risk standing up to see how he is advancing on us. Day after day, down in our private foxholes, we manage the night of our fears with thoughts riddled with desperation, regret, censure, fault-finding, resentment and pain. In relentless waiting, we hold our rifles to our chests, hoping that we will never have to use them and that the enemy will somehow pass us by.

I know what it's like to be hunkered down deep in the foxhole.

It was not too many years ago when death was waiting for me on the next ridge. Unlike Private Blithe, I did not realize it until way too late.

The night was little more than halfway over by the time I left the party. Although I felt a little guilty for leaving Aileen home alone so long, the food, wine and cocaine had been too tempting, and after a tough week of work I had willingly yielded to indulging myself.

The farthest thing from my mind that February night in 1981 was that my life was about to be over.

After all the goodbyes had been said, I climbed into my black BMW with a yawn, regretting that home was more than an hour away. The good news was that I knew the winding road well and traffic was guaranteed to be light. High from the cocaine and very wide awake, I pushed the car up to 70 mph.

Up until that night, my twenty-six years of living had been a lot like my sleek, well-tuned car. I was after the fully loaded package, looking for every available advantage that served me. I was hungry to be satisfied and, when out of control, could be dangerous. My vision extended no further than myself because seeing beyond the horizon never once occurred to me as a possibility.

I never expected to be hit head-on. But I was.

The other car's headlights came right at my face. In a moment that seemed removed from time, the BMW's steering column smashed into my chest, collapsed my lungs and cut my diaphragm like a knife. The brake, clutch and gas pedals bounced up into my jaw, breaking it into pieces. My right femur snapped like a twig and my liver ripped like paper.

Blood flowed out of me like a flood. I was dying.

My life was about to end, but I was not ready. I had chosen to live down in a foxhole, missing the opportunities to stand for what I longed for but thought impossible. Like Private Blithe, in the face of enemy fire, I had stayed in the mud instead of getting out and taking the ridge. Little did I anticipate that night driving home that my enemy had not only reached my foxhole but was about to jump into it.

As I lay dying in my crumpled car in the middle of the freeway, I was in a state similar to those moments between sleep and wakefulness. There, I found myself in a presence that I instinctively knew was Jesus. I felt Him stroking His fingers through my hair, like a father would his child.

I heard Him ask me, "Do you want to stay with Me or go back to work? You have much work to do."

I told Jesus that I wanted to go back. I wanted a second chance at creating a life worth living, and this time I wanted to live not for myself, but for Him and for others.

Instantly, I awoke to blaring sirens and ambulance lights.

In the midst of weeks of hospitalization and life-changing shifts, the love of God would continually speak to me just like Lieutenant Spears did to Blithe. Would I be a dead man walking?

Did I have a vision worth dying for? More importantly, did I have a vision worth living for? What would Daniel Tocchini's life contribute to this world? In my struggle to find answers to these questions, I discovered some resistance.

My own and some from the complaints of humanity, in general.

✡ ✡ ✡

The Wisdom of Solomon

✡ ✡ ✡

"I could not, at any age, be content to take my place by the fireside and simply look on. Life was meant to be lived. Curiosity must be kept alive. One must never, for whatever reason, turn his back on life."[3]
Eleanor Roosevelt

And I set my heart to know wisdom and to know madness and folly.
I perceived that this also is grasping for the wind.
I said in my heart, "Come now, I will test you with mirth;
therefore enjoy pleasure" but this was vanity.

✡ ✡ ✡

I made my works great. I built myself houses and planted myself vineyards.
I acquired male and female servants…I had greater possessions of herds and flocks than all who were in Jerusalem before me.

✡ ✡ ✡

I became great and excelled more than all who were before me in Jerusalem. Also my wisdom remained with me.

✡ ✡ ✡

Whatever my eyes desired, I did not keep from them.
I did not withhold my heart from any pleasure
for my heart rejoiced in all my labor;
and this was my reward from all my labor.

✡ ✡ ✡

Then I looked on all the works that my hands had done
and on the labor in which I had toiled
and indeed all was vanity and grasping for the wind.
There was no profit under the sun.

✡ ✡ ✡

Therefore I hated life
because the work that was done under the sun was distressing to me
for all is vanity and grasping for the wind.

✿ ✿ ✿

Then I hated all my labor which I had toiled under the sun
because I must leave it to the man who will come after me.
And who knows whether he will be wise or a fool?

✿ ✿ ✿

Yet he will rule over all my labor which I have toiled
and in which I have shown myself wise under the sun.
This is also vanity.

✿ ✿ ✿

Therefore I turned my heart and despaired of all the labor
in which I had toiled under the sun.

About 3,000 years ago, a man whom others have said was the wisest man ever to have lived embarked upon a quest to find the meaning of life. What King Solomon discovered was that life under the sun is meaningless.

Solomon unearthed the root of humanity's complaint, which is the fact that we are going to die, and, as I have already pointed out, we know it. We know that there is not enough resource to stop our own deaths and because death is inevitable, then life is ultimately futile.

What Solomon concluded may seem rather abhorrent and incomprehensible. Yet while you might consider him our equivalent of Donald Trump, Bill Gates and Warren Buffet rolled into one, Solomon was the kind of individual who used every resource available in his quest to fully seek out satisfaction and meaning in this life.

However, as his search for meaning here on earth repeatedly failed, Solomon descended deeper and deeper into despair.

In the place of justice, wickedness was there;
and in the place of righteousness, iniquity was there.

✿ ✿ ✿

And look! The tears of the oppressed,
but they have no comforter.
On the side of their oppressors,
there is power but they have no comforter.

✿ ✿ ✿

Again, I saw that for all toil and every skillful work
a man is envied by his neighbor

✡ ✡ ✡

There is one alone without companion…
But he never asks "For whom do I toil and deprive
myself of good?

✡ ✡ ✡

…when you draw near to the house of God…
draw near to listen than to give the sacrifice of fools,
for they do not know that they do evil…
…in the multitude of dreams and many words,
there is also vanity.

✡ ✡ ✡

All things are wearisome with labor;
man cannot express it.
The eye is not satisfied with seeing
nor the ear filled with hearing.

✡ ✡ ✡

What profit has the worker from that in which he labors…
God has put eternity in their hearts
except that no one
can find out the work that God does from beginning to end.

Just when you think that things can't get worse, Solomon comes
to the conclusion that it is better never to have been born than to
live here on earth under the sun.
Therefore I praised the dead who were already dead
more than the living who are still alive.
Yet better than both is he who has never existed,
who has not seen the evil work that is done under the sun.

✡ ✡ ✡

A good name is better than precious ointment
and the day of death than the day of one's birth.
Better to go to the house of mourning than to the house of feasting,
for that is the end of all men
and the living will take it to heart.

Ecclesiastes (NKJV)

As I pondered Solomon's thoughts, here's what I think he is saying in a nutshell:

The best that human wisdom and reason can offer is disappointment.

✿ ✿ ✿

All earthly pleasures are hollow.

✿ ✿ ✿

Gaining wealth is a doomed pursuit of emptiness.

✿ ✿ ✿

Injustice, envy, being alone, pretence in formal religion and all the flawed civil institutions are evidence of the futility of our days.

✿ ✿ ✿

*We are in something designed before time—
something that we do not understand.*

✿ ✿ ✿

We have control over very, very little.

✿ ✿ ✿

We will never be fully satisfied here on earth.

✿ ✿ ✿

Death is better than life here under the sun.

Sunburned here on Planet Earth, I live in a universal tension between my temporal condition and my eternal calling. As a spiritual being, I live in a temporal condition in which my death is inevitable. Because there is no way around that fact, life under the sun is colored by scarcity, inevitability and futility.

Seeing that my death is inevitable, I am faced with a complete contradiction to what God has promised. He has promised me eternal life; He has said that He will give us the desires of our heart. Yet, our greatest desire is to live forever in love and without suffering.

Yet, I do not know what His promises mean in this life. I live in a world where moments of love, intimacy and community overwhelm me. I also exist in a world where others are free to destroy all that I cherish including my life.

Down in this foxhole, under the sun, there is suffering, hatred, betrayal, injustice and absolute horror. Down in this foxhole called Earth, the Word has been sent.

I live in the tension between God's eternal promises and my temporal condition. If I am honest, I acknowledge the reality of that tension, and long to transcend the restlessness and despair of this world through faith and love.

✡ ✡ ✡

A Beautiful Mind

✡ ✡ ✡

"A man who has nothing for which he is willing to fight, nothing which is more important than his own personal safety, is a miserable creature and has no chance of being free unless made and kept so by the exertions of better men than himself."[4]
John Stuart Mill

After seeing the movie *A Beautiful Mind* (Universal Pictures, 2002), I realized, I am not so crazy after all.

Up until now my idea had sounded a little wild; even Aileen had done a double-take when I threw it out to her. Here it is.

What if I don't have my thoughts but my thoughts literally have me?

Let me give you an example of what I am tracking here. For a number of years, I used to believe unquestionably that women could not be trusted. No matter how hard I tried to find a woman whom I could trust, I couldn't find one. Each one of them gave me some reason that invariably substantiated my unquestioned belief system not to trust her.

How about being married to a guy like this? Talk about making your wife walk on eggshells.

One night, Aileen had had enough. She interrupted my entrenched belief system by pointing out that no matter what she did, I found reason to not trust her. She asked me to consider the possibility that trust was not a function of a person's actions as much as it was a function of my own power to decide. Hitting the nail on the head, she proposed that I was getting a lot out of proving myself right about women.

That conversation was one big wake-up call. Was it true that women could not be trusted?

As I stopped, examined myself and questioned my previously unquestioned sacred ideas, I realized that Aileen was absolutely right. I was getting a huge payoff from not trusting women. If a woman could not be trusted, then I was completely justified in doing what I thought I *needed* to do in order to protect myself including drugs, lying and withholding myself in the relationship. My belief system had made it acceptable for me to betray women before they could betray me.

Hunkered in that particular foxhole, I saw that the person who decided whether or not women can be trusted is me, *me and* no one else. Grabbing my rifle, smearing the mud off my face and starting to climb out, I wondered about other absolutes I was treating as sacrosanct in my head and how they were showing up and limiting the possibilities for a life worth living.

A number of years later, I got a huge clue through the movie, *A Beautiful Mind.*

The film is based upon the true story of Professor John F. Nash, a mathematician who was awarded the Nobel Prize in 1994 for his pioneering work in analysis equilibrium in the theory of non-cooperative games. Besides his brilliance, what makes John Nash's story so unusual is his battle with schizophrenia.

Professor Nash saw people who did not exist, except in his own mind.

These people were as real to John Nash as his own wife. He saw them with his own eyes. He spoke, interacted with them and believed what they told him was true. By all logic of sight, sense and reason, Nash had no basis at all to question their existence. It was beyond his comprehension to even consider the possibility that these people did not exist.

No one could convince him otherwise. His wife, doctors, friends and colleagues had little success no matter how hard they tried. Even with repeated forced hospitalizations, Nash argued that everyone else was somehow wrong.

And, it's hard not to blame him. You see, he *saw* these people. They were far from imaginary, and he simply could not find any reason to refute what appeared completely real.

In the 1994 Les Prix Nobel, Professor Nash gives us a glimpse into how he discovered that he was completely wrong.

...Now I must arrive at the time of my change from scientific rationality of thinking into the delusional thinking characteristic of persons who are psychiatrically diagnosed as "schizophrenic" or "paranoid schizophrenic."

While I was on the academic sabbatical of 1956 – 1957, I also entered into marriage. Alicia had graduated as a physics major from MIT where we had met and she had a job in the New York City area in 1956 – 1957. The mental disturbances originated in the early months of 1959 at a time when Alicia happened to be pregnant. And as a consequence I resigned my position as a faculty member at MIT and, ultimately, after spending fifty days under "observation" at the McLean Hospital, traveled to Europe and attempted to gain status there as a refugee. I later spent times of the order of five to eight months in hospitals in New Jersey, always on an involuntary basis and always attempting a legal argument for release.

And it did happen that when I had been long enough hospitalized that I would finally renounce my delusional hypotheses and revert to thinking of myself as a human of more conventional circumstances and return to mathematical research.

But after my return to the dream-like delusional hypotheses in the later 1960s I became a person of delusionally influenced thinking but of relatively moderate behavior and thus tended to avoid hospitalization and the direct attention of psychiatrists.

Thus further time passed. Then gradually I began to intellectually reject some of the delusionally influenced lines of thinking, which had been characteristic of my orientation.

...So at the present time I seem to be thinking rationally again in the style that is characteristic of scientists. However this is not entirely a matter of joy as if someone returned from physical disability to good physical health. One aspect of this is that rationality of thought imposes a limit on a person's concept of his relation to the cosmos.

However real the delusions seemed, they were ruining John Nash's life. So in order to have the future Nash wanted with his wife and son, he was forced into what was unprecedented for him.

He had to "intellectually reject some of the delusionally influenced lines of thinking." What he discovered was equally unprecedented, namely that the mind he trusted so much was making up fictional people.

With that stark interruption, Professor Nash heroically took on a reality different than he had ever experienced. He determined to *have* these fictional people more than these delusions *had* him.

Nash's road to freedom was far from smooth. Nash refused to acknowledge the existence of his delusional people but they continued to haunt him throughout the rest of his life.

By the end of *A Beautiful Mind*, we discover that Professor Nash has become keenly aware of his tendencies to see and talk to people who do not exist. However they no longer control Nash because he chooses not to give them the significance they demand. *He has them more than they have him.*

I think there is something tremendously significant in John Nash's experiences. As new as this idea might sound, I think each of us is just like him. I believe that the thoughts and feelings we have are something that we experience and not create.

I think we are born into a pre-existing conversation that *has* us.

Others seem to be on this same path. Look at what Dr. Barbara Fittipaldi, an international management consultant, cites in her article, *New Listening: Key To Organizational Transformation*[5]:

Do you believe your opinions are really yours? Tell me where you were born, into what kind of family, what your parents did for a living, how many other children there were, what profession you are in, and a couple of other things, and I can pretty well tell you your opinions.
So can anyone else who has done some research on this. This is because opinions are not a matter of thinking. We do very little real thinking a lot of having thoughts, but that's not thinking.

If this sea of pre-existing conversation is real and we are just experiencing thoughts, where did they come from in the first place? Is it possible that this sea comes from every speaking being before us including the One who established us? What if the nature of this sea is language, and as we learn to talk we enter into the thinking that is mankind?

For example, have you ever wondered why the Hebrew religious community did not see the Son of God, Jesus, standing right before their eyes some 2000 years ago? They were the academic, civil, theological experts and the personal growth kings of their day. They were the people who everyone else turned to for answers.

What blinded them to the possibility that Jesus was the fulfillment of the long awaited Messiah? Were they blinded by their historical assumptions of how the Messiah would come and what he would do for them?

I imagine that they were people like us: they had expectations about what *should be*. They believed that the Messiah would liberate their nation through the overthrow of the Roman government.

However, Jesus Christ the Messiah showed up completely different from their expectations. Again and again, He interrupted their logic and reason with statements and actions that were verified by the Scriptures, yet outside of the categories of their thinking and sensibilities.

The liberation that Jesus provided came through the unthinkable: He died on a cross right before their eyes and did it in an attitude of forgiveness in a society seeking revenge. Is it any wonder why so many didn't recognize Him?

And, I say as it was with them, so it is with us today.

If we don't examine the examiner, namely our own thoughts and perspectives, we will unconsciously live out our lives from those assumptions. Those assumptions will automatically drive our behavior in ways that will actually substantiate our complaint against life and our contempt for God.

And, doing so, we will never get out of our foxholes.

✧ ✧ ✧

Magnolia

✧ ✧ ✧

"When I resist suffering, all of my relationships—with God and myself and others -become shallow and unfulfilled. For if embraced, suffering can draw people together; otherwise it pushes them apart. When I suffer, I tend to judge myself, and so withdraw from others

in insecurity. When others suffer, I tend to judge them, which again distances me. In either case, the enemy is not the suffering itself, but the judgment. Judgment is a strategy for keeping suffering at bay. But the fruit of judgment is the greatest suffering of all: alienation."[6]

Mike Mason, Practicing the Presence of People

Wow. Talk about a collision of coincidence, human choices, past history and divine intervention. *Magnolia* (New Line Cinema, 1999.) What a movie.

Magnolia takes ten different characters, a dying father, a young wife, a male caretaker, a famous lost son, a police officer in love, a boy genius, a now-adult boy genius, a game show host and an estranged daughter and weaves them together into one story. In this film, you find everything suicide, redemption, inexplicable coincidences, impossible relationships as well as frogs falling from the sky.

Here's my interpretation of *Magnolia*. I think it is ultimately about God delivering us from the sins of our fathers *and* our own choices. In this film, as the fathers repented, the children were presented with a clear space to reinvent their future as they chose.

Within this context, *Magnolia* reveals how we are addicted to our complaint and our assumptions based on history. Every main character in the movie has a complaint, which is ruling their lives.

For example, notice the complaint generated by Frank T.J. Mackey played by Tom Cruise. Now Frank T.J. Mackey is at the top of his game as the Tony Robbins of seduction. A slick, leather-vested creator of *Seduce and Destroy* a high priced seminar that teaches men how to rule over women Mackey's life motto is "Respect the Cock."

What we discover is that Frank's father deserted him and his mother when she was dying of cancer. As a teenager, Frank was left alone to care for her until she died. As an adult, he turned into a sex guru who teaches men how to seduce women.

When Frank's mother died, we learn that she was still hoping that her husband might return. As the one who was taking care of her, Frank assessed his mother's longing to mean that he was not good enough. Out of that assumption, he decided that women are not faithful and that they will suck you dry.

As a chapter in his book, *How to Fake Being Nice and Honest*, reveals, Frank felt fully justified in doing what he did in order to get what he wanted from women. His complaint gave him permission to do what his father had done to him. He makes himself right on the basis of what had happened to him. In this, the sins of the father have now been transferred to the son. In some respects, Frank is ultimately worse than his father because he makes money by teaching men how to hurt those they should love.

Frank's complaint gave him a winning way to get what he wanted. However it never actually filled the holes in his life. This complaint blinded him to what was actually available and possible in his life. Just like our own complaints, Frank's complaint made him right and consequently the idea of giving it up was almost impossible, even if it meant having what he ultimately longed for.

Anything outside of the complaint anything that can provide greater joy or fulfillment than that which our complaint provides we see as a threat *because to admit our complaint is to admit that we could be mistaken about what we think is real and possible.*

As the movie continues, we discover that Frank is not aware that his father is about to also die of cancer and that his father regrets how he abused the love of Frank's mother by cheating and abandoning her.

Through the hospice nurse, Frank learns his father's final wish is to be reconciled with his son. Reluctantly, he goes to his father's mansion, not to show pity or remorse but to vent his years of unsatisfied anger. At the end of his raw confession, Frank breaks down weeping and saying, "Don't leave me."

In those words, he forgives his father and releases his complaint. In the final moments of the film we see Frank going to the hospital where his father's second wife is lying in intensive care. Unlike hours before, his complaint is no longer ruling him. Instead he is there for the purpose of reconciliation.

Frank's complaint rested on an assumption. Love must be scarce. Because he was not loved as a child that meant that there was not enough love in the world.

How many of us think that we, like Frank, are addicted to assumptions such as love is scarce? (If you are not raising both your hands, I would suggest that you are addicted to not knowing that you are addicted!)

I know about addiction from firsthand experience. As I have shared previously, a little over twenty years ago, I was a cocaine addict. By numbing out on cocaine, I protected myself from the helplessness of realizing that my life wasn't turning out as I thought it should be. If you have ever been addicted to any substance, you know for yourself how obsessive you become about getting the drug. The more addicted you are, the more your life gets consumed by when and how you are going to satisfy your craving instead of engaging those areas in your life where you feel helpless and out of control. Each time you "score," there is a temporary, hollow sense of victory over an abiding and undeniable reality.

I believe that as human beings we are so addicted to our assumptions that we rarely, if ever, investigate, explore or question them.

These assumptions define who we are and how we engage life. They show up in our assessments of the past and the future. Our assumptions are the superstructure upon which we hang our self-importance, and they comprise the rationale for our complaint. We are addicted to assumptions but like every good addict we swear that we are not hooked.

For instance, regarding Frank's assumption about scarcity, do you remember what you were thinking when reading those lines? How was your internal conversation voting? Were you looking for something right or wrong, good or bad, useful or not? Or were you exploring the different ways love, time or even life might automatically seem scarce for you?

Did you have an automatic conversation about scarcity and how it might be influencing how you perceive the world? Or did you evaluate my statements? Was your internal conversation, "That isn't right," "That's messed up" or "I don't want to waste my time."

Now we know that being right about certain things is critical to survival. Being wrong about your location in the mountains or deserts could cost you your life. Not preparing adequately for earthquakes, winter storms or even cooking food correctly could be devastating.

Being right is vital to survival, but as human beings down in the foxhole, we also assume that life is scarce. Like John Nash, we assume that the scarcity we see is real; we believe that our assumptions are telling us the truth.

Scarcity wakes up with us in the morning and shrouds our perspective and our behavior throughout the day. As a result, we act to protect and obtain more of what we believe is scarce, regardless of how much we have already. Inside our beings, we feel a never-ending sense of impending loss. We will kill ourselves trying to fill it or avoid it.

Here is how Solomon frames our addiction to the assumption of scarcity.

All things are full of labor; man cannot express it.
The eye is not satisfied with seeing,
Nor the ear filled with hearing.

Ecclesiastes 1:8 (KJV)

Try it on. Examine how you relate to love.

Is love scarce? Is there sufficient love available for everyone on the planet? If your answer is "yes," does your life reflect that sufficiency? Do you freely love or do you dole it out carefully to those who you think deserve it? Do you protect yourself by inauthentic conversation or cordial hypocrisy? Or are you free to receive whatever other people might say or do?

Let's try another one. Time.

Do you have enough of it? Does anyone? Notice your behavior when you have enough time to get to an appointment or to catch a plane. Are you acting as if you have enough time even when you do? How are you present in the now?

How about scarcity of ability?

As a trainer, I have been in countless situations where I go home after the first night of a training completely convinced that we are sunk. "Oh God, don't send me back there," I say. "I have no idea what to do here. It's hopeless. I think I'll call in sick tomorrow." Then by Sunday morning I am exuberant, saying, "Wow. This was the best training ever!" What happened? Somehow in a matter of days, abundance showed up in the face of my scarce abilities.

When we think scarcity is real, we control the little resource we assume is available. Then we maneuver to expand our knowledge so that we can predict our lives in order to get more of the little we think is available. Believing that no one including God has our backs, we must, at all costs, look out for #1. We devise winning approaches to life in order to get what we think God and others cannot be trusted to provide.

Just like the payoff I got from my belief that women could not be trusted, there are windfalls that we derive from our complaint. Besides making ourselves right, we gain the illusion that we have power over our lives. Anything that is unprecedented appears as impossible and as a threat because it informs us that there is more out there to live and learn than that for which we have settled.

Here's how this goes. We spend our lives telling ourselves and others that the decisions we have made were the only ones available, that there really wasn't anything else we could have done.

In this, we justify why we gave up on our dreams and convince ourselves to be satisfied with what we settled for in their place. Then, somebody crosses our path and demonstrates that what we have longed for was not only possible but available.

What is our response? Are we not disturbed, let alone threatened? Do you think we might get a bit defensive?

As the film *Magnolia* discovers, I am convinced that our complaint is a crime against who we really are. It ultimately separates us from having relationships with others and the Divine as we end up reducing people down to what skills, competencies or benefit they supply to us in our effort to get more of what we think we desperately need.

Only when we see a vision greater than our complaint will we risk getting out of the foxhole. Until then, we will settle for leftovers, resigning ourselves to inevitability and futility.

✡ ✡ ✡

Wedding Plans

✡ ✡ ✡

"If I were to wish for anything, I should not wish for wealth and power, but for the passionate sense of potential for the eye which, ever young and ardent, sees the possible. Pleasure disappoints; possibility never."[7]

Søren Kierkegaard

"Dan, you have got to talk to Elizabeth." Aileen was getting frustrated, and not only with our daughter.

"Honey, I have already talked with her," I responded, with a growing certainty that I had already lost the debate. "If I keep doing what I've been doing, I am going to get the same results. Talking in the way you are suggesting is not working. This is what Elizabeth and Tyler are choosing."

"Dan, I want you to talk to her again."

In December 2004, our eighteen-year old daughter announced to us that she and her fiancée, Tyler, were planning on getting married the following August. To say the least, all of Aileen's and my alarms went off.

None of our concerns related to Tyler or Elizabeth or how they had built their relationship with each other and us. They were in love and wanted our support in being married. However, as parents who have more life experience, our objections were a mile long.

The bottom line for us was that Elizabeth was too young to get married.

All the statistical evidence was against them having a successful marriage if they did it at such an early age. Having gotten married at a similar age, both Aileen and I knew the significant difficulties involved in keeping a marriage together when you have so much to learn about life and each other.

In my mind, marrying young was just not the right thing to do. Aileen's biggest fear was that she was about to lose her daughter. Although we had these objections, we also realized that Liz was the one who was going to make her own decisions. She was a free agent, and if she were going to choose marriage, then we would love her and share in her excitement.

However, driving in the car one afternoon, I broached the subject again with Elizabeth mostly to show Aileen that I was having *the conversation* with my daughter.

"Dad, why is this not the right thing to do?" she asked. "If this were a hundred years ago, you would be happy for me."

As I ran through the litany of reasons why marrying young is not the right thing to do today, Liz pointed to Aileen and me and others who have had successful marriages despite marrying at a young age.

"Dad, is it possible that you are only having a cultural conversation?" Lizzie asked. "Are you really looking out for my welfare or your own agenda? Are you seeking to protect me because of your own insecurity about me getting hurt or do you want to stand in the possibility of my own transformation and development?"

Egad. The apple doesn't fall far from the tree. I had raised a trainer. I let Liz's words sink in.

"Honey," I answered, "my concerns are probably cultural, but that doesn't mean there isn't wisdom in them. The culture is like a person; it has healthy and unhealthy conversations. Since this is a decision that ultimately affects everybody in your life, including us, I want to explore it thoroughly. I want to know you are making the most informed choice you can. I love you and Tyler very much, and I am not going to stand in your way."

Immediately I hear Aileen's voice ringing out from the back seat. "I thought you were on my side, Dan!"

As much as my father's love wanted to keep my child safe from any harm, I realized that I was dealing with my own inner thoughts about wanting to suspend time and keep my family. Underneath all the reasoning and logic, what Aileen and I were dealing with was getting out of the comfort of the foxhole and facing death.

Aileen and I could not suspend time. Even wanting to was as futile as trying to hold a wave along the sand. Our progression towards death was inevitable. Elizabeth was an individual past the age of consent. She was completely capable of living on her own, facing a crisis and gaining from it.

Did her mother and I own her? Was Elizabeth a tool to make me look good or feel better for my incomplete actions and failures?

Or is she a true and unique expression of God on the earth?

I realized that I had to forsake what I was holding onto for the unprecedented future of my daughter. I had to see my child as a human being separate from me, a gift of God whom I had the wonderful privilege of loving.

The bottom line was that I couldn't do for her what only God and she could do. Only Elizabeth could experience her own transformation in life. If she were going to experience that transformation, she needed to not only know the principles of transformation but also walk it out.

The weight of this decision needed to sit in her lap.

During our conversation when I asked her, "What happens if this or that happens?" Elizabeth replied, "I won't know, Dad, until I get there, but I am clear about how I am going to live for Tyler and our future together in the midst of what shows up."

Then she turned to Aileen, "Mom, I understand your fears, but I love you and I really need you."

I saw that instead of copping an attitude, Elizabeth was viewing her life from the perspective of a tangible future one that I could taste, feel and imagine. She was thinking now from the future of being married and having her mother and me close to her. She was showing up in her future now, and what she needed me to do was to disengage from my foxhole assumptions and show up as well.

As our conversations continued, I returned once again to Solomon.

That which has been is that which will be,
And that which has been done is that which will be done.
So there is nothing new under the sun.
Is there anything of which one might say, "See this, it is new"?
Already it has existed for ages which were before us.
There is no remembrance of earlier things;
and also of the later things which will occur,
There will be for them no remembrance
Among those who will come later still.

✡ ✡ ✡

"What is crooked cannot be made straight,
And what is lacking cannot be numbered."
Ecclesiastes 1:8 (NKJV)

Are we addicted?

If I said that you could go through the rest of your life without having another argument, would you believe me? As you're thinking something along the line of "You've got to be joking. Everyone knows that arguments are inevitable!"

How about this one? If I said that you could stop starvation in the world, would you believe me?

I don't know many who would tolerate twenty-one children dying every minute of starvation in their own neighborhood if they had some way to save them. Yet this situation is exactly what is happening every day throughout the world. The only reason that we tolerate these deaths is because we do not believe there is an answer to world hunger.

Is there a solution? Or do we just brush it off as impossible?

Futility is the assumption that there is no solution to our condition. Inevitability assumes that certain things are just going to happen.

They are either inherently true? Or could it be that both assumptions are part of our own *Beautiful Mind* conversation? I would suggest the latter.

People do not die from starvation or other tragic conditions because there are no solutions. We assume that there is no solution because the past has provided us with none, meaning that up until now *no one has come up with a way of thinking, structure or strategy to solve the impossible.*

When we believe there are no solutions, then any action is ultimately futile.

What we do instead is make a *gesture* such as donating money which doesn't solve the situation but keeps us at a comfortable distance from it. Through making a gesture, I am relieved of my guilt and any impact on me personally because I have done *something.*

The reality is that I have taken myself out of relationship with the problem because I believe it is inevitable and futile. My action or inaction is grounded in feeling right. I don't commit to possibility because I ultimately don't believe there is any.

Let's say that you have hurt someone. You know that they are hurt, and you have tried twenty times to restore the relationship. Nothing has worked. Finally you make the choice to avoid the person. Instead of being in the problem, you make the gesture of cordiality, pretending that there is trust between you where there is none.

Now, let's bring this closer to home. What did you want most in your life as a kid? How many of those longings and hopes are you still willing to dream about today? When did you simply choose to forget that which mattered so much to you before? What are those things that you don't even bother to discuss because you feel it is futile to consider any new possibilities?

The real question here is why do you think that you can't? Where does that *I can't* come from?

I know: taking on our assumptions is like looking through a pretty bugged up windshield. Yet what if the impossible were possible? What if we engaged seemingly unsolvable situations without our pre-existing assumptions? What would happen if we considered ourselves already dead, and participated as if there weren't anything to preserve or protect? Like that country song that exhorts us to "live like we were dying"?

Our lives, and this world, would be radically changed. We would go to the moon. Find vaccines. Discover America. Feed thousands with only a few loaves of bread and a couple of fish. Our expectations of this life would be transformed.

We would be transformed. Our families, our friends, our communities, our world, our future would be transformed. We wouldn't know ourselves.

In the Gospel of John, there is a story that happens at an unusual place in Jerusalem called the Pool of Bethesda. Every day hundreds of people all having incurable diseases or ailments would come and wait *for the moving of the pool's waters*. No one would know when the waters would stir but when they did, whoever got into the pool first was miraculously healed. From the Scriptures, we don't know if this movement happened often or every ten years. However day after day, people would come to the place as a last resort.

On the shore not far from the pool was a man who had been ill for thirty-eight years. Day after day someone would carry him to the pool. Day after day, the pool would be still, or even worse someone would get into the moving waters before him. Day after day, his eyes reminded him of the scarcity, inevitability and futility of his life. Then one day, an unusual man walks up and asks him a question. "Do you wish to get well?"

What do you think? If you had been in this man's shoes for a lifetime worth of years, what would you answer? Would you answer "Yes"?

Are you so sure? How are you answering "yes" to your lifetime of unanswered challenges right now?

Like you and me, the sick man answered out of his assumptions of scarcity, inevitability and futility. He responded from the foxhole. "Sir, I have no man to put me into the pool when the water is stirred up but while I am coming, another steps down before me."

Instead of engaging his assumptions, Jesus (the one asking him the questions) interrupts by telling him to do the unprecedented and the impossible.

"Get up, pick up your pallet, walk, and sin no more," is what Jesus says to the man who has been ill for thirty-eight years. And, at His words, the man does the impossible. Jesus ends with the peculiar command to sin no more. What was the man's sin? Perhaps it was the defeat in his response to Jesus' question about wanting to be healed.

The life, death and resurrection of Jesus has proven that nothing is scarce, inevitable or futile. He invites us to join Him outside the foxhole where, as dead men walking, we live out the beauty, awe and wonder of an unprecedented life.

✣ ✣ ✣

The Thin Red Line

✣ ✣ ✣

"War is not an altogether new situation, it simply aggravates the permanent human condition (what he calls living on the edge of a precipice) so that how precarious and uncertain life is cannot be ignored. He asserts that there is no such thing as normal life. A wise man recognizes how precarious life is and in times of war, even a fool does."
C.S. Lewis

What is this war in the heart of nature?
Why does nature vie with itself; the land contend with the sea?
Is there an avenging power in nature?
Not one power but two?
I remember my mother when she was dying.
She looked all shrunk up and gray.
I asked her if she was afraid. She just shook her head.
I was afraid to touch the death I see in her.
Couldn't find nothing beautiful or uplifting about
her going back to God.

Heard people talk about immortality but I ain't seen it.
I wondered how it'd be like when I died.
What'd it be like to know that this last breath now
was the last one you was ever going to draw.
I just hope I can meet it the way she did,
with the same calm.
Cause that is where it is hidden,
the immortality I hadn't seen.
Maybe all men got one big soul that everyone's a part of
All faces of the same man.
One big self.
Everyone looking for salvation by himself.
Each like a coal thrown from the fire.

These words of Private Witt in the film *The Thin Red Line* (20th Century Fox, 1999) stirred me. What is this existence in which we live?

"Hey, Dad," my son's words pulled me out of my thoughts, "Did you know that light is the constant of the universe?"

Danny was in the process of getting his degree in Engineering Physics and qualifying for degrees in Electrical Engineering, Computer Science and Material Science at the University of California, at Berkeley. Among his favorite hobbies is the study of light.

"Light is not in time," Danny added. "Light never changes its velocity no matter what is going on. Actually, space and time change in relationship to light."

I listened with both ears.

"For example there is so much light that we just don't see, Dad." he continued. "The range of the light spectrum that we can see with our eyes is exceedingly small, from about 300 to 600 microns. In that range, we see only the visible colors of the spectrum."

"Okay. Got it."

"Outside of the range that we can see, there are probably an infinite number of wavelengths of light that our eyes simply cannot detect. If we could see even a little more of the light spectrum, we would see such crazy stuff. We would see how a person's emotions affected them, or if they were hungry. We could see their bones and skin at the same time."

"Where does this lead us, Danny?

"Well, it shows us that there is a lot more that we cannot see with our eyes. Visually we are very limited."

Was God answering my wonderings through the words of my son? Could eternal life be like light?

If we could fully see, what would our eyes behold? Would we wonder (like Private Witt in *The Thin Red Line* wonders) if we are "all faces of the same man, one big self looking for salvation"?

I had seen the film once before. Based on the novel by James Jones, *The Thin Red Line* tells the story of C-Company, an Army rifle unit stationed in the Pacific Rim during World War II. Although the story revolves around their mission to take a small piece of land being held by the Japanese on Guadalcanal, to me this movie is not just another war film.

Watching it again, I found that it poignantly explored our lives here on earth in the foxhole and our desire for eternal life beyond the sun. Perhaps, too, this film reflects our conversation about death.

We see what is under the sun but intuit that there is more. Like the man at the Pool of Bethesda, we search everywhere but fail to find it. Like a lost coin in plain sight, we refuse to look in places that we think couldn't possibly contain our fortune. Instead we hunt for the coin in all the obvious places that have already been searched.

We say, "Why engage oppression, suffering and disease since death is their end result in our lives? Certainly this immortality we seek can't be found there."

Take this early scene between First Sergeant Welsh and Private Witt, which takes place after the private was recaptured for going AWOL (absent without leave).

Welsh sees one world. Witt, another.

WELSH: You haven't changed at all, have you, Witt? You haven't learned a thing. All the old man has to do is leave it to you, and you put your head in the noose for him. How many times have you been AWOL? You've been in the army, what, six years now? Ain't it about time that you smarten up and stop being such a punk recruit? I mean, are you ever gonna?

WITT: We can't all be smart.

WELSH: No we can't and that's a shame. Look at you. Truth is you can't take straight duty in my company. You'll never be a real soldier. Not in God's world.

Witt is silent at Welsh's rebuke.
WELSH: This is C-Company of which I am First Sergeant. I run this outfit. Now Captain Staros is the C.O. But, I'm the guy who runs it. You're just another mouth to feed. Normally you'd be court-martialed but I worked a deal for you. You should consider yourself lucky. I'm sending you to a disciplinary company. You'll be a stretcher bearer. You'll be taking care of the wounded.
WITT: I can take anything you dish out. I am twice the man that you are.
Welsh sneers at the proposition. He leans close to Witt's face.
WELSH: In this world, a man himself is nothing. And there ain't no world but this one. (How often are we as convinced as the Sergeant that the world we see is the only world there is?)
WITT: You're wrong there, Top. I've seen another world. Sometimes, I think it was just my imagination.
WELSH: Well, then you're seeing things I never will.
Welsh stands up to leave.
WELSH: We are living in a world that is blowing itself to hell as fast as everybody can arrange it. In a situation like that, all a man can do is shut his eyes and let nothing touch him. Look out after himself. I might be the best friend you ever had. And you don't even know it.

What if the salvation of eternal life is in a completely different dimension than temporal life? What if, like light, the eternal life of which we dream is something beyond what our temporal vision can detect?

Could it exist and be available now if we would only surrender seeing things through the temporal lenses from which we are trained to view life? What if salvation was an abundant life here and now?

By the word "abundant" I mean abounding in resource, which would include possibility, passion, presence, creativity, etc. rather than possessing large amounts of material goods a way of relating to God, others and life's circumstances that opens possibility to that for which you stand.

I wonder.

Notes:

[1] G.K. Chesterton, *Orthodoxy: The Romance of Faith* (Doubleday, 1990).

[2] 10-part HBO TV miniseries based on the book by Stephen Ambrose.

[3] Preface to *The Autobiography of Eleanor Roosevelt* (1961), p. xix.

[4] "The Contest in America," *Fraser's Magazine* (February 1862); later published in *Dissertations and Discussions* (1868), vol.1 p. 26.

[5] *When the Canary Stops Singing: Women's Perspective on Transforming Business* (Berrett Koehler, publisher).

[6] Mike Mason, *Practicing the Presence of People: How We Learn to Love* (Waterbrook Press and The Doubleday Religious Publishing Group, 1999).

[7] Søren Kierkegaard, *Either/Or*, Diapsalmata.

GOD'S SKIN

"Language is a skin: I rub my language against the other. It is as if I had words instead of fingers, or fingers at the tip of my words. My language trembles with desire."[1]
Roland Barthes

Day turns into night. Night becomes the new day. I breathe. I feel. I think. I touch. I grieve. I speak. I wonder. What is this existence in which I live, move and have my being? Who am I? Who are you?

Who is this God?

My son Danny and I were flying home from a training I had done in Dallas and normally the flight home was a long one but on this particular night our conversation made the hours pass like seconds.

"There are a million of these things we can't explain." Danny spoke like the scientist he was becoming. "Look, Dad," my son leaned over and said, "Here is how I describe God and the universe to my friends who can't seem to imagine the possibility of a God. I give them this scenario. 'Go buy a vacant lot. Put everything you need to build a house into one big pile. Wood, plumbing, windows, paint, shingles. You name it. Then blow the pile up.' Then I ask them 'Is it possible that everything you just blew up could land and turn into a fully constructed house by itself?'"

"Doesn't seem possible."

"Mathematically it is possible," Danny stated "but it is absolutely improbable given the second law of thermodynamics, which states that any system left to itself simplifies to a less complex system."

"Bottom line," I translated, "The blown-up pile is not going to somehow become a house."

"Right. Unless someone puts all the pieces back together and builds it."

"Sure. Common sense."

"But, get this," Danny said letting the cat out of the bag, "That is *exactly* what is happening on earth.

"How do you mean?"

"Our world is getting more complex, not simpler. The pile is landing as a house even though the second law of thermodynamics states it should not be doing that!"

"How do you explain it?" I wondered aloud.

"The only way something can get more complex is if there is intelligent and perpetual intervention."

"Intelligent and perpetual invention keeps it from simplifying?"

"Right." Danny smiled. "Dad, when you look into the physics of our reality, the structure and the order is so beautiful and so obviously designed that it is impossible to think that there is anything but an intelligence intervening in it. To think otherwise, you would have to consciously choose to deny what all the evidence suggests, which means that you would have to reject modern science."

Danny's words sank into my wondering. Who is this Intelligence intervening in our world?

✡ ✡ ✡

In the Beginning

✡ ✡ ✡

"I no longer demand answers from God, rather, I learn to enjoy living the questions, in time and by God's grace, I trust that I will live into the mystery of life in a way that is more fulfilling than simply getting solutions to my problems."[2]

Howard Baker, *Soul Keeping*

I was just an altar boy when I first starting asking. What's the point here?

It all arose out of a Conversation,
a Conversation within God.

In fact, the Conversation was God.
So, God started the discussion and everything came out of
this and nothing happened without consultation.
This was the life, the life that was the light of men
shining in the darkness,
a darkness which neither understood nor quenched its creativity.
John, a man sent by God, came to remind people
about the nature of the light so that they would observe.
He was not the subject under discussion
but the bearer of an invitation to join in.
The subject of the Conversation, the original light, came into the world,
the world that had arisen out of his willingness to converse.
He fleshed out the words but the world did not understand.
He came to those who knew the language, but they did not respond.
Those who did became a new creation (his children);
they read the signs and responded.

These children were born out of sharing in the creative activity of God.
They heard the Conversation still going on, here, now, and took part,
discovering a new way of being people.
To be invited to share in a Conversation about the nature of life, was for
them, a glorious opportunity not to be missed.
John 1:1-14 Clive Scott Translation

What is the purpose for all these rituals? Are we playing a game or is there some reality within the words? I go to church. I pray and even fast. Yet, my life is still full of problems I don't know how to solve. Where's the power to live this stuff out? Is this all there is to life? Does anyone have a clue?

Tell me, someone. Anyone.

Nothing but blank stares. Shrugs with polite dismissals. Placations: "If you simply keep the faith, Dan, God will do the rest." Comments so vacuous that even I could see the emperor had no clothes on.

During most of my childhood and teen years, I was looking for someone or something to tell me that I was going to make it.

You see, my mom was bi-polar and manic-depressive. Most of the time she terrified everyone but me. One minute, Mom was crazy like something out of the *Twilight Zone,* the next seemingly normal. She would have high swings, zooming a million miles an hour, making the house spotless. Then, boom! The bottom would fall out and she would lie in bed for long periods of time, getting up only to make sure we kids had what we needed.

In the midst of Mom's illness, my father sought refuge in gambling and the nightlife around town. After dinner, Dad would go to work at the movie theatre he owned, while we kids watched TV or fought Mom when she attempted to put us to bed.

It wasn't surprising that before my sophomore year of high school, I found refuge in drugs. Soon I earned a reputation as a partying athlete with a hot temper. More than once my dad and I got into some major battles, which ended with my storming out of the house.

As soon as high school was over, I blew out of my hometown bound for Santa Clara University to play football. Happiness and peace at last, I thought. Life was on my terms now.

I had no idea that I was already living life on my own terms.

Within a few weeks of making Santa Clara's football team, I got sidelined for the entire season due to a broken foot. Then, my favorite aunt died of cancer and my grandfather, the other rock in my life, died right behind her. Shortly afterward, on the same day, I found out that my parents were getting a divorce and that my girlfriend of four years was leaving me.

Life completely rolled over on me.

All that I had planned and dreamed was at a complete dead end. My aunt and grandfather were dead, and my parents were living a life that didn't make any more sense to me than my own messed-up existence. The fabric of my life was falling apart, and I struggled with despair, wondering, *does anyone really know what they are doing in this life? Where is God in all this?*

I quit college and grew so depressed that I wondered if I were going crazy like my mom. I was so despondent that she would ask me repeatedly if I was thinking of killing myself. "Of course not, Mom," I would respond but the truth was that I was contemplating suicide.

From every indication my life was not turning out the way it should, and I had no reason to think anything was going to change.

In my darkness, I searched for meaning, understanding and hope. Why would God allow all these bad things to happen to me? Is anyone really happy in this life? Why am I doing things that I know will hurt me and others? Why is love so transient?

For a long time, I had no answers. As days turned into years, day jobs into the fast track career and pot into cocaine, I was swimming down around the bottom of my soul. Although I had the beautiful experience of meeting Aileen and eventually marrying her, these circumstances did not interrupt the despair that I felt inside.

For many years while she slept, I would do cocaine while reading the Bible, orbiting most often around the Gospel of John. One night, the writer's mystical words reached me like never before.

In the beginning was the Word,
and the Word was with God and the Word was God.
John 1:1

As I read, John's words penetrated deep into my body. *What is drawing me here?* I wondered. *Why am I so captured by these seemingly enigmatic passages? The Word was with God and the Word was God? God is the Word? What does that mean?*
Inside my thoughts urged me. "Find out what *Word* means."

✡ ✡ ✡

Yet Unseen

✡ ✡ ✡

"The important thing is not to stop questioning. Curiosity has its own reason for existing. One cannot help but be in awe when he contemplates the mysteries of eternity, of life, of the marvelous structure of reality. It is enough if one tries merely to comprehend a little of this mystery every day. Never lose a holy curiosity."
Albert Einstein

"**D**an. It's Danny on the phone for you."

"What's up, son?"

"Hey, Dad. Parent's Day is next week. Are you coming?"

"Absolutely."

As I walked around the University of California Berkeley campus the following weekend and met some of Danny's professors, I had this sense that I was about to learn something myself. Sure enough, the lesson showed up during a tour of Danny's physics lab.

"You know Dad," Danny said, "science is really about learning everything you can about something and then *questioning* what you have learned."

"Wait a minute. I thought the whole point was to discover the answer?"

"But Dad, that's the point. When you assume that you have landed, then you stop discovering. Only through questioning 'the answers' can new possibilities and breakthroughs open up. It all starts with a belief that there is something out there that you know you don't know. In other words, we don't know everything about anything."

"It's all a bit crazy making, but I understand it from experience. It seems like the more I learn the less I know."

"Well, I think it is crazy making when I have to be in control. Dad, most people don't get it about science. They think scientists know what they are doing. *Not*. Great scientists strive to understand everything they can about something, and then they do the unthinkable."

"What's that?"

Danny answered, "They question everything they have learned. They ask themselves, 'What am I missing here because I think I know everything there is to know? I guess in that way they do know what they are doing!'"

Dan went on, "Copernicus and Galileo both questioned the status quo of the earth being the center of the universe. For that questioning, Galileo was sentenced to life imprisonment because his assertions directly contradicted the scientific, religious and political systems of his day. In more recent times, Oppenheimer and Einstein looked at Newtonian physics and wondered why certain principles worked in Newtonian physics but not on the atomic level. Because they questioned Newtonian physics, the discovery of quantum mechanics happened."

"You have to be willing to get to the edge of what you think 'is' and then leap."

"Totally. I think you have to take on the mindset of a beginner. Otherwise you will ignore anything outside the status quo what you already know and expect. You will invalidate or criticize any new possibility out of fear of being proven wrong."

Driving north from Berkeley towards home, I realized that Danny's observations went far beyond the field of science. Ask anyone who dares to believe in something that we think is impossible, something so important that they are willing to fail in the process of achieving. What do they get from their peers? Often what they receive is that critical, skeptical look or that offhand comment.

I thought about this great book, *The Art of Possibility*,[3] which points out that "A cynic is a passionate person who refuses to be hurt again." How aptly that describes our reaction to impossible horizons. So often we allow the hurt of the past to invalidate the potential reward of the future.

To see the yet unseen, we need a beginner's mindset.

✧ ✧ ✧

His Being

✧ ✧ ✧

"A bird doesn't sing because it has an answer, it sings because it has a song."
Maya Angelou
"In the beginning was the Word."
John 1:1

What does *Word* mean?
My hunger to find out grew as my cocaine-laced nights reading the Gospel of John continued on. In the original language of the New Testament writers, *Word* means *Logos*.

Logos (log'-os): from New Testament: something said (including the thought); by implication a topic (subject of discourse), also reasoning (the mental faculty) or motive; by extension, a computation; specifically (with the article in John) the Divine Expression (i.e., Christ).

Account, cause, communication, concerning, fame, have to do, intent,
matter, mouth, preaching, question, reason, reckon, remove,
say(ing), shew, speaker, speech, talk, thing, tidings, treatise,
utterance, word, work.

What is *Logos*?

Something said. By implication a topic, Reasoning.
The Divine Expression.

What was I looking at here? What was hiding behind this veil of words, words and more words?

A Greek by the name of Heraclites was among the first to pursue
the meaning of Logos. He along with other Greek philosophers
defined it primarily as Reason. In its most important sense in
philosophy, Logos (to the Greeks) refers to a cosmic reason
which gives order and intelligibility to the world. In this sense,
the doctrine first appears in Heraclites, who affirms the
reality of a Logos analogous to the reason in man that
regulates all physical processes and is the source of
all human law.

So I tried on John 1:1 using their definition.

In the beginning was Reason
and Reason was with God and Reason was God.

Reason was *God*?

Something seemed off here. I wondered. Did the Greek philosophers articulate a puzzle while having only a few of the pieces together?

About three hundred years after Heraclites, the Stoics expanded on the Greek view of *Logos*.

The conception is developed more fully by the Stoics who conceived
of the world as a living unity, perfect in the adaptation of its
parts to one another and to the whole, and animated by an
immanent and purposive reason. As regulating all things, the
Logos is identified with Fate; as directing all things toward the good,
with Providence and as the ordered course of events, with Nature.[4]

For the Stoics, *Logos* was a celestial, all-present power resident in every created thing. Common, everyday expressions such as "Well, it must be fate," "Must be Providence," and even "Mother Nature," are rooted in the Stoic perspective.

Then I stumbled upon the insights of a contemporary author, Paul Tillich.

Logos means "word." But it also refers to the meaning of a word, the reasonable structure, which is indicated by a word. Therefore, Logos can also mean the universal law of reality. This is what Heraclites meant by it, who was the first to use this word philosophically. The Logos for him was the law, which determines the movements of all reality. For the Stoics, the Logos was the divine power, which is present in everything that is. There are three aspects to it, all of which become extremely important in the later development. The first is the law of nature. The Logos is the <u>principle</u> according to which all natural things move. It is the divine seed, the creative divine power, which makes anything what it is.

Secondly, Logos means the moral law. With Immanuel Kant, we could call this "<u>the practical reason</u>," the law which is innate in every human being when he accepts himself as a personality with the dignity and the greatest of person.

When we see the term "natural law" in classical books, we should not think of physical laws but of moral laws. For example, when we speak of the "rights of man" as embodied in the American Constitution, we are speaking about natural law.

Thirdly, Logos also means man's ability to recognize reality; we could call it "<u>theoretical reason</u>." It is man's ability to reason. Because man has the Logos in himself, he can discover it in nature and history. From this, it follows that the man who is determined by natural law ("practical reason")… is the wise man. But the Stoics were not optimists; they did not believe that everybody was a "wise man." Perhaps, there were only a few who ever reached this ideal. All others were either fools or stood somewhere between the wise and foolish. So Stoics held a basic pessimism about the majority of human beings.

In the middle of this discussion, Jesus came to the earth. He lived, died and rose from the dead. John, the writer of the Gospel of John, knew Jesus on a firsthand basis, and what he wrote in John 1:1 blew history right out of the water.

John said that *Logos is God.*

Logos is divine self-manifestation Word of God. He is Jesus Christ, who is the exact image of God manifested in flesh. John expressed what the Greeks would not have discovered through reason. Jesus was the human expression of divinity.

He was saying that *Logos* is not an object or principle. Rather, *Logos* is a Who that reveals Himself in language, in Word.

> *The idea that the universal Logos became flesh could never have been derived from the Greek thought. Therefore, the church fathers emphasized again and again that while the Greek philosophers possessed the idea of the Universal Logos, what was peculiarly Christian was that the Logos became flesh in a personal life. The Logos is God manifest to Himself in Himself. Therefore, whenever God appears, either to himself or to others outside himself, it is the Logos which appears. This Logos is in Jesus as the Christ...the self-manifestation of God, the Self Manifestation of Being.[5]*

What John discovered through his personal relationship with Christ was that when God expresses who He is, He does so in self-manifesting speaking and then acting congruently with those declarations. God speaks and then He does. This is quite frankly all we know of Him. In Jesus, the Word made flesh, God fully manifests Himself as humanly divine.

My mind was spinning with something I had never imagined before. If Word is the manifestation of God, could language, then, be where God dwells?

As I considered this thought, all my resistance showed up. "Such a suggestion trivializes God! God is more than 'self manifesting through speech,'" I rebuked myself.

As I listened to my own conversation, I realized something. Because God uses language does not mean that it is all of who God is. Rather, it is suggesting that language is the way He chooses to reveal Himself and what He uses to create.

His *Being* is apprehended through speech acts. God reveals Himself, His Being, through His speaking...through language.

✡ ✡ ✡

The Matter of Substance

✡ ✡ ✡

"Love does not alter the beloved, it alters itself."
Søren Kierkegaard[6]

"**A**re you saying that the electron knows what you are doing?" Danny and I were getting our usual cups of coffee at the Flying Goat Cafe. Mine was a double-Americano espresso with a sugar. Danny was having his black.

"Yeah. Kind of," Danny explained. "Let's say I'm doing a subatomic experiment where I am measuring an electron's spin. The spin is either up or down. If one person measures it spinning up on the first measurement, the second measurement will record it with a down spin. So, if I measure it and it is down. Then, when I am not there, some other dude comes along and does his own measurement of the electron. When I return, I will know that someone has been messing with my experiment because the electron I measured will be spinning up because the other guy measured it. By somebody simply looking, it changes the direction of its spin."

"No way. That's amazing."

"Light does a similar thing. Light takes on one of two forms that you measure for."

"I heard this before?" I chimed in.

"Yeah. If you measure light as a particle, it shows up as particles. If you measure light as a wave, it shows up as a wave. It is as if light chooses how it is going to relate to you based on how you are relating to it."

My mind went a little wild at the thought. Here I live in light; I am contained in it like a fish in the sea. Yet I know so little about it.

"What do you mean by showing up?" I asked Danny. "How we perceive it?"

"When you measure an electron it has a fifty percent chance that it will be spinning either up or down. 'Showing up' is the state of the electron that is revealed by the measurement," he answered. "Even though light is both particles and waves, it shows up as one or the other in its relationship to us. Which makes you wonder how light would show up if neither system of measurement were used."

"That's wild. What are your thoughts on light responding to how you are observing it?"

"Well, Dad, there are three schools of thought trying to explain what we can't explain. The realist school proposes that light acts this way regardless of our system of measurement. In essence, their view is that the system of measurement did not create anything; we simply have not yet determined the cause. The orthodox school holds that the system of measurement created the attributes that we are observing. The third perspective, the agnostic school, tries to ignore the issue completely, saying that since we don't know what's going on, we're not going to bother with trying to figure it out. The agnostic view tosses it all up to some kind of a metaphysical thing where the attributes were created by some unseen force. From a mathematical perspective, each school of thought is valid and has equal probability."

"What do *you* think, Danny?"

"I think the electrons are showing us that we as human beings are not neutral observers of the universe and that we are actually in a *relationship* that literally influences the world around us. I feel strongly that we affect matter in ways we do not yet perceive."

Who is this *Logos* that I try to measure, observe and define? Could it be possible that I am measuring Him as particle, not realizing that He could also respond to me as a wavelength or as something I cannot even imagine?

How is my system of measuring God limiting what I know about Him?

✡ ✡ ✡

Another Voice

✡ ✡ ✡

"Don't seek God in temples. He is close to you. He is within you. Only you should surrender to Him and you will rise above happiness and unhappiness."

Leo Nikolaevich Tolstoy

As months passed, I journeyed through history hunting after *Logos*. One afternoon, these words snagged my attention.

I utterly dissent from those who are unwilling that the sacred Scriptures should be read by the unlearned translated into their own vulgar tongue. I wish that even the weakest woman should read the Gospels, should read the epistles of St. Paul. I long that the

*husbandman should sing some portion of them to himself as he
follows the plow. Do you think that the Scriptures are fit only for the
perfumed?*[7]

He was quite a fellow, the man who expressed himself so passionately. I soon discovered that he caused quite an upheaval in his day. "The chief evil of the day is formalism, a respect for traditions, a regard for what other people think essential," he said, "but never a thought of what the true teaching of Christ may be."

One thing was for certain: Desiderius Erasmus was a thorn in the side of the religious status quo of his day.

Born in 1466, Erasmus was one of the most prolific writers of his day and he brought transformation to the world through language. The son of a priest who had taken the vow of celibacy, Erasmus and his brother lost both parents to the plagues rampant in England during his childhood. It wasn't long before his uncle shipped the young Erasmus off to a monastery. Quickly gaining a reputation for his intelligence and wit, Erasmus eventually became a priest.

But he behaved in ways that were quite unusual for the Augustinian order. He didn't keep the vigils, never hesitated to eat meat on Friday and berated the overt wickedness of the papacy. Although a sometime favorite of the Pope, he was a constant critic of Pope Julius, the priesthood and the overindulgences of the monks, stating that they would not touch money but were not so scrupulous concerning wine and women. Furthermore, he rebuked the Roman Catholic Church for how it dealt with so-called "heretics."

One of Erasmus' harshest dissensions concerned the Church's doctrine of salvation based upon works and not faith alone. Complaining of the influence of Greek philosophy in the Church, Erasmus bemoaned that "Aristotle is so in vogue that there is scarcely time in the churches to interpret the gospel." Despite his outspoken nature, Erasmus' wit and diplomacy enabled him to keep his head on his shoulders, which was no mean feat at that time.

Erasmus' greatest gift to the world was not his rebuke to the religious status quo of his day. Rather it was his translation of Scriptures from the original Greek into the language of everyday, common people.

During Erasmus' time, the Scriptures were reserved for clergy *only*. There was only one version of the Scriptures, called the Latin Vulgate, and it was completed a thousand years before Erasmus.

Erasmus objected not only with the accuracy of Latin Vulgate but he differed strongly with certain passages that gave pivotal substantiation to the papal authority claimed by the Roman Catholic Church. With the help of printer John Froben and after combing through hundreds of original manuscripts, Erasmus translated the first relatively complete text of the New Testament in Greek and Latin.

Because Erasmus' translation challenged the infallibility of the Latin Vulgate, it soon became a dangerous book to own. Nevertheless, his New Testament was smuggled deep into England where it found warm reception among the scholars of Oxford and Cambridge. Among those scholars was William Tyndale, who had dedicated his life to getting the Bible into the hands of the ordinary people of England.

Erasmus' translation eventually became the basis of the King James Version of the Bible, and thus the quality of Erasmus' work stood the test of time. It wasn't until 1930 that his work was essentially repeated when scholars Westcott and Hott undertook to translate manuscripts from the fourth century.

Would Erasmus have some keys to my quest? Could he help me with *Logos*? What I discovered was something so subtle that I almost missed it. Erasmus didn't translate John 1:1 *Logos* as *Reason* like the Greek philosophers.

No. He translated *Logos* as *Conversation*.

In the beginning was the Logos
(Conversation)
and the Logos was with God
(Relationship)
and the Logos was God.
(The Trinity)

If *Logos* is not simply Word but Conversation, what does that mean? First, God is a speaking Being who converses and dialogues in relationship.

And, second, God's skin is language and I live in it.

The Trinity carries on a dialogue, and from that conversation all living things are created and established. As beings born into *Logos*, we inherit His conversation and even more, are free to invent our own conversations.

In essence, I live in God's skin.

The words I speak, hear and think are constructed with the substance of the conversation that is the great I AM. The conversations and thoughts I have exist in the *Logos*. They float about along with all the others that are going on even those from before time. He is the audience of one each time we make our being evident as we use His flesh, *Logos*.

God is the Speaking Being. What if He is never more than a conversation away from you, or me, or anybody? I am able to see what He has revealed about Himself and commune with Him if I choose to live in His conversation.

Think about times when you wanted to be intimate with someone. Didn't you want them to tell you their thoughts? Wasn't it through conversation that the person became evident to you, with each interaction drawing you deeper into an understanding of how they were being, how they "saw" things, "felt" about things or people?

What if God *is* the very language we are speaking? What intimacy could be possible! How are we making ourselves manifest in our conversations with Him and others?

What if Jesus, the *Logos*, is much different than we imagine or interpret?

He is the spoken Promise who through His death and resurrection made Eternity available to all who choose Him. Jesus declared Himself as "the Way, the Truth and the Light." What would be possible if we join Him in His conversation? Would it be possible for us to live in this temporal world from an eternal conversation?

Let's go one step further. What if the Scriptures and the theology we make of them were never intended to be used to prove the existence of God or to make right what Jesus said? What if they are meant as a doorway, a tiny piece of God revealing Himself to us so that we might relate, commune in our humanity with the Divine?

What if He gave us His word so that we can relate to all people of all races and be all things to all men? How might the eternal word of Jesus open divine and eternal possibilities to us?

What if our system of relating to God is only a sliver of what exists in Him? What if we are measuring God as a particle, from a survivalist point of view, when there is a wavelength aspect of God that we are not seeing?

If we got this, how would our reality shift? What would we see?

Perhaps, a completely new reality.

✡ ✡ ✡

New Ways of Seeing

✡ ✡ ✡

"There is nothing more difficult to carry out, nor more doubtful of success, nor more dangerous to handle, than to initiate a new order of things. For the reformer has enemies in all who profit by the old order. This luke-warmness arises partly from fear of their adversaries who have the law in their favor; and partly from the incredulity of mankind, who do not truly believe in anything new until they have had the actual experience of it."[8]

Machiavelli, *The Prince*

The game was over before it started. Our San Francisco Giants were getting pummeled once again. So, our thoughts and conversation went elsewhere.

"Such a proposition can be a bit confusing to people at first," Danny said. "What you are proposing, Dad, is really different from how we understand life and God."

"I guess so," I wondered back at him.

"But the same thing happened in physics when quantum mechanics hit the scene." Danny mused. "Quantum mechanics challenged the cultural assumptions in a way that hadn't been done up until that point and it took scientists some years before they would even consider the possibilities that it revealed."

"How so, Danny?"

"Since the philosopher Descartes, the guy who said 'I think, therefore I am,' Newtonian science sought to reduce the world into progressively smaller and 'more accurate' properties. Also known as 'the Cartesian approach.' Now when Newtonian scientists discovered quantum mechanics, they found that they had to stop reducing matter to its smallest characteristics. Instead, they began to realize that in order to understand the subatomic world, they had to consider *relationships* to explain, define and predict probable outcomes. In other words, because I could identify and prove that something exists doesn't mean that I can tell you how it will behave."

"So, in real English here, are you saying that the old Newtonian way of science was inadequate?"

"Exactly. In order to understand how particles related to each other, they had to throw away their previously held Cartesian assumptions. Namely, that they, the observers, were subjects objectively observing and measuring a phenomenon."

"What happened next?"

"Major conceptual revolution. They were proposing the idea that the observer actually was influencing that which it observed because the observer through observation has entered into a relationship with what was being observed."

"Say again?"

"Okay, here goes. Instead of Descartes' 'I think, therefore I am,' the system approach looks like 'I become what I think about what I observe.' If I think that what I observe is a lie, I become suspicious. I transform with my assumptions about what I observe."

"So, what you are saying here," I asked, "is that a non-Cartesian or transformational approach has replaced the Cartesian model."

"Yes, but despite being proven irrelevant, Cartesian models persist. For example, Cartesian explanations of psychological reality inevitably lead to reducing observations and understanding of the individual to rigid and fixed characteristics that can be measured and counted like peas in a can. 'You are A, therefore you could never be B.' Hence, we see the dominance of Cartesian thought in contemporary psychological research and explanations for being. In other words, 'Cartesian' explanations of human beings and their social lives together ultimately lead us to descriptions, diagnosis, remedy and explanations of individuals as if their characteristics were fixed and permanent rather than an expression of how they are relating to others and life as a whole. A non-Cartesian approach, on the other hand, suggests that individuals do not, in fact, exist like a fixed, isolated, separate entity with predetermined characteristics. In essence, human persons can only be understood in the context of their relationships."

"That sure makes sense to me," I said as I thought about *Logos* being conversation, implying more than one Being and more than one way of being human. "Haven't you ever noticed how you are 'being' changes from one relationship to another, depending who you are with? Could it be that we are in a process of becoming, rather than a fixed state existence that never changes?"

"Yeah, Dad. Sounds a bit like what Erasmus was referring to in John 1:

They heard the Conversation still going on, here, now, and took part, discovering a new way of being people."

"In summation, Dad, viewing human beings and society itself as a creative, pulsing, changing, adapting system is a radical departure from how we are taught by our culture. The challenge appears to be to probe the depths and dimensions of a divinely created way of relating, a series of conversations of human existence in community."

"Translate, please."

"Here goes. The Cartesian 'conversation' as it manifests itself in today's churches traditionally interprets social order as an organizational chart with positions defined by God in Scripture. In contrast, a relational, non-Cartesian model suggests that society is more like a flow chart of relationships that are evidenced by conversations, assumptions, attitudes and ways of relating. Approaching human beings in a non-Cartesian way means that you seek to open up possibility in relationships between people rather than reduce, describe or formulate interactions into a religious system that dictates the right way to be."

"In a nutshell, it sounds like you are saying that Jesus is more concerned with how we relate to Him and others rather than some position, appearance or form. Like He said, 'Love, or relate to, one another even as I have loved, or related to you.'"

"Dad, you never cease to amaze me!"

Although the Giant's game was over, our conversation was not. Aileen and Liz had given up on us guys, leaving Danny and me to our musings about the nature of the universe.

"Here's another one, Dad."

"Okay, hit me again."

"It's wild when you think about the fact that we measure *what we don't know* from the limited principles that we *do know* here on earth. Take light. For years, physicists tried to figure out what light travels through because, here on earth, everything we know travels through a substance. Sound waves travel through particles hitting each other. Waves pass through water. However, scientists couldn't figure out what light waves pass through. Then we got it. Light is independent of anything. Light needs nothing to pass through."

"Nothing?"

"You see, Dad, light has no mass. It's pure energy. Light does not change its velocity. Instead, space and time shift relative to light. Light is the overall constant of the universe. It transcends time. What gets me excited is that we are made of light. Our cells are made up of atoms, and atoms include electrons. In essence, light. I am convinced we are unaware of how divine we really are and what is really possible. Dad, the bottom line is that we can explain so little because our system of interpretation is so hugely incomplete. For example, our eyes can detect a tiny sliver of the light where we see colors in the visible spectrum, such as the rainbow. However, there are many, many colors and stuff outside that range that we cannot see but know exist. Like X-rays or ultra-violet, gamma rays, infra-red, for example. We just don't understand what exists beyond our own capabilities. We can only analyze light through what we do know."

"No wonder the Scriptures say in 1 Corinthians 13:12: 'For now we see in a mirror, dimly.'" I pondered, "Gives you a whole new understanding of humility doesn't it!"

✡ ✡ ✡

Living in His Skin

✡ ✡ ✡

"Life, is not a having and a getting, but a being and a becoming."9
Matthew Arnold

"He was in the beginning with God.
All things were made through Him
and without Him nothing was made that was made."
John 1:2-3

I exist in what I cannot explain.

I live in the mystery of *Logos*. All I know is what He has revealed through His skin of language:

He is the image of the invisible God,
the first born of all creation.
For by Him, all things were created,
both in the heavens and on earth, visible and invisible,
whether thrones or dominions or rulers or authorities
all things have been created through Him.
He is before all things
and in Him, all things hold together.
He is the head of the body, the church;
and He is the beginning, the firstborn from the dead,
so that He Himself will come to have first place in everything.
For it was the Father's good pleasure for all the fullness to dwell in Him,
and through Him to reconcile all things to Himself,
having made peace through the blood of His cross.

Without *Logos* there would be nothing but profound silence.

Complete void. No earth, no animals, no man or woman, no family. No words. No emotions. No beauty. There would be no understanding, right or wrong, good or evil, angels or demons.

Everything has been created through Jesus, the *Logos*.

Everything. All that is visible and invisible, known and unknown, love, hatred, death, life, the universe itself would not exist outside of Him. Even freedom.

In *Logos*, God has also given me complete freedom. I can question everything, including my own existence as a human being. I can invent, speculate, imagine and exalt myself above the knowledge given in *Logos* Himself. I have the freedom to choose whether or not the Conversation will run my life. I can choose the language that brings life or a conversation that brings death. I can even make *Logos* in my own image.

God's skin has me and everything else, including the Anti-*Logos*.

I am in a Conversation that contains not only the Word made Flesh but also that being who opposes the *Logos*. This Anti-*Logos*, the anti-Christ, is a created being and lives in the *Logos* as a free being. God through Christ created beings free to interpret themselves through *Logos* and this Adversary, Satan, was one of God's created beings who chose to make evident his being as evil or Anti-*Logos*. He has freely chosen to identify himself as "against" *Logos*.

The Anti-*Logos* finds his meaning only because of *Logos*. Like me, he exists as freely to construct his own conversation. He is the father of the conversation of death and darkness. And, we can hear him.

What if being in God's skin is like being fish in the sea? Like the water that circulates from the skies to the oceans and back to the skies again, what if all the conversations that have happened throughout time are the conversations that we as human beings are swimming in?

And our only choice is choice itself.

What if "I" in *Logos* is like a person sitting in a chair in the middle of a room listening to many others who are speaking? In this room, I get to choose which conversation I am going to listen to or not. I get to decide which voices will empower me, and how I will empower them.

In *Logos*, could it be that I am only a chooser? That "I" am not what I hear, only the listener who chooses what to make up about what I hear?

When I hear a conversation of anger and choose to be angry, *I am not anger* but the chooser deciding to be empowered by that *anger conversation*.

If I try to ignore the choice I have as a chooser, then what happens next is that the conversations that are the loudest influence me. Because I have resisted, ignored or denied my role as the chooser, I default into thinking that "I am angry" or "I am lustful" or "I am an addict." What if I am nothing more than a chooser in the middle of the sea of conversations passing through the room? The thoughts and feelings are not me, the "I," but something "I," the chooser, swim in like a fish swimming in the sea.

In this light, take a look at Paul's exhortations in 2 Corinthians 10:4-5 (NIV):

We demolish arguments and every pretension that sets itself up against the knowledge of God, and we take captive every thought to make it obedient to Christ.

Paul is telling us that *arguments and pretensions have set themselves up* against the knowledge of God. What we do is take every thought captive to make it obedient to Christ. In saying that arguments and pretensions are themselves to be obedient, Paul is speaking as if they have their own being.

Could he be onto something?

Could "I" be the chooser who knows when "it" was born, yet not when "it" began? Who knows that I will die but not when "I" will end? Who knows not itself but merely the shadows it casts in the light of the ever-continuing conversation?

Consider further what God has said in Deuteronomy 30:19-20:

I have set before you life and death, blessings and curses.
Now choose life, so that you and your children may live.

If I am the chooser and not the origin, what does this mean? I think the word is transformation.

I think that we could truly be changed, transformed, in the "twinkle of an 'I'" through shifting in our choice. We could cease from confusing the "I" with what has chosen "me" in God's skin and, as the chooser, decide which thoughts will define "me," the "I," to others.

How precious to me are your thoughts, O God!
How vast is the sum of them!
Were I to count them,
they would outnumber the grains of sand.
When I awake, I am still with you.
If only you would slay the wicked, O God!
Away from me, you bloodthirsty men!
They speak of you with evil intent;
your adversaries misuse your name.

Psalm 139:17-20

Day turns into night. Night becomes the new day. I breathe. I feel.
I think. I touch. I grieve. I speak. I wonder. What is this existence in which
I live, move and have my being? Who am I? Who are you?
Who is this God?

Notes:

[1] Roland Barthes, *A Lover's Discourse: Fragments*, translated by Richard Howard. (1979), p. 73.

[2] Howard Baker, *Soul Keeping: Ancient Paths of Spiritual Direction* (NavPress, 1998).

[3] Benjamin Zander and Rosamund Zander, *The Art of Possibility: Transforming Personal and Professional Life* (Penguin Books, 2002).

[4] Dagobert D. Runes, *The Dictionary of Philosophy* (Citadel Press, 2001), p. 324.

[5] *The History of Christian Thought*; "Lecture 2: The Readiness of the Ancient World to Receive Christianity" (Touchstone Books, Hannah Tillich 1967, 1968) (can be found at http://www.religion-online.org/showchapter. asp?title=2310&C=2308).

[6] Søren Kierkegaard, *Philosophical Fragments [1844]*.

[7] Paraclesis, Basel ed. V. 117 sq; quoted in *History of the Christian Church,* Volume VI: The Middle Ages. A.D. 1294-1517.; §77. The Study and Circulation of the Bible. http://www.ccel.org/ccel/schaff/hcc6.ii.x.vi.html?highlight=the,9,parts,of, bible - highlight#highlight

[8] Machiavelli, *The Prince*, translated by Luigi Ricci (Signet Classic, 1999), p. 49.

[9] Quoted in *Letters of Justice Louis D Brandeis*, by Louis Dembitz Brandeis, Melvin I. Urofsky, David W. Levy (SUNY Press, 1971), p. 94.

IMAGO DEI

"In a word man knows he is wretched. Thus he is wretched because he is so, but he is truly great because he knows it." [1]
Blaise Pascal

✧ ✧ ✧

Monsters in the Dark

✧ ✧ ✧

The memory of that night is burned into my body.

I awoke with a start, hearing my eight-year-old son screaming out my name. I rushed down the hall into Danny's room to find him sitting straight up in bed, his eyes big as saucers. His face was red and covered in tears; his thin baby hair pasted to his head with sweat. As I entered his room, he said, "Daddy, I killed a monster in you."

"It was just a bad dream, son," I replied as I held him tight.

"No, Daddy. There was this mean monster in you, and I had to kill it so you could come alive again."

"Well, Danny, I did have a monster inside of me called 'cocaine,' and it was my love for you that killed it. But see? I'm here now and everything is all right."

"Will you stay with me?"

"I'm not going anywhere." I assured him as I rocked him back to sleep.

Years passed from that night but not the pattern. As he grew up, Danny would give offhand comments from time to time about the nightmares he was experiencing. I knew that my son was not only very intelligent but also exceedingly intuitive in a prophetic way.

During his teenage years he would often sit silently and withdrawn. I could tell he was in deep thought with his eyebrows furled in a pose that gave the impression that he was on the verge of something very important. When I would ask him what he was feeling he would look at me and say, "Feeling? What do you mean?" There was truly a sense of not knowing exactly what I was referring to. He would think about my question and just answer, "I don't know what to say, Dad."

Fifteen years after that horrid night, I gained some insight into what it was all about.

Danny had turned twenty-one years old and had decided to participate in The Discovery Seminar for the first time. I had developed Discovery in 1999 out of the recognition that there was a demand for a faith based educational model dedicated to people breaking through to unprecedented levels of fulfillment and satisfaction in their lives. During Discovery, participants examine attitudes and assumptions that limit their relationships with God and others. The process is a powerful inquiry into what kind of character is called for to transform purpose into reality.

During this particular Discovery, I had invited the participants to consider Logos and our existence as an ever-continuing, pre-existing conversation. As the participants and I engaged this possibility of our being, I continually interrupted the Cartesian ideas about "I" as the subject originating their thoughts. Instead, I introduced the possibility that some of the thoughts were having us, instead of us having them.

After Discovery, I found out that Danny had been tremendously impacted during the conversation. For days, he had pondered the implications of being in Logos like a fish is in water, and what opened for him was monumental. Unbeknownst to me, through the years he had been much more plagued with violent dreams and dark thoughts than I realized.

He explained that often his silence as a teen was the result of guilt for having violent, lustful, and sometimes angry thoughts, adding that he could not find a reason for why he was having them.

He had assumed that there was something fundamentally wrong or evil about himself.

During Discovery, Danny had come to the revelation that the oppressive dreams and thoughts he was experiencing may be part of that ever-continuing, pre-existing conversation that we are swimming in as human beings. What opened up for him was that *he* wasn't evil for experiencing those dreams and could choose not to make them significant or have them define his existence.

For the first time since he was a child, my son was free from his oppressor. The guilt was gone, and now Danny had tools to disengage and even learn from his dreams. If they did occur again, he could choose not to signify them and "rest in the presence of the One who established him."

Talking to me after Discovery, Danny said, "Dad, you used to say something to me I never really understood until now. You would say, 'Son, significance breeds resistance.' Now I am clear what that means for me. When I make these dreams significant, you know, saying that 'because I am having them there must be something wrong with me,' I resist life as it shows up for me I am ashamed because I believe there is something wrong with me, and who wants to be with somebody who is defective? Then I withdraw from life, which isolates me from others!"

Soon after we talked, Aileen remarked how she had never seen Danny so animated and talkative. It was as though Danny had discovered his voice.

His freedom, that's what I call it.

✧ ✧ ✧

...As He Is...

✧ ✧ ✧

"Prepare yourself for the world, as the athletes used to do for their exercise; oil your mind and your manners, to give them the necessary suppleness and flexibility; strength alone will not do."
Lord Chesterfield

"**D**an! Mom is going to kill herself!"

I shut the front door behind me, hot and covered in sweat from my high school football practice. What had greeted me was my sister, Cindy, in tears. Upstairs, white as sheets, I saw my little brother, Leo, along with Corey, my other brother, standing in front of the upstairs bathroom just outside my mother and father's room.

"Mom won't come out of the bathroom. She said she's going to kill herself."

Putting my gear down, I said, "Hey, you guys, it's time for dinner. Get everyone into the kitchen and get the table set. I'll get her out." As the three scurried into the kitchen, I took the stairs two at a time and put my face next to the bathroom door.

I knocked. No answer.

Putting my face inches from the door, I said loudly, "Look, if you're going to kill yourself, get it over with because we have to get dinner ready. I'll call the ambulance now and get your body out of here."

Immediately, the door opened. There was Mom, all primped up with her hair and make-up immaculate. "I was just wondering," she said smiling sweetly as dove, "if anyone out there cared."

There you have it, my bi-polar, manic depressive mom. Back then, you never quite knew what to expect. High. Low. Someone you knew. Or another person, a mystery guest, altogether.

Another wild moment happened between us when I was still a teenager. Coming home, I found her at 1:00 p.m. in bed and under the covers. "What are you doing!?" I asked.

"I am Jesus Christ," she answered me from under the sheets.

"You're not Jesus Christ," I said back to her. "You're Jeanette."

Sitting up, Mom, with a dead-serious expression on her face, told me once again, "I am Jesus Christ."

"Yeah. And I'm Captain Kangaroo. Now let's get going."

It didn't take a second for Mom to start laughing, I knew she was back with us, at least for the time being.

There are few heroes in my life like my mom. I have watched my mom meet her fair share of challenges, as someone who had to work through mental illness. Despite every temptation to call it quits, Mom has never given up or compromised her high moral standards. She doesn't care if you are the richest man on earth or even the Pope himself, she is tough as nails when it comes to the truth, especially when it comes to herself.

As an adult, I have come to realize that our relationship has prepared me for life in ways neither one of us anticipated. Through our many experiences together, I learned not to be afraid or intimidated by how people were acting or the process they were in. Through having a mom who was sometimes crazy like nothing you have ever seen, I was taught how to listen and discern what someone with or without a mental illness was trying to say to me. And I learned to say sometimes, "Yeah. And, I'm Captain Kangaroo. Now let's get going."

Similar to my mom's road to recovery, my own personal transformations, kicking drugs, trusting others, becoming a husband and father, pursuing loving my neighbor as myself, have come through listening, discerning and shifting my internal conversations.

By becoming aware of what conversations I was choosing to define me, I realized that I could change what I was saying outwardly about myself and others. As my conversations shifted, so did my behavior. New and unprecedented possibilities emerged in my life.

Noticing this link between my thoughts, words, behavior and new possibilities, I stumbled upon something profound. I realized that for most of my life I had assumed that I was the originator of my own thoughts.

Let me explain. One day I was having a conversation with my friend, John Hanley. He simply said, "Hey, Dan. What are you thinking about?" I told him I was feeling guilty about something.

Then, he hit me with a zinger. John said, "What if those thoughts were having you, instead of *you having them*?"

What? Now that's a crazy idea, isn't it? I create my thoughts and even control them. Don't I?

He suggested that I try a simple experiment. If I were the author and finisher of my thoughts, then logically I would have the power to stop or start my thinking anytime I wanted.

Right? Wrong.

The experiment alone almost drove me nuts. I was shocked. I could *not* stop thinking. I had thoughts continually and without interruption 24/7; waking or sleeping, my thoughts were like a TV that would not turn off. As much as I wanted to stop thinking, *I couldn't*.

Time and time again, my internal conversation would merrily wander off into some thought about *something*. No matter how hard I tried, I could not stop thinking. Even when I sought to be meditative, still and silent inside, I would discover that I would be thinking about *not* thinking. I asked the Lord to help me and then think about how He might help me out.

Finally it dawned on me that if I stopped thinking, I wouldn't know it because I would have no thoughts. Egad. If I can't stop my thoughts, what else can I not stop having?

Feelings.

I had no control over the fact that I had feelings. They didn't ask my permission first. Some are great; others make one wonder from what pit they had escaped. Weird or elated thoughts hit me from out of nowhere, leading me to ask, "Where did *that* come from?"

Whoa. I had not realized this before.

All of a sudden, I became acutely aware that other people were in the same boat as I was. In the trainings, I would hear otherwise "normal" men and women talk about their own demoralizing thoughts, and like me they would reveal their shame, guilt and anguish over what they assumed they were generating from some mysterious dark recess inside of them.

"I don't know where these thoughts are coming from," they would say, meaning "I don't know what is wrong with me."

Then when I started doing trainings overseas in foreign countries, the same phenomenon would happen. It got to the point where I did not need a translator to understand the inner struggles that our training participants were experiencing. The themes, the drumbeats and the heartaches were identical around the globe. Individuals in different cultures were having the same experiences!

Curiously, I asked, "Why are we having the same conversations, simply dressed up in different personalities and cultures? Were any of us really thinking? Did other generations experience what we are experiencing now?"

Re-reading some of the Ancients, such as St. Augustine's writings about how his thoughts had led him into sin, I questioned the nature of our internal thought life.

Is it possible that we were living in a world similar to the one portrayed in the film, *The Matrix* (1999), where we show up in a conversation of language that pre-existed our appearance on the scene? If so, does that mean I am *not* the one who is thinking and feeling?

As I explored these ideas, the circuits of my Cartesian mind were overloaded and blown out by the implications of all this!

Is *something else* thinking and feeling and I am *just having* those thoughts and feelings? Am I like a fish swimming in an ocean of thoughts and feelings? Like a radio picking up a bunch of stations all at once? Could that *something else* be related to my being made in the Image of God?

My questions led me back to the beginning.

In the beginning, God created the heavens and the earth. The earth was without form and void and darkness was on the face of the deep. And the Spirit of God was hovering over the face of the waters. Then God said, "Let there be light": and there was light. Then God said, "Let there be an expanse in the midst of the waters and let it divide the waters from the waters." Then God said, "Let the waters under the heavens be gathered together into one place and let the dry land appear"; and it was so.

Genesis 1:3, 6, 9

Nothing existed before God spoke.

All of Creation everything, absolutely everything we see, touch, taste, sense, smell, hear, think, feel, know, imagine and experience was in the being of God before He articulated it into substance and meaning. He had thoughts. Through His speaking those thoughts, Creation was manifested.

Then God said, "Let the earth bring forth grass, the herb that yields seed, and the fruit tree that yields according to its kind; whose seed is in itself, on the earth": and it was so.

Then God said, "Let there be lights in the expanse of heavens to divide the day from the night and let them be for signs and seasons and for days and years and let them be for lights in the expanse in the heavens to give light on the earth."

Then God said, "Let the waters abound with an abundance of living creatures, and let the birds fly above the earth across the face of the expanse of the heavens."

Then God said, "Let the earth bring forth the living creature according to its kind: cattle and creeping thing and beast of the earth, each according to its kind"; and it was so.

Genesis 1:11, 14, 15, 20, 24

Layer after layer of dimension everything was given its meaning through God's voice. His spoken-out words, His conversation!

Finally like a crescendo in a symphony, God put Himself into what He had created. Out of His Being, the Trinity spoke the image of Himself into existence.

He spoke us into being.

> Then God said, "Let Us make man in Our image according to Our likeness; let them have dominion over the fish of the sea, over the birds of the air, and over the cattle, over all the earth and over every creeping thing on the earth."
> So God created man in His own image; in the image of God He created him; male and female He created them. Then God blessed them and God said to them, "Be fruitful and multiply; fill the earth and subdue it..."
>
> Genesis 1:26, 27

As I took a look at Genesis 1, my imagination went wild. As human beings created in the image of God, we are speaking beings who have the capacity to converse like the Godhead!

What does that mean? As I pondered this question I began to imagine that Human Being has been in a conversation for thousands of years. It has its own concerns: looking good, feeling good and being in control in essence, survival. And those concerns seemed to automatically be at the root of our conversations. Further, it appears that Human Being is using us, and it isn't using us for love!

✧ ✧ ✧

Untying the Knots

✧ ✧ ✧

"One of the major signs of despair is distraction, because it cannot even stand itself."
Søren Kierkegaard

Aileen didn't want to talk about it. Every time I broached the subject she became very upset at me. But I kept having these ugly, fearful thoughts.

What would happen if Danny and Elizabeth died?

As this thought and subsequent fears became stronger, I hid them from Aileen. In the process, I felt more and more isolated from her. Compounding my anxiety was the statistic I had heard on a public education channel that reported ninety-seven percent of marriages end in divorce after the death of a child.

"I could lose everything" (survival), I thought (automatically).

Even though I tried not to pay attention to these thoughts and fears, they grew more persistent. As I resisted and kept them in the dark, I became increasingly distracted, apprehensive and isolated.

Then what I feared happened to two good friends of mine.

Their young son died from leukemia, and soon after the ordeal they divorced. As I talked with them, they both confessed that while they knew nobody was to blame, they still found themselves blaming the other. The feelings and thoughts they were having only compounded their grief, and eventually they got to a place where they could no longer bear being together.

Hearing their story, I was in anguish.

Could there have been a different outcome if they had talked about the potential death of their son before it happened? Were they having the conversation or was the conversation having them? If they had brought their fears to each other, could the tragedy have united them instead of tearing them apart? Seeing my friends' marriage turn into a shipwreck, I couldn't stop wondering when the marriage actually began to unravel.

In the book, *The World According to Garp*[2], the character, Garp, admits that once in a while the thought of losing their children would pass through his and his wife's conversation. Neither one would talk about it except to refer to their thoughts as "the Turtle" or some other such animal. This was their little signal that kept them from engaging those unpleasant thoughts.

I realized that, as human beings, this death conversation is having us.

We are so terrified of its potentiality that we instinctively resist the conversation. However, refusing to look at what we are thinking about death meant that it already had us, instead of us having it. Through our mutual resistance, Aileen and I were divorced and not one with each other.

So I jumped in. "Aileen," I said, "What do you think would happen to us if Danny or Elizabeth died?

Immediately Aileen became livid. "Dan, just you mentioning that thought makes me even more afraid that it might happen."

Hearing Aileen's fearfulness, I realized that both of us had been dogged by the same fear. And, I got ticked off. Big time. This fear had us around the throat.

I refused to let Aileen isolate herself from me. We got back into the conversation, and as we talked it through, we were able to start dismantling our fear of "What if…"

The more we talked, Aileen and I saw "it" had "divorced" us, and in that separation we had made up things about each other. We had assumed an unbearable future, instead of even considering the possibility that tragedy could have made us more passionate about each other and about living.

We had never considered the possibility that suffering and loss could bring deeper meaning to our lives. I saw that I had been only thinking about myself and Danny and Elizabeth. They would have wanted their lives and deaths to bind us together and not tear us apart.

That night, Aileen and I learned a couple of great lessons about freedom.

First, I learned that the conversation of death was here way before Aileen and I arrived. I thought again about what the Apostle Paul writes in Ephesians 2:1:

And you were dead in your trespasses and sins, in which you formerly walked according to the course of this world, according to the prince of the power of the air, of the spirit that is now working in the sons of disobedience.

Moreover, I learned that Aileen and I were having the same conversation internally. One was, "Let's not talk about this and everything will be okay." The other one was, "If we talk about death, then that could bring what we fear to happen." This conversation had us so deeply entrenched inside we had isolated ourselves in fear and distraction, hoping that the anxiety would somehow disappear into the background of life's activities.

This experience with Aileen changed everything.

✧ ✧ ✧

Making the Invisible Visible

✧ ✧ ✧

"Passion, it lies in all of us, sleeping... waiting... and though unwanted... unbidden... it will stir... open its jaws and howl. It speaks to us... guides us... passion rules us all, and we obey. What other choice do we have? Passion is the source of our finest moments. The joy of love... the clarity of hatred... and the ecstasy of grief. It hurts sometimes more than we can bear. If we could live without passion maybe we'd know some kind of peace... but we would be hollow... empty rooms shuttered and dank. Without passion we'd be truly dead." [3]

Joss Whedon

Our discussion opened a possibility that I hadn't seen up until this time. The more Aileen and I brought our private conversations into the light of external examination, the less they had power, significance or sway over us. By making what was invisible visible, we could start untying the knots around our wrists. We could be free.

The conversations I tend to resist are the ones that persist. By hiding it, I empower it. By revealing it, I open the possibility of transforming by gaining some distance between the conversation and the one who can observe it, which gives it less and less control over me.

There by I keep myself from making things up about me that are not true and allow myself to agree with the possibility that God has made up for me.

All things are possible for those who believe.

Jesus, from Mark 9:23

It was becoming clear to me that I have inherited a number of "I"s.

I was starting to suspect that the pronoun "I" that we use to speak about ourselves such as "I am sad," "I am alcoholic," or "I am just this way" has us.

If I argue for my limitations, then they are my inheritance. Human beings act congruently with who or what we think we are.
As a man thinks, so is he.
Proverbs 23:7

Let's take a common conversation we have all heard others use when they break their word with us. "I know I am late a lot, but it's just the way 'I' am. I can't help it!"

When we use strategies like these to survive, we are simultaneously revealing as much as we are covering up. Subtext: *"So, don't expect from me what I don't expect from myself, even if I promise it!"*

My words say "I can't," which means I don't have the ability. As if I am unable, victimized by my nature to do anything about what is hurting you. It is a statement of fact that indicts anybody who dares to question it. Think about it. Logically, it would be a very insensitive and cruel thing of you or anybody else to require of me what is not possible. At the very least it would be inhumane, and it would make you look bad. So, others tend to go along so they will survive as well. I mean, who wants to look bad?!

And should anybody dare to demand the performance or forbearance of what was promised, they will experience the indignation and contempt that they deserve for making fun of me in such a sadistic way for being crippled!

Words are revealing because they give us clues that we are hiding something. In the above conversation, I cover my need to protect myself by framing what I have promised as impossible because I don't have the ability.

What happens when people give up on what it is they long for? Don't they get apathetic, angry, dispassionate, resentful, etc?

✿ ✿ ✿

Signs of Resistance

✿ ✿ ✿

"There is only love; everything else is our resistance to it."
Terces Engelhart

When we think we will not survive which always shows up in one of these domains: physically dying, looking bad (socially dying), feeling bad (emotionally dying), out of control (relationally dying) then we resist what is happening and that resistance shows up like so many different strategies. These strategies become ways of telegraphing what is being covered up or hidden.

What happens when we sense we are vulnerable to somebody who could hurt us? I notice that I tend to omit or minimize the subject if possible. If that doesn't work then I may try to completely obfuscate it by changing the subject or focus of the conversation. Notice when you don't want to talk about something because it is threatening to you in some way and it comes up. How do you tend to "show up"? Do you avoid, obscure, not say anything or even misdirect the conversation so as not to bring to light that which you fear can harm you?

Could this be Human Being's way of using you? The phenomenon is universally human. That is why I can write about it, and you can relate to it. We have all been used by it.

We may verbally attack what is being said. Other times we agree with others just to avoid getting into what we assume will be an argument that could reveal things we don't want talked about. We develop strategies to avoid or drive danger or threat out of our immediate experience. We have become so familiar with these winning ways that we end up rarely examining the price we pay for the immediate relief we get from such actions.

Sometimes we hide out in selfishness and intentionally create distance between ourselves and others. At other times, we resign ourselves to whatever the status quo will provide. Whatever we do to survive, it imprisons us from the inheritance of an unprecedented future. We are impotent to transform any purpose into reality except just surviving. We dare not dream or long for anything more than what those romantic sensations we inherited from humanity known as our opinions tell us are possible.

What if the first act of freedom is speaking our longing for life when the opinions of the ages inform our experience that death is all that awaits us?

As one of my favorite authors, C.S. Lewis, writes in his fictional book, *The Great Divorce*[4]:

Our opinions were not honestly come by.
We simply found ourselves in contact with a certain current of ideas
and plunged into it because it seemed modern and successful.

At College, you know, we just started automatically writing the
kind of essay that got good marks and saying the kind of
things that won applause.
When, in our whole lives did we honestly face, in solitude, the
one question on which all turned: whether after all the
Supernatural might not in fact occur?
When did we put up one moment's real resistance to the
loss of our faith?"

✧ ✧ ✧

Being Un-Had

✧ ✧ ✧

"Three times in my life I have been captured: by the orphanage, by
school, and by the Army. But I'm mistaken. The fact is I was captured
only once, when I was born, only that capture is also setting free,
which is what this is actually all about."[5]
William Saroyan

It was an important introduction made by a close and influential friend to a successful organizational development expert who had worked with international ministries such as our Association for Christian Character Development. However, from the moment Aileen and I were introduced to the man, I knew we were headed right for the ditch.

Why? Because I was driving.

Seconds into the meeting, I found myself being defensive, edgy and irritated but not with the advisor who had agreed to talk with us. Rather, the one I wanted to put a gag order around was my own dear wife, Aileen. With a force that caught me by surprise, I started to interrupt her rudely.

Getting increasingly angry at my behavior, Aileen returned a round or two in my direction. Soon the whole atmosphere of the room went south, leaving our host and invited guest a little embarrassed and amused at our right-out-there-in-the-wide-open-range marriage.

After the dust settled, I asked myself, *What triggered my irritability?* An honest moment with God soon gave me my answer.

I was attached to the thought that my wife should think the way I thought, especially in public. Prior to this meeting if you had asked me outright if Aileen always had to agree with me, I would have replied, "What planet are you living on?" I would have confidently told you that unity is not conformity. We could have differing opinions but still be one in a common purpose and mission.

My behavior, however, revealed what I really thought.

The truth was that I believed that Aileen should agree with me at all times and on all issues. When she did not agree, I interpreted her actions as desertion and betrayal you know, do what it takes to survive.

The more I saw how I had aligned my thoughts and behavior with this "blind loyalty to Dan" idea, the more I felt that deep bitter sting, like a fool taken for his money. I saw the meaning that I had created with that thought, and I had to work to undo the negative affect it had generated on my wife and that unprecedented future we were committed to in our lives and work.

I had been had. And, I did not like it at all.

So, now what?

I had to take this on with rigor. First, I needed to become much more aware of what was going in my internal conversation. Then, I had to consider something about my free will, namely if *something else is thinking* and I am just *having* those thoughts, then my free will is not what I had assumed it to be.

Could it be that I am not as free as I thought?

I think I am infinitely free in a tiny sliver of space. I am seeing that free will and real thinking happens only in the space between me, the chooser, and what I am experiencing as thoughts and feelings. My freedom lies there, in that clearing where I choose how I am going to respond to those thoughts and feelings. In other words, I am not my thoughts nor am I my feelings.

Only I observe that I am having certain thoughts or feelings. The minute I observe I am having them, then the clearing is created between the thought and the one observing and inquiring into it.

I become aware of my opportunity to choose. Until I recognize that certain thoughts and feelings are occurring, they will appear *to be me*. In this scenario, there is no choice, only automatic reaction.

Existing in *Logos*, the one thing I *can* control is *what I do with my thoughts and feelings*. Although I cannot keep them from happening, I do possess the freedom to choose how I am going to relate to them.

Remember Professor John Nash and *A Beautiful Mind* once again.

When Nash believed that he was being had by these delusional people, then he could have them more than they had him. Only after he acknowledged that he was seeing imaginary people could he develop a different relationship with them.

Professor Nash's transformation did not stop after he realized what was going on. Rather, he had to rigorously disengage himself from these delusional people on an on-going basis. He had to continually not give them significance even though they would still haunt him. Day after day, year after year, Nash had to humbly and continually persevere in his commitment not to give these fictional people meaning, even though he still saw them and experienced their presence. Only until he chose not to engage them did their influence decrease.

What did it take?

Love. It was Nash's love for his wife and their future together that compelled and sustained him.

To me, this old Zen metaphor seems to say it all. A perplexed young pupil approached his master with a question. "Master! Master! I have these two dogs the past that limits me and the future that inspires me fighting inside of me. Which one will win?"

With a smile, the Master calmly replied, "The one you feed the most."

Just like that pupil, we have these two dogs inside of us barking for attention. The one we feed the most will win.

I can release the burden of having thoughts and feelings. I can stop obsessing or feeling condemnation over what I should or should not be experiencing. Rather, I can learn to disengage from what is distracting me from the future I am committed to having.

The key distinction here is that I have a choice. I am neither helpless nor omnipotent. Free will has given me the opportunity to choose who I will be in any circumstance. No matter what happens, as long as I am breathing I can go again.

A number of years ago, I came home from a business trip. As I was walking towards the front door, I noticed that I was extremely irritable. Just that second, Aileen opened the door and immediately asked me to help her put our five-year-old daughter Elizabeth to bed.

Instantaneously, I began to complain. I was tired. I had been away for so long. I needed time to unwind before jumping back into home life. Whine. Whine. Whine.

With each word I spoke, I noticed myself complaining but I allowed it to continue. When I finally took a breath, Aileen looked at me and said, "Would you like a do-over?" I laughed. I knew exactly what she meant. She was saying, "Would you like to stop making your complaint significant and invent a new possibility that will work for us right now?"

I smiled, did a 180-degree turn and walked out the door. Then, I turned around and walked back in with, "Hi honey! How are you? I missed you so much. Where are Liz and Danny? I can't wait to see them. Is there something I can do to help you?" Though I was being facetious, my commitment to shift started to transform me. Before I knew it, we were both upstairs having a great time putting the kids to bed.

As I become more familiar and aware of my internal conversations, I find that they have much less significance or power over my behavior. I become open to subtleties and motivating thoughts, while learning in the ambiguity of the questions they may raise. I can be a detached observer of my feelings and not their slave.

As I identify and choose, I can be un-had.

✧ ✧ ✧

In Whose Likeness You Are

✧ ✧ ✧

"Each of us literally chooses, by his way of attending to things, what sort of universe he shall appear to himself to inhabit."[6]
William James

"This was the life, the life that was the light of men shining in the
darkness,
a darkness which neither understood nor quenched its creativity."
John 1:4, 5

What if *subdue* means to bring every conversation out of
darkness and into the light? After all, wasn't everything made
spoken into existence? What if dominion talked about in Genesis 1:28
happens through our words?

As I wrestled with understanding what it means to live in *Logos*,
I continued to ask questions that often led to more questions rather
than yielding answers. How much will God have me? I can give
myself to Him, but how much will He have me? How much will
others have me?

I looked to Jesus.

Jesus, the *Logos* made flesh, was a declaration. He is *the Being*
who is the complete Image of God. He was and is the Imago Dei.

However, I believe 100% that Jesus lived in the same tension between darkness and light as we do. He was in *Logos*, just
like us, but as the "I," the chooser; Jesus Christ always chose the
Father's will.

In the Garden of Gethsemane, I think He experienced thoughts
and feelings that we would have experienced if we had been in His
shoes such as thoughts and feelings that urged Him to save Himself.

However Jesus Christ disengaged Himself from that survival conversation and embraced another conversation the one that spoke
to Him about His Father's sacrificial love. He made His declaration.
Jesus' declaration of love was possibility and joy in the face of death.

He showed up in the world *as* His Word. And, because He did, we
know Him.

As a speaking being made in the Imago Dei or Image of God,
I am also free to declare meaning through my words and my actions.
I have power over my own speaking and, like Jesus, I can show up in
the world as my word.

Without my speaking, I am not.

For centuries now, the focus of the theological inquiry into the
Imago Dei has been from the perspective of "what's in it for us?"
From "bodily form" to "mental and moral endowments" to "rationality

and freedom" regarding the inquiry into what "image" means, human beings have put themselves at the center of attention instead of seeing that we are paupers before the Great King.

The one beautiful exception is Jonathan Edwards, the great American scholar and theologian of the New England colonies in the eighteenth century. Recently I discovered an unpublished essay written by Edwards on the Trinity.[7] In it, Edwards gives us significant revelation about the nature of the Godhead and what it means to be made in the image of God.

The knowledge or view which God has of Himself must necessarily be conceived to be something distinct from His mere existence. There must be something that answers to our reflection. The reflection as we reflect on our own minds carries something of imperfection in it. However, if God beholds Himself so as thence to have delight and joy in Himself, He must become his own object. There must be duplicity (duality). There is God and the idea of God if it be proper to call a conception of that that is purely spiritual an idea.

What Edwards is expressing here is something we also experience.

He is saying that we have an idea of ourselves while at the same time being ourselves. Because the *reflection* of ourselves is flawed, we are made painfully aware of the difference between the two. This condition does give us the idea of the "duplicity" or the duality that Edwards is talking about.

The key distinction here is that to have an idea of oneself, one must be having a conversation with oneself. Otherwise there is no idea to be considered.

Therefore as God with perfect clearness, fullness and strength, understands Himself, views His own essence (in which there is no distinction of substance and act but which is wholly substance and wholly act), that idea which God hath of Himself is absolutely Himself.

This representation of the Divine nature and essence is the Divine nature and essence again: so that by God's thinking of the Deity must certainly be generated. Hereby there is another person begotten, there is another Infinite Eternal Almighty and most holy and the same God, the very same Divine nature.

And this Person is the second person in the Trinity, the Only Begotten and dearly Beloved Son of God; He is the eternal, necessary, perfect,

substantial and personal idea which God hath of Himself; and that it is
so seems to me to be abundantly confirmed by the Word of God.

I believe Edwards is saying that when God thinks, it is life. As God formulates His thought into language, the idea has being or it lives.

In essence, the Speaking Being creates through language.

What I discovered from Edwards was that God's image is a particularly distinct conversation in the sea of conversations that He has in His grace allowed to be generated by His creatures.

The Godhead being thus begotten by God's loving an idea of Himself
and shewing forth in a distinct subsistence or person in that idea, there
proceeds a most pure act, and an infinitely holy and sacred energy
arises between the Father and Son in mutually loving and delighting
in each other, for their love and joy is mutual. "I was daily His delight
rejoicing always before Him" (Prov. 8:30).

This is the eternal and most perfect and essential act of the Divine
nature, wherein the Godhead acts to an infinite degree and in the
most perfect manner possible. The Deity becomes all act, the Divine es-
sence itself flows out and is as it were breathed forth in love and joy.
So that the Godhead therein stands forth in yet another manner of sub-
sistence, and there proceeds the third Person in the Trinity,
the Holy Spirit, viz., the Deity in act, for there is no other act
but the act of the will.

Edwards distinguishes the Holy Spirit as the "Deity in act." The acts of God are in and of themselves a person of the Godhead. These are not acts of utilitarian nature but of abundant love, appreciation and rejoicing. In other words, the Godhead's love and joy are made evident in acts toward the beloved.

This is confirmed by the symbol of the Holy Ghost, viz., a dove, which is
the emblem of love or a lover, and is so used in Scripture, and especially
often so in Solomon's Song, "Behold thou art fair; my love, behold thou
art fair; thou hast dove's eyes": i.e., "Eyes of love," and again 4:1, the
same words; and 5:12, "His eyes are as the eyes of doves," and 5:2,
"My love, my dove," and 2:14 and 6:9; and this I believe to be the reason
that the dove alone of all birds (except the sparrow in the single case of
the leprosy) was appointed to be offered in sacrifice because of its
innocence and because it is the emblem of love, love being the
most acceptable sacrifice to God.

It was under this similitude that the Holy Ghost descended
from the Father on Christ at His baptism, signifying the infinite

love of the Father to the Son, Who is the true David,
or beloved, as we said before.

His image is revealed in relationship—love, delight, joy, mercy, kindness all the generous acts of love. By definition, love requires another being. In our relationships with others, joyously delighting in them, we make evident the image of God.

It is a confirmation that the Holy Ghost is God's love and delight,
because the saints communion with God consists in their
partaking of the Holy Ghost.

The communion of saints is twofold: 'tis their communion with
God and communion with one another. "That ye also may have
fellowship with us, and truly our fellowship is with the Father and
with His Son, Jesus Christ" (1 John 1:3).

Communion is a common partaking of good, either of Excellency or
happiness, so that when it is said the saints have communion or
fellowship with the Father and with the Son, the meaning of it is that
they partake with the Father and the Son of their good, which is either
their Excellency and glory (II Peter 1:4), "Ye are made partakers of the
Divine nature", Heb. 12:10, "That we might be partakers of His holiness;"
John 17:22, 23, "And the glory which Thou hast given Me I have given
them, that they may be one, even as we are one, I in them and
Thou in Me"; or of their joy and happiness: (John 17:13) "That
they might have My joy fulfilled in themselves."

But the Holy Ghost being the love and joy of God is His beauty and
happiness, and it is in our partaking of the same Holy Spirit that our
communion with God consists: (II Cor. 13:14) "The grace of the Lord
Jesus Christ, and the love of God, and the communion of the
Holy Ghost, be with you all, Amen."

Once again, Edwards leads me to one conclusion. God explains us, not the other way around.

We speaking beings perceive very little. Here and now, we only catch a little bit. I suspect that we will never know absolute Truth in this life and, as some suggest, we will spend eternity still on the adventure of discovering Who God is.

For me, this is awe-inspiring because the infinite God had turned off the "Why" and the "How" signs and points us to a bright neon one, "Who." God has taken the heat off of us being right. We don't have to watch the scoreboard to see who has figured God out.

Because no one will. Not here, under the sun.

Instead, through His beyond-words love, God has given us Imago Dei beings freedom to ask and search out what might seem the craziest or most heretical questions.

Although our small egos want so desperately to say, "Look at what I did," or "Look at what I know," the simple reality is that it is all a gift, not an achievement. We have no real control over much of anything beyond how we choose to be in relationship with God and one another.

I can't change a hair on my head. I can only relate to how the hair *is* (or in my case isn't) on my head.

As human beings, we look for the answers or responses that will make "it" (life, children, work, the result, ourselves or what we want) turn out the way we want. We do this instinctively, as if it's wired into our being. We draw from what we have experienced, read or believed from what others have told us. Although our past should be honored, revered, understood and appreciated, God never meant it to be the basis for our future.

He has intended for us to be in awe and wonder of "Who" *is* our future.

It gets more mind-blowing. Take a look. If God is in Conversation, in thought and in speaking as I suggest, then He can be spoken in and through my words. Consequently, there is something alive, creative and unprecedented in being made in the image of God, which is evidenced by my speaking.

I suspect that few of us get this but God has opened up the largest, most eternal clearing imaginable. You and I can be like Him. We can speak Him, His life, in such a way that it comes to others through us. What if conversion meant we transform from an isolated individual into an individual in community with God and others?

In this infinite possibility, my heart explodes. What is for me to declare? How do I access the eternal potentiality of God in this life? Who is this "Who" that calls me to glory?

I turn once again to C.S. Lewis, my questions waiting.

For if we take the imagery of Scripture seriously,
if we believe that God will one day give us the Morning Star
and cause us to put on the splendor of the sun....At present we are on
the outside of the world, the wrong side of the door.
We discern the freshness and purity of morning, but they don't make
us fresh and pure. We cannot mingle with the splendors we see....

When human souls have become perfect in voluntary obedience as the inanimate creation is in its lifeless obedience, then they will put on its glory, or rather that greater glory of which Nature is only the first sketch.[8]

C.S. Lewis, The Weight of Glory

Notes:

[1] Blaise Pascal, *Pensee* 122.

[2] John Irving, *The World According to Garp* (Random House; Modern Library Edition, 1978). Movie adaptation released by Warner Bros. Pictures in 1982.

[3] American Screenwriter, Producer and creator of the television show *Buffy the Vampire Slayer*; also known for *Toy Story, Alien Resurrection,* and *Angel.*

[4] C.S. Lewis, *The Great Divorce* [1946/1973] (HarperCollins Publishers, 2001).

[5] William Saroyan, *Here Comes There Goes You Know Who* (Simon and Schuster, 1961).

[6] William James, *Principles of Psychology* [1910].

[7] Jonathan Edwards, "An Unpublished Essay on the Trinity" (http://www.ccel.org/ccel/edwards/trinity/files/trinity.html).

[8] C.S. Lewis, *The Weight of Glory and Other Addresses* [1949/1976] (HarperCollins Publishers, 2001).

BE YE TRANSFORMED

✧ ✧ ✧

A Future Worth Having

✧ ✧ ✧

"It is not because the truth is too difficult to see that we make mistakes. ... We make mistakes because the easiest and most comfortable course for us is to seek insight where it accords with our emotions—especially selfish ones."[1]
Alexander Solzhenitsyn

"What is a 'future worth having,' Dan?"
My friend had heard me use this phrase a number of times.

"Is a 'future worth having' a pie-in-the-sky theory to make people feel better about their lives not turning out as they thought they should, or are there possibilities of being in the world in such a way that would make a difference in life?" Can you actually *live* a future worth having?

C.S. Lewis captures it best in *The Weight of Glory* when he writes, "At the end of all things ... the Blessed will say 'We have never lived anywhere but Heaven,' and the Lost, 'We were always in Hell.' And both will speak truly."

When God created us as human beings, we were given His image. We live in His skin in this world. We were also given complete freedom and, as free beings, we became marred by the suffering we experience through our own as well as other people's free choices. The losses we suffer or the things that we want but have not known personally become the longings of our soul.

Those longings constitute a large part of the foundation for our future worth having. I say, out of our deepest longings springs our desire for transformation.

For me, the vision for a future worth having is rooted in a longing to have a close family where people communicate their struggles, call on each others' strengths, appreciate the individual and celebrate community. This longing grew out of the loss I experienced as a child when my own family disintegrated. In the midst of that pain and loss, a paradox occurred to me. God seemed to be calling me into a future worth having, one that was unprecedented compares to anything I had previously known. That future required that I deny myself, climb out of the foxhole of survival, come out from behind what I think should be and move beyond my self-interests. It meant engaging reality from the perspective of a future that seemed impossible in light of the many failures I had gone through up until that point.

As a child, I grew up in an Italian-American family in Northern California where my Tuscan-born grandfather was the family's patriarch. From my earliest memories, I can recall our family life centered on my grandfather's house and the family. Every holiday, birthday or special occasion, we were there with him and my grandmother. All of my grandfather's six children, including my father, lived near one another, and as a young child I experienced the warmth of a large extended family.

I first noticed my parents' relationship falling apart when I was about twelve years old. My father became more and more absent from the house, being present with us kids only at dinnertime. As the arguments between my mother and father grew more severe, the warmth that was once ours dissipated.

By the time I reached eighteen, my family had completely unraveled. My grandfather died. My parents divorced. Our house was sold. Mom struggled with her mental illness. My dad was always at work or on the town. The family life I had known and loved as a child completely died.

The loss launched a deep bitterness and anger into my emotional life. For a long time, I harbored hatred and anger, especially towards my father. I became very cynical about the institution of marriage and the idea of family. As an adult, I nursed a complaint that my parents had done me wrong.

I felt entitled because I was ripped off. My attitude communicated my entitlement in every relationship. My wife, or anyone else I let into my life, existed essentially to fit my agenda. All I knew about my wife was what she did for me. Aileen served me so that I could have the career I wanted. She cooked dinner, took care of our son, washed my clothes and cleaned the house. She made love to me when I wanted.

Without any thought, my complaint justified my behavior—the occasional affair, the cocaine and the lies—as my own personal business. "What does Aileen care?" was my comeback to myself. "No one is getting hurt." In my mind, we had a functional partnership where we both got what we wanted. I worked hard and made the money. Aileen got to stay at home with our infant son and be a mother.

When Danny was about six months old, I found myself resisting going home to be with him and Aileen at the end of the day. When I would reach the front door, all I wanted to do was turn around, get in the car and leave. Danny's diapers, crying and demands on my time didn't serve me and, besides, taking care of him was Aileen's job.

Then came the day when Aileen said she was going to leave me. It was the first of many wake-up calls in my universe.

It challenged me to answer the question, "Who am I and what I am living for?" Would I live to gratify myself in the comfortable, self-seeking hell I had created? Or would I shift for the possibility of the future I thought was worth having? When Aileen interrupted how I was living, I knew I was at a crossroad in my life. I could not tell you where any of it would lead.

During that time period, I arrived home one night to find Danny teething and Aileen sick as a dog. As minutes turned into hours, Danny's crying drove me crazy. Aileen and I got into a big argument, and she went to bed angry and disappointed with me.

After she fell asleep, Danny went for another round.

I knew that if I got Aileen up we would fight again. With that being more burdensome to me than facing Danny's wails, I reluctantly dragged myself down the hall to Danny's room. As I opened the door, I saw my tiny son and my irritation melted.

As I picked him up, minutes turned into hours and something wonderful happened between us.

I said to myself, *Why did I think this would be horrible? The truth is that I am missing out here.* Hour after hour, I held my son and got lost in him—his sweat, his breathing, his wonderful smell. Why had I not wanted to do this? As we finally fell asleep, all I could think about was how much I loved my son.

Love, in its uncomfortable disguise, had drawn close to me. I was seeing what I had never seen before.

Transformation.

✡ ✡ ✡

Metaschematizo

✡ ✡ ✡

"You can clutch the past so tightly to your chest that it leaves your arms too full to embrace the present."[2]

Jan Glidewell

The word, *transformation*, has two distinct meanings in the original Greek.

The first is *metaschematizo*, which means, "the changing of form, the schematic, scenery or appearance." The second, *metamorphoo*, means something completely different. *Metamorphoo* involves the Divine. This kind of transformation entails *a complete change that— under the power of God—finds expression in character and conduct.*

If you change a Japanese garden into an Italian garden, this would be an example of *metaschematizo*. The appearance of the garden has changed but it is still a garden. Another example of *metaschematizo* is how the Apostle Paul describes his willingness to shift his packaging in order to win those who did not know Jesus Christ.

For though I am free from all men,
I have made myself a servant to all that I might win the more.
And to the Jews I became as a Jew that I might win Jews;
to those whose are under the law, as under the law, that I might win those
who are under the law; to those who are without law, as without law
(not being without law toward God but under law towards Christ)
that I might win those who are without law;
to the weak I became as weak that I might win the weak.
I have become all things to all men that I might by all means save some.
I Corinthians 9:19-22

Paul's willingness *to be all things to all men* flowed out of his radical love for God and others. His vision of a future worth having began with his relationship to Jesus, and it produced in him a transformation that transcended his natural self-interest of looking a certain way. His future worth having compelled him to be whatever he needed be in order reach others.

Unlike Paul, our motives for changing our appearance are often about ourselves. We assign our happiness to the forms and contents of our lives, such as looking good, being able to control circumstances, or being accepted. This kind of self-interested, *metaschematizo* effort casts us into the endless pursuit of more, better and different. "I just need to work more on controlling my temper." "I want a better relationship than what I have now." "I think I would do better work if my manager had a different style of managing me."

Where do we get this idea of "more, better or different?"

One place. Our past!

We *try* to be *more* patient than yesterday; we *seek* to be a *better* husband or wife. We *commit* ourselves to having a *different* attitude towards those things that tick us off. When we are in a personal growth mode, which is the context of "more, better, or different," we assume certain things are true based on what has happened to us. All these history-based assumptions form our present actions.

Unless we break with that history, we tend to perpetuate only "more, better or different" versions *(metaschematizo)* of what we have always had. How we are *relating* to the situations, circumstances or relationships hasn't shifted, only the way we package it.

Like rearranging the deck furniture on the Titanic, the "more, better, or different" approaches, methods, strategies, and tactics only change the content or form of life, not the destination. Put another way, there are infinite ways to end up arriving where we come from.

Personal growth utilizes competencies, trained skills and human effort. I am not saying the past is a bad thing or that we should ignore it. We can learn from and honor the past because it has taught us that transformation is possible.

However, that is distinct from using the past to determine our future or to justify an undesirable or unacceptable present state. While a rearview mirror is valuable to use when driving, it will be disastrous to use it to determine where you want to go. Unless you want to drive in reverse.

A future worth having demands a new way of thinking. This new way of thinking comes *from the future*. It is a partnership with God to bring forth something unprecedented; it is the process of freely choosing something new regardless of history or circumstance.

✡ ✡ ✡

If We Walk in the Light

✡ ✡ ✡

"Love is not consolation. It is light."[3]
Friedrich Nietzsche

About a year had passed since that night I cared for Danny.
     Although my eyes and heart had been cracked open, I was a work-in-progress. I hadn't committed myself fully to the future

that I longed to have. I was still a shadow in my own home. I was off cocaine but I hated the cocaine-free life. I was still having one-night stands with other women, justifying it with the story that "what Aileen did not know wouldn't hurt her."

Bottom line: I was still committed to living for myself. Love for God and others was a tool to gratify myself.

Just prior to our second child, Elizabeth, Aileen decided to start a daycare center in our home. Instead of being supportive and happy for her project, I hated the daycare children intruding into my privacy and diverting Aileen's attention from me. Every morning, I would wait in bed for the "Brat Pack" to go outside to play. Then like a troll, I would emerge from the bedroom and resentfully eat my breakfast.

One particular morning, I was grumbling once again while eating a bowl of hot cereal. I was miserable. I felt stuck on an endless merry-go-round, and I had no desire to go through the motions anymore on any front. I was done being the fool rearranging the deck furniture on the deck of the Titanic. I begged God to hear my complaint; that unless something grabbed me now I was sure that my ship was going down.

For the previous few nights, I had been unable to sleep. Each night I had gotten up to read the Bible and begged God to pierce my isolation. In the presence of my family, I was divorced from their company. As I prayed that morning, two verses from the Gospel of John moved me.

"And this is the condemnation, that the light has come into the world and men loved darkness rather than the light, because their deeds were evil."

John 3:19-20 (NKJV)

The second was like the first:

"...if we walk in the light as He is in the light, we have fellowship with one another and the blood of Jesus Christ His Son cleanses us from all sin."

1 John 1:7 (NKJV)

Looking out the window, I saw Aileen playing in the backyard with the Brat Pack. She was sitting on the ground with the kids dancing around her, pulling her hair and teasing each other. They laughed and laughed and laughed, free as birds. The morning sun bathed Aileen and the children with such warmth that they radiated.

Suddenly, I stopped breathing and realized something incredible.

Tears filled as my eyes began to see, as if for the first time, the overwhelming beauty of my wife. In her lap sat two children, Danny and another boy named James, and a third one named Zach danced about her. Aileen's tenderness towards the boys showed no favoritism in her love for *any* of them. My wife loved those children, all of them, with simple, unconditional love, just like I imagined possible with God.

Jesus Christ was answering my prayers right before my eyes.

Like the blind man seeing for the first time, I saw the truth about myself. All I knew about my wife was what she did for me. I had absolutely no idea what Aileen aspired to be or do in her life or why any of it was important to her. I thought about some of our conversations around our family activities. I remember Aileen saying, "The only reason I went skiing was because you like it. I don't mind, but it isn't my favorite thing to do." However, when Aileen would talk about the kids in the day care or the elderly woman next door, I would cut her off by saying that I didn't bring work home and neither should she. Our fights were over what I wanted, not what was best for Aileen or our family.

Until that moment, throughout our marriage I had been seeing Aileen in the light of my own self-interests.

Suddenly the words in John's letter made sense to me, and the weight of what I saw overwhelmed me. I did not have fellowship with Aileen, God or anyone else. I had chosen to live in darkness, cut off from others except for when they served my needs. I was alone, even when I was in their company! Time and time again, God had given me choices and I turned my back on them.

I had chosen to cover up and withdraw in isolation and had reaped loneliness, emptiness and futility. I had cast myself out of relationship and was separated and isolated from life, God and everyone who mattered to me. I was empty and isolated due to my insistence on how life should be. If there is a hell I certainly had been living there and up until that moment not even realizing it.

The philosopher Søren Kierkegaard calls this state of being "despair not knowing itself as despair." The symptom of this despair is when a human being finds a level of despair that is tolerable and calls it happiness.

I had chosen myself right into hell. Choice after choice, I saw that no matter how much *more* I got, how much *better* I felt and how *different* life was, it had more often than not been hell and it rarely turned out anything like I had planned it to turn out!

The only bright spot in my anguish was the fact that God was giving me another opportunity to choose. I could stop lying and blaming everyone else for my situation. I could start choosing to love instead of insisting on being loved. I could walk in the light as He is in the Light and have fellowship with Him and others.

Seeing the opportunity, my heart sank. To choose the light, I would have to confess my affairs to Aileen.

To be that honest meant putting everything on the line. If I told Aileen what I had done, she might leave me and take Danny with her. Then what would I do? My body winced at the possibility of such grief!

The thought, *Trust God*, came to me. "Trust Him for what?" I responded. An answer came. If the worst happened and Aileen left me, she and I would have a relationship based upon the truth and not deception. "But, she would surely leave, and so what would I have accomplished by being so honest? Was I just thinking this because I felt guilty and wanted to relieve myself?" When I considered that question I noticed my mixed motives, but it wasn't the primary one. I was just desperate and tired of living this way- suspecting people as being as dishonest—a projection of my isolation, anger, cynicism and sarcasm.

I thought, *"Am I crazy? What could be the benefit of living so honestly?"* What immediately occurred to me was the possibility for us to be together in unprecedented ways- ways I could have never considered until entertaining this possibility. I was blinded to such ideas because of how inauthentic I had been being with Aileen. But now, if there were any possibility of us having the kind of relationship I was longing for, it would emerge from the trust that an authentic relationship where love of reality is understood and appreciated in real terms such as honesty, trust, respect and power. How many times had I wanted to be with somebody who loved me for who

I am while standing for all I could be? How could that happen if they really didn't know who I was and what I was struggling with? The possibility of intimacy was emerging from considering what would surely be the end of my relationship up until that point. There was no guarantee of what it would be afterward. However, the possibilities were intoxicating and the reality of remaining in what I had created represented more of what I really didn't want.

Before I left for work that morning, I asked Aileen if she would set aside time when I got home because I had some difficult things to say. Hesitantly, she agreed.

I will never forget the hours at work that day. For the first time in a long time, I felt alive. I had a new anticipation towards the future despite not knowing what that future looked like. I was excited and afraid at the same time and seemed to bounce between the two as my thinking shifted back and forth about the different ways of relating to my life. I was beginning to see light where I thought there was only darkness.

After putting Danny to bed, I walked into the living room where Aileen was waiting with tears already in her eyes. As I fumbled my way through my confession, Aileen's first question was "With whom did you have this affair?" I told her but then she asked more questions, "Where did you do this? How many times? How come? Who else knows? What did you do exactly? Did you love her?"

After about the third question, I raged and headed for the door.

Aileen's next question stopped me like a brick wall: "Just *who* are you confessing for, Dan?"

Who was I confessing for? Me, myself and I.

My motives were surfacing, particularly the motive to relieve my guilt and preserve my image of myself. She looked at me with tears in her eyes and asked, "If you really want to change, why don't you humble yourself and account for your broken promises and the devastation they have caused in our life together?"

The fire of God's light had come. Any good thought I ever had about myself now reeked like rotting garbage.

I sat down and we walked through some of the most humiliating moments of my life. As I answered every one of Aileen's questions, I felt a growing regret for what I had done to her and an uncontrollable longing for Aileen to forgive me for the pain I had caused her and the damage it had done to our relationship as a family. As the night drew to a close, I felt like I didn't deserve to be in Aileen's presence, let alone share a bed with her.

How long would it take for her to trust me again? I knew it could happen in a twinkle of an eye should she choose, but that was up to her. The reality was she might choose never to bestow trust for me again.

All I knew to do was to choose the light. Each day, I could choose the truth, fulfill my promises and account when I fell short. I could choose to listen, love and communicate honestly with her, believing that God would bring us into a fellowship with Himself and each other if we continued walking in the light learning to be new ways of being together.

Difficult? Yes.

Hell? No.

Rewarding? Absolutely!

As I tasted the shame that my actions had brought upon my wife and family, something mysteriously paradoxical occurred. It was a cup of burning hot soup, which if spilled would scald me but if sipped would take the chill from my body and set me free from the freezing reality of isolation and cynicism.

✿ ✿ ✿

Metamorphoo

✿ ✿ ✿

"God will become visible as God's image is reborn in you."
St. Bernard of Clairveux

God's kind of transformation is called *metamorphoo*, the word from which we derive metamorphosis. It is the realm of where "all things are possible for those who believe in Jesus" and through it, we are set free from ever seeking to improve anything.

Transforming is first about dying to our need to protect ourselves or in the traditional Christian vernacular, "denying self." In it, we become unified with God in His conversation, forsaking complaining as a way of justifying not joining in the Conversation that is God so that we might have a future worth having.

Often it is messy, uncomfortable and downright tough because our fallen nature can't be transformed through mere human effort yet at the same time it requires we live like it does. Moreover God has no interest in renovating- making more, better or different- our fallen image. Instead, He is after freeing us from the endless futility of our striving into the realm of being in relationship with Him.

Transformation is all about the death of ourselves- our expectations, the way we think we should look, how life should turn out, how we think people should treat us, how we should perform—and instead about living purely for the sake of others. Transformation finds its heartbeat in God's love for you, me, and the world.

Metamorphoo is all about relating, not self-effort towards more, better and different, experiences, images or material possessions. When we transform the way that we relate to the past, our present circumstances and others from the perspective of the unprecedented, then unimaginable possibilities open up.

During my confession to Aileen, I shifted from relating to her as somebody I owned to someone who was a complex and eternal gift of God. In my new way of relating, I was compelled to investigate her loves, fears, desires, hopes and dreams. In the process, I found myself more and more intrigued to experience and know who she is and what our future could be together.

And, as I drank deeply of the cup of shame that I had so fiercely attempted to avoid, I found myself in the middle of an intimacy and union with God and others I had so longed for.

To me, transformation is like heading for California from New York State. Although you may have never been to California, you do know that after a lifetime of snowy winters, the land of sunshine on the other coast is where you long to be. Although you may not know exactly what California is like; you know what you see on a map, in the movies, on TV, or in magazines and what you have heard from others.

As you follow the map and drive down the highway, you suddenly come upon a raging river that has completely washed out the road.

You search the map; neither the river nor the washout is listed. Technically, they shouldn't be there. Any idea that your road trip would be a smooth, problem-free ride has vanished. Seeing many other drivers sitting in their parked cars, you are also tempted to throw up your hands and say, "I can't have my vision."

The truth is that California is still waiting for you.

The journey has just turned out to be different than you thought. On the banks of that raging river, you are still free to choose your future. You can turn around or set up your tent. However, in order to have the future worth having, you are going to have to tackle this river. You will have to navigate it from the perspective of getting to California and be open to any way that God is going to help you get to the other side.

Even if that means that He floats your car.

That's transformation. It is where you discover that the menu is not the meal. The map is not the territory, and your journey to your destination will probably be radically different from everyone else who has preceded you.

As human beings, we tend to live moment to moment, never thinking about where all the moments are taking us. I suspect that we want to live oblivious to where these moments are leading us because we see life not turning out the way we think it should. So we live with the short-term attitude of "eat, drink and be merry, for tomorrow we die."

A future worth having makes the journey awe-inspiring even when it is challenging. By anticipating the fulfillment of our longings, we can turn from our scams and, instead, face our Maker with our deepest groaning. We can be reconciled to Him, to one another and to all that we have been eternally deprived.

Including creation itself.

I consider that our present sufferings are not worth comparing with the glory that will be revealed in us.

All creation waits in eager expectation for the sons of God to be revealed. For the creation was subjected to frustration, not by its own choice, but by the will of the one who subjected it, in hope that the creation itself will be liberated from its bondage to decay and brought into the glorious freedom of the children of God. We know that the whole creation has been groaning as in the pains of childbirth right up to the present time. Not only so, but we ourselves, who have the first fruits of the Spirit, groan inwardly as we wait eagerly for our adoption as sons, the redemption of our bodies. For in this hope we were saved. But hope that is seen is no hope at all. Who hopes for what he already has? But if we hope for what we do not yet have, we wait for it patiently.

Romans 8:18-25 (NIV)

✡ ✡ ✡

Two Steps

✡ ✡ ✡

Even at ten months, our little Elizabeth had a stubborn streak and was already giving her mother a run for her money. It showed up just as Lizzie was starting to walk.

She loved going up and down two steps that lead out of our kitchen and into the sunroom. One suppertime, as Aileen was getting Danny into his high chair, I came in the kitchen to find Lizzie going up and down those two steps.

"Elizabeth, time to sit for dinner," I said.

"No," she answered like a CEO of a Fortune 500 company.

"Time to sit down for dinner," I said more firmly.

"No."

"Elizabeth, when I say it's time for dinner, we eat together. This is our time as a family."

"No."

"Okay, if you don't want to sit down for dinner, then you go to your bedroom."

"No."

As Elizabeth threw down the gauntlet, I calmly picked her up and put her in the crib in her room. For the next four and a half hours, she threw a tantrum. She cried so loudly that I wondered if she was waking up the whole neighborhood. About every fifteen minutes, I would go into Lizzie's room and ask her if she would like to eat dinner with us. Burning a hole in me with her stare, she would yell, "No!"

Throughout the four hours, Aileen wanted to just get Lizzie, but I was able to persuade Aileen not to yield to her wailing by discussing what the future would be like if she thought she would always get her own way. We found ourselves consoling each other by saying, "This is what we need to do right now for Elizabeth's sake," even though we were hurting deeply and wanted nothing more than to relieve the pain she was suffering. I could so relate to her rage about not having life the way she thought it "should" be!

Aileen was surprised. Up until this point in our marriage, I had taken a back seat in the training of the children. However I was taking the initiative as a father in ways that would benefit the growth and development of our children and our lives together as a family. The old me would have said, "Aileen, just deal with her. Don't let her climb up and down the stairs when I'm eating."

At the end of four and a half hours, I sneaked into Elizabeth's room. What a precious sight I saw. My little girl had thrown everything out of the crib, including the crib's mattress. Her clothes were on the floor. Her diapers were off. Still red faced and from crying and exhausted from her tantrum, Lizzie was sound asleep on the springs sitting in the corner of her crib. Her head was bent down with her chin on her pudgy little chest and her thin baby blonde hair pasted to her round head resting on her little Buddha like body.

In that crib was my future worth having.

In the years to come my love for my daughter would transform my life from the bitterness of self-protective entitlement into open, vulnerable depths of grateful appreciation for others, even my worst enemies!

✿ ✿ ✿

Hope in a Vision

✿ ✿ ✿

"Now the Lord is the Spirit
and where the Spirit of the Lord is, there is liberty.
But we all, with unveiled face, beholding as in a mirror,
the glory of the Lord, are being transformed
into the same image from glory to glory, just as by the Spirit."
2 Corinthians 3:17-18 (NKJV)

Jesus Christ has been to California and back. He is inviting you and me to let Him revolutionize our lives from the inside out.

"Do not be conformed to this world," writes the Apostle Paul in his letter to the Romans, "but be *transformed* by the renewing of your mind" Romans 12:2 (KJV). Said another way, "Let the Spirit of the Logos do in you what you can never do on your own- to love God and others as He loves them."

How does this revolution show up? Many times, like a death threat.

For example, let's take a look at a relationship that stops you cold. As you consider it, describe how you are relating to the breakdown in the relationship itself? Do you have a functional or dysfunctional relationship with the breakdown?

Do you relate to the breakdown in a way that opens up possibility? Or do you just chalk everything up as futile?

What happens when something is not going as you expect? Do you get stuck? Do you get defensive, attacking, depressed, withdrawn, shy, angry or reactionary? What words and actions come out of you when life presses you? Do you quit, feel sorry for yourself or chase your friends, family or team away?

If any of the above ring true, please consider how your behavior may be revealing your points of resistance. This resistance, and resulting withdrawal, will keep you from recognizing the resources that are available to resolve the breakdown.

For example, I have a fun, hospitable friend who was robbed once by a beggar in Italy. After the incident, I noticed how he would become rude and angry if we encountered someone asking for a handout. When I pointed this out to him, he saw how what had happened to him was making him prejudiced towards the homeless. After we talked, he saw what was going on inside of him, and he was able to shift how he was relating to others around him.

As Paul writes in Romans 12, transformation by the Spirit manifests itself in our lives through our relationships with others. "Associate with the lowly. Love without hypocrisy. Repay no one evil for evil. Bless those who persecute you and do not curse. Rejoice in hope. Weep with those weep. Honor one another. Don't set your mind on high things but associate with the humble. Do not be wise in your own opinion. Don't avenge yourself. Do not be overcome with evil but overcome evil with good."

Said another way, "Examine and dis-empower the conversation that brings significance to your identity based upon success: education, connections, big income, good looks, and fame. Die to that old conversation where you have to be right and look good. Die to your own thinking and self-effort conventions for the sake of others having a future worth having."

Jesus is telling us that the game is finished. You don't have to strive to self-improve, rise higher, be more, better or different. Instead, choose to live in Him.

I am fully persuaded that Jesus is the heart of transformation, the key to the mystery. Through the creative Spirit of God, you can die to all that you have declared or chosen to believe about yourself up until now. In an instant, you can have a new life with God and others through the life, death and resurrection of Jesus, because God has reconciled man to Himself through the Savior.

What will enable us to go through the inevitable pain involved in the process of transforming?

Some transformations are volitional; some are not a matter of our will. For myself, I have found three anchors that have kept me on course when the price of transformation was more than I wanted to pay:

Love for and faith in God.
Knowledge of Jesus and His kingdom.
Love for others.

Vision is seeing the future, not present at the moment, as if it *is*, now.

You have probably heard the saying in Proverbs 29:18, "Where there is no vision, people perish." The way this is often worded can leave you thinking that vision is some undefined, subjective force. Furthermore, it gives the impression that vision determines survival, which is not what Solomon, the writer of Proverbs, means.

A more careful rendering of the Hebrew text gives us a better picture of what "vision" is all about.

Where there is no revelation (prophetic vision),
the people cast off restraint or purposeful living (discipline).

Consider *vision* as a way of relating to the present from the unprecedented future. Instead of vision being something we possess, like a car or a house, what if vision is a way of relating *to now from where* I long to be?

With a future-looking-to-the-present vision, things such as comfort, looking good, feeling good or being right are insignificant in comparison. We would find ourselves willing to delay or forsake immediate gratification for the rewards of the future. We would be clear in purpose, directed in thought, and resolved to act.

The vision I have for my own life is a way of relating that makes possible what we as a family long to have together a legacy of celebrating the gift of life in the context of what Jesus called the kingdom, the rule of love, justice and mercy. With this perspective, I move from living to please myself to being directed and intentional in loving others.

✧ ✧ ✧

Needing to Be Home

✧ ✧ ✧

"**H**oney, I need you home with the kids. I can't have you on the road right now."

A number of years had passed since that night with Lizzie, and during that time Aileen and I had built a successful ministry organization called the Association for Christian Character Development. During the building process, I was away from home for one or two weeks out of each month. Aileen and I agreed that, if she ever needed me home, I would get off the road for as long as was wanted and needed.

Now was such a time.

"Elizabeth is starting to hang out with the wrong crowd and is making choices that aren't good for her," Aileen told me. "You need to be here so that she can talk to you."

Together we decided that I needed to be off the road for at least a year. Despite the cost to the ministry for my absence, I took a sabbatical from ACCD without any second thoughts. Aileen and I had declared our vision of a future worth having with and for the children many times. When she asked me to come home, I knew Aileen would only ask if I were needed.

Right from the start, I saw that Aileen had been dead right about Elizabeth. Our normally outgoing daughter would come home after school withdrawn and moody. It was evident that Elizabeth was facing situations among her peers, such as drugs and sexuality, which represented a turning point in her character development. That she had these challenges was expected; how she related to them was what I was committed to working with her on. Right before my eyes, she was turning into stone, and I didn't know what to do.

One night, Aileen pushed me out of bed.

"You go talk to her," Aileen insisted. Terrified, I resisted but she still insisted. "You talk to her, or tomorrow she is going to that school to talk to some kid about what is troubling her and they are going to give her some teenage advice. I can't get through to her, Dan, but she's listening to you. Will you talk to her?"

I got up, irritated but dutiful.

I thought, *"Damn. Why do ""I" have to do this?"* Catching myself, I realized that attitude would not work. Lizzie would pick up on my resistance, I would be stiff and un-resourceful and get mad at Aileen. Although I was tempted to let Aileen be the bad guy to get myself off the hook, I realized that I was just in survival mode. "No," I said to myself, *"this is about Elizabeth. This is not about me. I need to talk with her, so that she has the benefit of my relationship with her. She needs to know that I am with her in what she is going through."*

As I walked down the hall towards her room, I had no idea what to say or even how she would receive me, given we had not really talked like this about these subjects before. To say the least, I was getting in touch with how out of touch with my daughter's life I really was.

I opened her door, and she was doing some homework at her desk. I sat on the bed and asked her if she wanted to talk about anything. She retorted in a very sarcastic tone, "Oh, is this your attempt at being a good father?"

I felt the truth of that comment like a wound deep in my body. I winced and caught my reaction to strike back. Instead I heard myself say, "Fair enough. You're right that is probably part of the mix, but the greater part of my heart is to know you and be with you."

Without looking at me she said, "I don't want to talk now. I am busy." I sat on the bed for a couple of minutes, which seemed like an eternity until I decided to leave and regroup.

In desperate straits, I called my good friend, Harry, who I deeply respected for how he fathered his children. "Harry," I said, "my family is out of control and I don't know what to do. Elizabeth is shutting us out. I know she is up to stuff that could potentially hurt her, but I don't know what to say or do."

"Dan," Harry said. "I can't tell you what to do but let me remind you of one thing—your purpose for being a family."

As Harry continued, I let my fears listen to his counsel.

"If you remind yourself and Elizabeth of your love and your purpose for being together, I think it will make a big difference. Even if you don't know exactly what to say, remember to be with her from the perspective of your purpose together. She will take great comfort and security in your willingness to reach to her even when she has been mean or vindictive, especially when she sees that even though you don't have the answer, you are going to stand with her for that purpose."

With Harry's words ringing in my ears, once again I took the long walk to Elizabeth's bedroom. Although I was afraid of failing, each step I took reminded me of my daughter's future and the gift that she was to me personally, to our family and also the world.

I saw something else.

The difficulty of this situation was actually doing me a good service. Elizabeth's dilemma and the subsequent suffering and pain were like logs on the fire of my passion for my children and our future worth having.

With one last step, I reached the door and knocked.

✧ ✧ ✧

Faith That God Will

✧ ✧ ✧

"Now faith is the assurance of things hoped for,
the conviction of things not seen."
Hebrews 11:1 (ASV)

Faith is being fully persuaded that things hoped for will be realized.

Faith is living out a future worth having in the present moment, upholding it through the tests of circumstance, history and culture in the knowledge of the ideas and experiences of what is possible with God. We have faith because we have a certain body of knowledge about reality that God has given us and which has born itself out in our experience. From this foundation, we choose our faith—or maybe it chooses us?

Dr. Dallas Willard author of *The Divine Conspiracy* says it this way in his book *Knowing Christ in the Modern World*[4]:

A life of steadfast discipleship to Jesus Christ can only be supported upon assured knowledge of how things are, of the realities in terms of which that life is lived. As in any arena of real life where knowledge is essential, infallibility is not required, of course, and numerous things to which ordinary Christians (or even lengthy traditions) have subscribed could be erroneous or, so far as their knowledge extends, groundless. Still, a steady life directed, in a communal setting, toward the good and right, can only be supported within a framework of basically sound knowledge and understanding.

What I am saying here might sound a little different than others. To me, faith is a way of relating and not a quantitative thing that we do or do not possess.

Consider when the disciple Peter was fully persuaded that, if Jesus commanded him, he could walk on water. Obviously Peter had the knowledge of what Jesus was capable of doing, and from the knowledge he was willing to step out in faith. Earlier in the day, Jesus had miraculously fed five thousand people near a place called Bethsaida, which was located near the Sea of Galilee. As the evening drew near, Jesus told his disciples to go ahead of him across the lake in the boat. Heeding his command, the disciples started to cross over, rowing late into the night. However amid the crossing, the sea became very rough and the disciples strained at the oars as the wind was against them.

Then Jesus did something unprecedented. He walked on the sea, heading right past the boat. When the disciples saw Him walking on the rough surface of the waves, they were terrified. Thinking He was a ghost, they cried out in fright.

But immediately Jesus spoke to them, saying "Be of good cheer! It is I; do not be afraid."

And Peter answered Him and said, "Lord if it is You,

*command me to come to You on the water." So He said,
"Come."
And when Peter had come down out of the boat,
he walked on the water to go to Jesus.
But when he saw that the wind was boisterous, he was
afraid; and beginning to sink he cried out, saying "Lord,
save me!" And immediately Jesus stretched out His hand
and said to him, "O you of little faith, why did you doubt?"*
Matthew14: 27-31 (NKJV)

With Peter, Jesus was dealing *not* with quantity but with how Peter was relating to the circumstances, Jesus and himself. Jesus was showing Peter how much he was persuaded. In effect, Jesus was saying to Peter, "I have given you a 1,000-watt bulb with a dimmer switch. Why did you hesitate and wonder, leaving the dimmer switch on low, instead of turning it up high?"

Jesus shows us that we can choose how much we will be persuaded. But, which personal experience of what Jesus can do with us will we draw from? Personally, I have drawn from personal experiences of good that have emerged in times of difficulty and tragedy. I have noticed that they follow the patterns Jesus discusses in the Bible with his disciples. I can see my character failures in the experiences depicted in the Bible as well. And finally, I have experienced the presence of good in the possibilities that have emerged in the most difficult situations I have faced as long as I have been willing to look for them.

We can choose to be fully persuaded of God's provision for our vision in the face of our history, circumstances or culture. When we are fully persuaded from the perspective of listening for and searching out our future worth having, our feet start to walk on water.

I will never forget how terrified I was of some school bullies when I was in the fourth grade. At that young age, I was already almost six feet tall. Because of my size, I was the target for every sixth grade bully. Some days, I was so scared that I would pretend to be sick so that I could stay home from school.

One day I was lamenting about my situation to a friend. She asked me how I knew that the sixth-grade bullies could beat me up. My response came from what I had known up until that time, "Well, they are older!"

"Do you feel you can't defend yourself against anyone older than you?" she asked.

"Well, no," I said.

"Then why do these sixth grade boys scare you so bad?" she persisted.

"Because they are big," I replied. "They look stronger," I insisted.

"That might be true," she answered. "But do you know if that's the truth for them? You look to me as strong as they are. What if they are thinking the same way I am?" I kept on whining until my friend added something that changed me. "What if *they* are afraid of you?" she asked. "Is it possible that they want to fight you because they aren't sure about how strong or persistent you are? If they do get hurt, they probably won't want to fight again even if they could win."

With her experience and ideas as a body of knowledge for me to consider, I thought about what was possible. Walking home, I became persuaded that I *could* put up a good enough fight that would make these bullies think long and hard before they ever bothered me again.

I will never forget going to school the next day.

As I walked down the street, I found myself looking forward to the confrontation that had paralyzed me the day before. Being armed with this knowledge and fully persuaded by the possibility it opened up, my way of being in the situation transformed. I was set free to be with these bullies in ways I had never been before. After that day, they never bothered me again.

✡ ✡ ✡

The Rewards of Purpose

✡ ✡ ✡

"Age wrinkles the body, quitting wrinkles the soul."
General Douglas MacArthur

Aileen was at the kitchen sink when the premonition happened. The 50th birthday celebration for our close friend had been terrific. He and his family had enjoyed the party, and we were in the process of cleaning up. As she was washing dishes, Aileen had this strong thought that our friend's teenage son was upstairs kissing Elizabeth.

The boy was Danny's best friend. We had come to know him and like him. What we didn't know was that he was making passes at Elizabeth, even though she will still only twelve and he was sixteen. She was letting him kiss her because she didn't know what to do, and she wanted his approval and affection.

The night of the party and Aileen's premonition at the sink came just days after the incidents had begun. Following her intuition, Aileen went immediately upstairs and caught the boy kissing Elizabeth.

What happened next made me grateful for the times I made that long walk to Elizabeth's room.

The incident opened conversations that we might have otherwise missed. All of us including the boy and his parents talked with each other about respect, dignity, honor and love. Aileen and I had long conversations with Danny about his relationship with our family and the relationship he had with his friends. In the messy ride, we developed an intimacy that was unprecedented for us, and a bond we continue to share to this day.

A few days after Danny's friend's father's 50th party, Lizzie and I were riding together in the car. Looking out the window, she began to speak about what had happened. Starting to cry, she said to me, "Dad, I was afraid that you were going to send me away for what I had done. I felt dirty and ashamed. Before it happened, I didn't know I would feel that way. After I got into it, I didn't know how to stop it!"

Stopping the car, I turned to her and said with tears in my eyes, "Honey, I love you and that love is stronger than anything you do or don't do. Please forgive me if I ever gave you the impression that you could do something that would change that."

With those words, she leapt across the seats and into my lap. Grabbing me around my neck, she buried her face into my chest and, together, we wept and forgave one another until we laughed.

My friend Harry's words of advice had proven true. As Elizabeth and I remembered our love for each other and our purpose together, the character of our lives individually and together were transforming and the future worth having of a loving, intimate family was showing up.

During those early conversations with Elizabeth, I would tell her how much I was struggling to know how to be with her in what she was experiencing. As best as I knew how, I told her that I recognized that she was going to make her own choices but that I wanted to be in the conversation with her.

More than anything else, I let her know how much I loved her. I did this through taking time to sit with her after school. Sometimes I would help her with her homework, but most of the time I would hang out in her room with her, listening to her music. Even when she got angry at me for something I did, I just kept on hanging out with her. Our relationship grew stronger as we learned each other's language.

As each day built on the last, Elizabeth would tell me about some of the things she had done. Instead of her choices pulling us apart, we drew closer in the process of listening to each other's point of view. Our trust and love grew so much at one point Elizabeth gave me her unedited diary to read because she felt she could not articulate verbally the things she was feeling.

I learned a huge lesson being with my daughter.

I saw that Danny and Elizabeth were human beings. They are not my property. Their job is not to become what I wanted them to be, like some kind of trophy or expression of my life. No. Their destiny is to become who God has established them to be. They were to be a unique expression of the kingdom on earth.

I was to be their champion, standing with them for their own future worth having. As they fail along the way, I will suffer with them instead of being disconnected from them. I will rejoice when they rejoice. I will weep, laugh, mourn and dance with them.

Most of all, I love them.

✿ ✿ ✿

Love for Others

✿ ✿ ✿

*"Is your love growing and becoming softer, brighter,
more daring and more visible?
Or is it becoming more discriminating,*

I will never forget walking into Notre Dame Cathedral in Paris.

For thirty minutes, I stood at the front door in complete awe. The arching stone ceilings, the ornately sculpted walls, the statues and the atmosphere alone took my breath away. I was overwhelmed as I imagined the blood, sweat and tears invested into building this indescribable place of worship.

As I remembered my European history, I wondered about the wave of passion and commitment that caused cathedrals to be built across Europe. What conversations were happening inside the spirits of those who gave themselves so sacrificially to constructing these immense structures?

To build a cathedral, one had to have vision beyond their years. You see, it took between 80 and 200 years to build a cathedral during a time when the average person's life expectancy was about 35 years.

However, they still built them.

Out of hope for a future worth having for their children's children, they did what was wanted and needed for those who would follow after them. These builders pulled together all the financial and material resources necessary, even planting trees that would mature in time for the later years of construction.

In my life, I am committed to being a cathedral builder.

Whether I am the first generation planner sowing into the generations I will never see, or the one who lays the last stone into place, I have dedicated my life to count for something that will outlast my time here on earth.

To me, cathedral building means relationship building, choosing to walk in the light as Jesus is in the light. He says that if we walk in the light we will have "fellowship" (relationship) with Him and one another. When He commands me to love God with all my heart, soul, mind and strength and to love my neighbor as myself, I don't hear His command like a threat or even something I have to do. I hear it as a call to live the way He has designed for me to optimally experience life. He is offering me a future worth having. He is inviting me to detach myself from the cultural conversation that taunts me to "Take care of #1 because nobody else will."

He stands together with me and that cloud of witnesses, who through their flesh and blood, life and death were used by God to reveal God's passion to the generations that followed, those who engaged conversations of God's love, grace and mercy, who had ears to hear and eyes to recognize the living Logos so that I, who came after, could walk in an unprecedented future today.

As I gazed upward at the distant vaunted ceiling of Notre Dame, I asked myself, *"What are we, in my generation, passing to the next? What conversations of a future worth having are we fostering with them? What legacy of vision and faith are we imparting to following generations? Are we leaving our children another version of the past or are we declaring the possibility of the unprecedented future that Jesus lived and died to make available?"*

I have found that Love is Logos. In the face of that Love, all theological and philosophical debate looks very small to me.

Jesus expressed His Love to us by being a ransom. In ancient times, it was a common practice for two warring kings to exchange hostages in order to achieve peace. The kings would exchange a son or daughter to live at the other's court. The hostages were the ransom or guarantee for peace. In the process, the hostages obviously risked their lives in order to maintain that peace.

Jesus had paid the ransom Himself.

When we love, we participate in His being, making ourselves a ransom for a future worth having for others. For me, this is the legacy I'm committed to leaving.

We become transformationalists, and cathedral builders.

✧ ✧ ✧

One Night

✧ ✧ ✧

"There are thoughts which are prayers. There are moments when, whatever the posture of the body, the soul is on its knees."[6]
Victor Hugo

About four years ago, Elizabeth and I had an interesting conversation, one that caught me by surprise. "Dad," she said, "I want to ask you to forgive me."

"For what, sweetheart?" I answered.

"When I was little, do you remember how much I hated the ministry and how it took you away from me and the family?"

"Sure, I do."

"Well, Dad, I want to thank you for everything we have been through. I have traveled the world. I have met such great people. I have more friends that I can count and feel like I have family everywhere. I know I am loved. I am not afraid of living my life. I trust God, and I believe it is because of the way you have been with me even when you didn't know what to do. You didn't do it perfectly. You made a lot of mistakes, but you allowed me to be in relationship with you through the process and you kept talking about why we were together. I feel so honored by our relationship."

As my daughter spoke, I realized I was a wealthy man.

Our relationship is the future worth having right now a future that was unprecedented in my life until Aileen and I met. I thanked God for my companion, warrior wife and our children who together, instead of seeking to be sheltered from dangers, have had the courage to face them.

When I seek to still my pains, my wife and children have the heart to conquer them. When I crave in anxious fear to be saved, they persevere for freedom. Their attitude inspires wisdom and courage when cowardice knocks at our door. In our weakness and in our success, His mercy has been ours.

And, for that, I am grateful beyond words.

Notes:

[1] Solzhenitsyn: *A Documentary Record,* "Trials in D'tente," *ed. Leopold Labedz (1974).* "Peace and Violence," *sct. 2, Index, no. 4 (London, 1973).*

[2] Jan Glidewell blog (http://www.janglidewell.com/?p=3).

[3] Quoted in *Emperor of the Earth* by Czeslaw Milosz, Chapter 7: "The Importance of Simone Weil," p. 93. "Gravity and Grace," quoted in *Time* by

Jonathan Westphal, Carl Levenson, Carl Avren Levenson, Chapter 18: Simone Weil, "Detachment," p. 163.

[4] Scheduled to be published in late 2008.

[5] Francis Frangipane, *The Three Battlegrounds* (Advancing Church Publications, 1989).

[6] Marius, in *Les Miserables*, part 4, book 5, chapter 4 (1862).

ALL EARS

✡ ✡ ✡

A Divine Wake-Up Call

✡ ✡ ✡

"To greed, all nature is insufficient."[1]
Seneca

It was a gorgeous, sunny day when Aileen, Davide (a dear friend and ministry associate in Florence, Italy) and I were driving south toward Italy's Amalfi Coast after finishing a Breakthrough Training in Rome. The four days of the training had been very exciting, and we were in the midst of a lively conversation when a call came through on Davide's cell phone.

After hanging up Davide told us the good news.

Somebody on the freeway had seen the "for sale" sign on his van that we were driving and had asked us to pull over at the next rest area so that they could take a look at it. As we approached the exit, we saw that the rest stop was a big one with a restaurant, gas station and delicatessen.

As Davide went to get gas and Aileen shopped inside, I noticed a small crowd of people surrounding what looked like a Las Vegas blackjack table. As I took a step or two closer, I saw that they were playing "the shell game," that old-time gambling game with three shells and one pea that usually spells bad news for any player crazy enough to take on the dealer.

To my surprise, there were a number of folks actually betting on the game. As the dealer moved the shells around and players laid money down, I knew the best bet was not to get involved. So I innocuously slipped by the crowd to start to look for Davide. After seeing him still at the gas pump and knowing that Aileen was going to be a few more minutes, I hesitated thinking, *"Why not relax and watch the fools play a game that is guaranteed to be fixed? This could be fun."*

So I took a position behind the dealer where I could see the faces of the people playing at the table. As I watched the action, my attention was soon caught by a tall, swarthy fellow who had just lost his money.

The guy was absolutely livid.

Throwing his hands in the air, he raged in a thick New York accent as he headed straight at me. "What a bunch of thieves!" he said right at me. Feeling an affinity for the guy (i.e., as a "sucker"), I nodded but kept quiet. Despite my silence, the guy stood next to me and kept on talking like we were long lost friends, insisting loudly that the whole game was just one big con to rip tourists off.

"Couldn't have said it better myself," I thought.

Then the guy suggested something to me that smelled like a plan. He proposed that from where I was standing I could see where the dealer was putting the pea. Sure enough, just as he had said, I saw the dealer slip the pea under the far left shell.

As the guy continued talking to me, I kept getting this quiet but pressing feeling that I should leave. So heeding that urging, I smiled at him and started heading towards Davide and our vehicle.

I had not gone two steps when the guy literally raced back to the gambling table. He slammed his hand down hard on that far left shell and shouted to the dealer, "Don't move. I am prepared to bet $500 dollars right now." Surprised at the force and certainty of his actions, I turned in amazement and, sure enough, the guy threw five U.S. $100 bills on the table.

Thinking that the guy had just nabbed the dealer, I laughed and turned once again to leave. As I did, his thick New York accent barked at me again. He said, "Hey, man. Come here. Quick."

What did I do?

In a moment of temporary insanity, instead of running for the hills (as any sane person would do), I did exactly what the guy requested. Like a sheep being led to the slaughter, I walked right over to the gaming table and when the guy said, "Put your finger on this for me will you?" I put my finger on the far left shell.

With every step I took, I got more and more hooked on the idea of seeing the tables turned on the crooked dealer. Then the guy added, "Come on, man. Get your money up while you can. We have this f_____ pig!"

Money? That's another story. When I answered, "I am not interested in betting," he reacted with a look that shouted, "Are you nuts? Put your money down."

Taking another look at the guy and my finger on that shell, I thought, *"Hum. He might be right. Sure would be nice to score some easy money off this scam."* What were the odds I was wrong? None. I was absolutely sure where the pea was located. I had seen with my own eyes where the dealer had put it. The guy saw the answer in my eyes and smiled as I put five $20 bills on the table.

Yes. I am telling you there's nothing like a bit of vigilante justice mixed with greed to help you think clearly. (Not!)

Seeing my $100 bet, the guy responded like I was some ninety-pound wimp on the beach. He reacted by saying impatiently, "Hey if you have any more in your pocket, get it out. Shit. This is it. I have been waiting all day for this." Then, as if to flex his biceps in my face, he pulled out another $100 and slammed it on the table.

"All in!" he yelled.

At that second my savior, Aileen, walked up to the table. Seeing what I was doing, she asked with a tone that whacked me across the face, "What are you doing, Dan?" However, before I could respond, the guy interrupted me like he had known Aileen all her life.

"You must be his wife," he cut in like he was thrilled to let her in on our grand scheme. "If you have any money, this is the time to get it out. We have this game where we want it." After the guy added a few disarming comments, Aileen decided to put $100 down and I added another $50 to the table.

As our combined $250 hit the table, I was absolutely sure that we were about to double our money or better. For goodness sakes, my finger was still on the shell.

Then Truth showed up to teach me a valuable lesson.

I heard the dealer say something, and it was not in some obscure Italian dialect. Rather, the dealer spoke exactly in the same New York accent as the guy who supposedly lost his money in the first place- the guy who had quite successfully hooked both Aileen and me into betting in the first place. At that instant, I realized that the dealer and the guy were working together as one very well rehearsed team of scam artists.

There would be no pea under that shell beneath my finger.

There wasn't. I had been played like a fiddle, and the only person I could blame was me. I had been so sure I was right. The truth was that I was completely wrong.

After many hours of reviewing the tape on my $250 lesson, I still wondered how I could have been so predictable. This was not my first trip overseas. I was fairly savvy- at least I thought I was- about the intents of others. I *knew* that the game would be fixed. Yet I had gotten hooked like a hungry fish jumping for a flashy lure.

How did these con artists predict so accurately what was going through my head? How had the guy been so able to win my trust?

Clearly I had underestimated their skill level when it came to understanding how Americans think. While I stood off at a slight distance watching, the pair must have adeptly sized me up as an American businessman or tourist who would think that the game was rigged.

As the charade commenced, the decoy won my trust by agreeing with my own thoughts that the game was a con. Then he enrolled me subtly by suggesting that the con could be beaten. Influencing me with the strength of his actions, he got me into a position that greatly increased the odds of me betting. Once my finger was placed so assuredly on that shell, he had me.

The only thing left to do was to take advantage of the obvious.

I had put my money down on that gaming table because I had chosen to agree with the internal conversation that said what I owned in life was not enough and that I needed more. At that table, the guy tapped into my own version of that well-sung American rendition of greed, fear of poverty and beating the bad guys at their own game. Not only could I win money, but I could make myself look like the good guy in my own eyes. In retrospect I realized I was no different from any other person I had judged as hypocritical.

The truth is that if I hadn't been attached to the idea that something was missing (in this case, money), the con would have never succeeded against me. It was my own internal beliefs that had hooked me for $250. I had been cemented to the "more is better" cultural drift of thinking and, until that painfully revealing moment of Truth, I had not seen how powerfully I had *been had* by it.

The truth is, I don't need anything.

I am loved by the Maker of heaven and earth and all I possess comes out of His generous giving to me. Yet just like Adam and Eve in the Garden, I had been caught red-handed looking for something other than what God Himself had provided.

I had chosen to believe a lie and was not as free as I thought I was.

As we traveled towards the beautiful Amalfi Coast, all I could ask God was how much of the rest of my life was drifting along in this earth's culture like some ox being lead around by a ring in his nose?

This was one Divine wake-up call that I was not going to ignore.

✡ ✡ ✡

Drifting Along

✡ ✡ ✡

"Jesus said, "'For judgment I have come into this world,
so that the blind will see and those who see will become blind.'"
"Some Pharisees who were present
asked, "'Do you mean that we are blind?'"
"'If you were blind,'" said Jesus,
"'you would not be guilty, but because you claim to see,
your guilt remains.'"
John 9:39-41 (NKJV)

As a minister and trainer I am often engaged assisting others when they are holding onto things that are causing them hurt and injury. Have you ever considered why we do this?

I have. Quite often.

Recently I was getting a cup of coffee in my favorite coffee shop in Healdsburg when I overheard a mother anxiously discussing with another woman her teenage daughter's current romantic relationship. As the mother continued expressing her doubt about the wisdom of the relationship, her friend asked whether she had talked to her daughter about her concerns. With a roll of her eyes, the mother responded with a bit of that all-knowing grimace.

"Love is blind," she said implying that the couple was so captivated in love that they would reject any insight she might offer them. Having a daughter myself, I had a hard time not laughing out loud in agreement.

Long after getting my cup of coffee, the mother's remark continued to gnaw at me. *Is it true that "love is blind"?* I wondered.

Thinking about it, I thought of Jesus. In Him, I can't find a better example of love.

Now. Was *He* blind?

Here was a guy who healed the sick, raised the dead and got scores of people angry at Him. Yet He did none of these things for His own personal satisfaction or notoriety. Rather He paid for the sins of our fallen humanity, not His own, by dying on the Cross. Out of His radical love, Jesus went through the agony of the Cross for the possibility that human beings might choose to receive and participate in His love.

To me, Jesus was more clear-sighted than anyone who has ever lived. He was completely free in dimensions I can only dream about. He loved, even while knowing that the ones He came to save, even His best friends, would ultimately betray Him.

Jesus knew the character of His own disciples would fail Him. Still He chose to love.

The mother at the coffee shop was echoing what the culture had taught her, not the truth. She had attached herself to a conversation, holding onto it like a piece of driftwood in the river. Instead of talking directly with her daughter, the mother was making herself right about who her daughter was or wasn't being. It seemed like a con, designed like all cons that allow us to live in an illusion of control over our lives. Even if that control includes being right about avoiding the difficult questions that can save! Instead of pulling hard to shore where she could be free to have constructive dialogue with her daughter, the mother was drifting along in the cultural bog. She could hold onto empty pieces of debris that allowed her to be at ease with the thoughts that *the situation is inevitably going to fail, there is not enough time, energy or whatever to do anything about it.* It allowed her to justify not attempting anything because *it's all futile anyway.*

I believe this mom is a lot like you and me.

Think about times when you have experienced anger, despair, anxiety or confusion because you did not get something that you felt you deserved. What goes off inside when you are forced to realize that some relationship or situation is not turning out as you had anticipated? What do you dread or desire? Or think about a time when you were in love with someone but were rejected. Remember how you obsessively focused on that person? Was it as though no one else existed?

When this happened to me, I was a mess. I did not eat, shave, do my laundry or even wash my dishes. All that mattered was avoiding the disastrous prospect of this person not being in my life. I was completely destitute. I could not imagine any new possibility ever coming into my life.

Do you want to know if you're attached or not? Stop for a second. Step back from yourself and pick one thing that is troubling you. Take a look at yourself from the perspective that you *are* attached to something that is hooking you just like those con artists hooked me for $250. What is it? What are you refusing to give up? What are you holding onto? How is the attachment you may have to how life is supposed to look, feel or happen blinding you to other possibilities? How do you react internally when you are around those who don't serve or agree with those things, circumstances or individuals that you consider essential to your survival?

What are you clinging to in the river of cultural drift? Where in your belief system are you drifting along, clinging to a piece of Styrofoam?

Here's one way to find out. How would you spend your time if you found out you had only a few days left to live? You would probably spend each minute on certain, highly valued things to the exclusion of everything else. Things such as personal gain, being rejected socially, being fabulously famous or being right would probably mean much less to you if not becoming completely meaningless.

Take away that imminent death, and what do you have?

How are you listening in life? In the process of transformation, I say one of the first things we need to do is to become aware of what is rattling around in our heads. When Jesus said, "I have come into this world so that the blind will see," I believe that He was inviting us to see the world outside of ourselves. His words are an invitation to transcend the everydayness of our circumstances and familiar interpretations of those circumstances and move deeper into the abundance of His kingdom.

To see, we first need to recognize how we filter what we hear.

✡ ✡ ✡

Fingers in the Ears

✡ ✡ ✡

"When He called all the multitude to Himself,
He said to them. '"Hear Me, everyone and understand:
There is nothing that enters a man from outside which can
defile him;but the things which come out of him, those are
the things that defile a man.If anyone has ears to
hear, let him hear!"'
Mark 7:16
"Then He said to them,
"'Take heed what you hear.
With the same measure you use, it will be measured to you
and to you who hear, more will be given.
For whoever has, to him more will be given
but whoever does not have, even what he has will be
taken away from him.'"
Mark 4:24-25
"Nearly all wisdom we possess, that is to say, true and sound
wisdomand sound wisdom consists of two parts; the
knowledge of God and of ourselves."2
John Calvin

You could have cut the tension with a knife.

It was a good sign for me as the group's trainer; such tension meant that we were close to breaking through to a new way of being with each other. As Erasmus might say, "a new way of being people." The room had gone dead silent and all eyes were fixed on an unpretentious young couple. Inside I knew that this was the couple's moment if they would be willing to investigate and explore the way they were talking to themselves about what was happening.

This second morning of the Breakthrough Training had hit the skids right out of the gate over something innocuous- a piece of unfinished homework. As the day started, I had asked the young man if his wife had completed her homework. The young man's body language, his eyes, his sentences and energy, all communicated that he really didn't know if she had done it or not.

As I experienced all my alarms going off, everything about him conveyed, *"Don't bother me with what I have been trying to avoid!"* With growing agitation, the young man answered me, "I don't know if my wife has completed her homework."

It was becoming clear to everyone that the couple had not completed their homework from the previous night, something they had promised to do. As the tension continued to increase, I could tell that something else was being revealed.

My heart was pounding. I felt that familiar but indescribable emotion of being with someone in a way that partners with the Holy Spirit in opening up unprecedented possibilities. Over the years I had learned to be at ease in that "uncomfortable air" as I invited people to explore possibilities other than the ones that were so familiar to them.

I asked the couple if they had come to the Breakthrough Training to work on their relationship. They both replied, "Yes." "Had they stayed together that night?" Again, an affirmative answer. "How about breakfast?" The young man acknowledged that they had been together and had talked. "What did you talk about?" I inquired.

The young man's tight response included the weather, some bills, things about their three kids and other business they had as youth group leaders and daycare managers for their church.

At this point, the proverbial elephant in the room was obvious. And as my mother used to say, "If there is an elephant in the room, you might as well introduce them to everybody." I asked if he thought his attitude was an example of the attitude he uses in life when he comes up against the unknown and, specifically, as it relates to his wife.

"How might that be?" the young man replied with increasing defensiveness. "What does your question have to do with the training?"

"Well, you have this homework from this training," I answered. "A training that you chose to attend for the purpose of working on things that you say you are committed to in your relationship with your wife and with God."

"You get this homework," I continued to observe, "that is directed toward those outcomes you say are paramount for this weekend. Yet when you and your wife are together, instead of talking about the issues raised by the homework and how they may apply to your lives together, you talk about what? All these other things. My point isn't to make you wrong about what you did, but to open a possibility you may not have considered before. What if your not talking about the issues the homework raises wasn't an accident? What if it was part of a larger system that has you and that you are not completely aware of? Even though you say you care about her, which I believe you do, just not like you think you do."

"You never got to finding out if your wife's homework was done, let alone what she was experiencing while doing it. What I have been wondering about is whether or not you are even in touch with what is really going on in her life beyond the superficial performance kind of things. If you aren't in touch and aren't aware of it, then by becoming aware you could make new choices that could more powerfully contribute to what you say you really want with your wife."

At this speculation the young man went ballistic, accusing me of calling him a bad husband.

"Hang in here with me," I invited. I asked him to tell me if I had in fact called him a bad husband. Still hot, the young man said I had not called him a bad husband but that I had implied it. At least, this was what he made up about my assessment.

I replied, "Do you see possibility for deeper intimacy with your wife in what I have speculated?"

With that last question, he shut down. "I don't see it. I don't want to talk about it anymore. This is too frustrating and not worth the effort!"

I persisted, "What if your assumption of being judged as 'not a good husband' is what you hear inside your head whenever your wife points to things that aren't working for her in your relationship? To avoid the feelings of inadequacy that would follow, you divert conversations with her by changing the subject or attacking her as you are doing with me right now? Further, if what I suspect has an ounce of truth in it, could recognizing this be an opening for what you really want with her?"

His response was nothing but silence—until the next day when his wife broke down during one of the training's exercises. With tears she revealed that she been molested as a child and was currently molesting and mutilating her own children. As she wept, the wife became so distraught that our team captain (who was also a pastor in her church) took the couple to a psychiatric care unit. Together, as an extra precaution, we persuaded the couple to come forward to appropriate authorities even though none of the children of the daycare facility had been molested.

Days after the training, the young husband asked to meet with me. When we met he was so unlike the man I had known in the training. Outwardly he looked like he hadn't slept in days but there was something very different with him now. He was at peace, free and willing to discuss what he had resisted just a couple of days before. He asked my forgiveness for reacting to my questions, adding that my assessment had been completely accurate. For some time he had suspected that his wife was molesting their children but he didn't want to see it, feeling inadequate to deal with it. Even when his children had come to him complaining of pain around their genitals, he did nothing.

To avoid the fear and pain of finding out the truth, the young man kept conversations with his wife superficial and detached. He chose to deny all the signs that were interrupting him at every corner, ignoring what his own intuition was screaming to him.

He had refused to have ears to hear and, as a result, had blinded himself. Out of fear of the inconceivable, he had chosen denial and ignorance instead. As a result of those choices, he couldn't provide what was wanted and needed in order to have the future that he desperately desired for his family.

Here was a young couple working in a church with a youth group and even managing a daycare facility for children. They knew the Bible, even taught it. Yet despite all the outward masks of "good Christianity," the wife had struggled with the torment and self-hatred of mutilating and molesting her own children. Her pastor of more than seven years had no clue what was going on, and her husband was detached, defensive and lost in denial.

Signs of their troubles had shown up all over the place, especially in how they communicated with friends, family and each other. Yet they had been extremely unaware of themselves and where they actually stood in relationship to living out the very concepts they taught every Sunday at church. They had been disconnected from those others they had called "community."

To make matters worse their community had not acted upon any of the signs that indicated something was wrong. How come? What was missing from their fellowship that something of this nature could have existed undetected for so long?

After years of his wife struggling with her inner suffering and outward actions, everything had finally come into the light. All it took to blow the lid were some questions about a piece of incomplete homework and a willingness on my part to persevere through some immediate discomfort while gaining more knowledge by asking about details that would allow us to meet the elephant in the room. Up until the homework encounter, the young man couldn't alter the disaster he was headed into because he had resisted hearing, seeing, or even considering the evidence that was shouting at him. All the strategies he had employed to protect himself had kept him in denial, detached from his most intimate concerns. As a result, he couldn't identify what was going on. He was impotent to know how to ask for what was truly wanted and needed to bring forth healing and reconciliation for his family.

Given the type of reaction I received during the training when I encountered the young man's unwillingness to even look at the possibility of what I was interpreting, I began to understand why those who had known him for years were in the dark about the couple's problems. I think that as human beings, we relate to breakdown sometimes by seeing it as adversarial. So, we resist engaging in it or anything we think will eventually lead to it.

Our culture teaches us that what people do in their lives is none of our business. In fact, the cultural conversation further accuses those who care enough to inquire as foisting their beliefs on others.

Yet society inherits the legacy of such uninterrupted tragedies, the results of which have been studied for years. In cases of sexual abuse, for example, a stunningly high percent of abused children end up abusing children in their adult life. Unless someone cares enough to see the signs of trouble and help others bring these kinds of conversations into the light so they can be reinvented, I suspect that there is little hope for reconciliation or healing for those who have been victimized.

In this case, the young man's attachment to staying blind almost destroyed everything he wanted the possibility of a great marriage and a loving family. He had allowed himself daily choices that had kept him super-glued to a lie and therefore helpless to do anything about it, until the day somebody was willing to risk his disapproval for what he said mattered most in his life. Only then did he allow the Truth to break through. To have life, the young man had to face dying to the lie; he had to let go of the denial that he had hoped would save them all.

When he did let go, the young man had a new possibility to act on and new resources to utilize in the journey. He could choose to be with his wife and children in a way that would powerfully contribute to the future that he had always wanted. By having those tough conversations, which he had long avoided, the young man found his life.

I think that to become free from what enslaves us and prevents us from seeing the unprecedented future, it is critical that we get a clear perspective on how we are listening to our internal conversation and what actions we are taking because of that listening. We do this is examining ourselves for the purpose of discovering how we have already made up our minds about who we are and what we hear.

This is easier said than done.

As human beings, we talk at the average rate of about 125 words per minute. Inside, however, we have conscious thoughts at a rate of around 600 words per minute. Some experts speculate that our actual thoughts (both conscious and subconscious) run more like 1,500 words per minute.

Right from the start there is excess capacity in our processing abilities. Small wonder that our minds wander all over the place and we make up things that are not true or relevant to what is being said.

Another component here is that we don't process information through language alone. We use our eyes as well as our ears to interpret communication. Researchers tell us that body language accounts for a significant portion of what we listen to when someone is speaking to us. In addition to body language, we process vocal tone, meaning we decipher by how someone is saying it. Words themselves account for a much lower percentage of what we hear than we think.

In addition, human beings listen like a radar machine.

Radar works by producing and transmitting electromagnetic waves. When these electromagnetic waves strike a moving or fixed object, the waves bounce back to the radar antenna. The key thing about radar is that it receives only those signals on a wavelength or frequency that it is designed to receive. Radars filter out what doesn't fit their metrics or, said another way, what they aren't tuned to listen for.

Just like us.

When we listen, we listen for the sound of our own ideas, interests, and fears bouncing back to us. We interpret, make assumptions and filter what is being said to fit what we have programmed ourselves to hear. Sometimes these filters are based upon our past experiences, our self-image or the current cultural drift. In essence, we are always listening for our own version of reality.

Like this young couple, sometimes this can cost us everything we hold dear.

✡ ✡ ✡

Cleaning the Filter

✡ ✡ ✡

"The more I work in the area of organizational transformation, creating learning organizations, the more convinced I am that what is already '"heard"' or known, before anyone speaks or acts, is what we have already '"listened to"' and that will shape and determine the future far more powerfully than any action taken."[3]

Barbara Fittipaldi

Researchers like Barbara Fittipaldi have studied for years the dynamics of how we as human beings listen, and she has observed a number of distinctions about our internal radar systems. Among her distinctions, four will especially help us become aware of how we are listening to others as well as how these filters affect our showing up for others.

ASSESSMENT

Assessment is another way of expressing the word *judgment*.

Judgment is an interpretation based on little or no facts. It can be based on a version of the truth that reflects opinion or our own declaration (whether spoken or not) about a person or situation. When we judge, we dissipate our power to act and we withhold ourselves in a posture of observation instead of giving ourselves fully to the conversation we have with others and thus to the relationship.

A judgment is often based upon past experiences and shows up as some form of defense mechanism, which keeps us focused on ourselves and not others. I become what I declare. If I declare a judgment, I become attached to that assessment and act accordingly, usually divorcing myself from others in some manner to preserve myself from what I have judged as damaging about that person.

What I am alerting you to here is that we automatically judge and assess in our listening. Because it is so automatic, our judgments don't become obvious until we begin to question ourselves and listen for assessment in our internal conversation.

For example, let's say that a friend kills his spouse. The fact is that he has committed murder, and I know that his actions are wrong. However, if I continue to relate to him as a murderer, there is little of myself that can be available for him. Only after I stop withdrawing myself in judgment can I extend myself in love.

When we resist someone through judgment, we withdraw our participation. When we judge something or someone as evil, wrong, bad or broken, we pull ourselves back as a natural fight or flight reaction. The problem with judgments is that through them we make ourselves right about how the world *should be*. Often we are simply creating a convenient illusion.

The reality is that if you are breathing, you have thoughts that lead you to an assessment about everything, including yourself. Try to stop for a second. Try stopping those thoughts of assessment, *"Do I agree or disagree?" Is this right or wrong? What is good or bad here?"*

No can do.

What you *can do* is disengage those thoughts by asking yourself, *"What is actually being said?" "What am I not seeing here?"* or *"What does the person really mean?"*

Sometimes the person we judge the harshest is ourselves. How many times a day do we judge what we have said or done as a negative declaration of ourselves? Our self-judgment shows up in "I am" statements that we hold as truth. When we say "I am short-tempered" or "I am someone who doesn't commit," or as 12-step programs tend to emphasize, "I am an alcoholic or drug addict," we are making a self-judgment defining ourselves based upon the past and not from the future worth having. The truth is that our self-judgments have no power to determine our future outside the power we yield to them.

One of my favorite interruptions is three little powerful words, that a good friend often uses on me.

"Up until now."

In my life, I am continually aware that "up until now" is a declaration from the perspective of my future worth having. "Up until now" wipes every slate clean. It is a way of being cognizant of the past yet not bound by it. "Up until now" is a simple but powerful adjustment to our habit of assessing. It is a practical way to listen so we avail ourselves of the unprecedented.

PERSONAL

"Personal" is another way of describing how conversations can have us.

Being in *Logos*, we as humans live within a conversation filled with thoughts and feelings that existed long before we arrived on the scene. The key is realizing that we are in this sea but that it doesn't have to take us under.

The real trap in the *personal* filter is that I imagine that the rest of the world actually sees the world, people and God the way I do. If they don't, then they must be lost, stupid, out of touch or something like that. The personal filter causes me to be blinded to the limits of my own interpretations. I am sucked into the river of my own judgments as if they are reality. Once there, I have little to no resource outside the tradition of my own cultural thinking.

I do not have to engage my thoughts as if they are me personally.

Although this proposition can be disconcerting, consider the possibility that your personal thoughts are not a reflection of you but of something else. For example, if you tell me where you were born, your race, what your home situation was like, what your parents did for a living and what you do for a living, I will be able to zero in on your likely judgments.

During the trainings, participants will often ask a trainer how they could see so clearly into what they were saying. They will say things like, "Wow. How did you know that?" or "Did you read my forms before you talked to me?"

I realize that the idea that we are *in* something that *has* us goes against our cultural characterizations of the individual being free. However, there is a distinction between being free and being in control. Although we want to be in control, I suspect we are not. I believe that the possibility for *true* thinking comes only with recognizing that we are not doing the thinking in the first place.

Consider what Paul says in Romans 7:15-23:

> *I do not understand what I do. For what I want to do,*
> *I do not do, but what I hate I do.*
> *And if I do what I do not want to do, I agree that the law is good.*
> *As it is, it is no longer I myself who does it, but it is sin living in me.*

I think Paul is describing how "it" is thinking and he is "having" the thoughts.

When we identify a thought, we create a space or clearing between our having the thought and the thought itself. In that clearing lies the possibility for a whole new thought or conversation.

When we realize that there is the possibility of a space between thoughts and our awareness of them, then we have some control over our attachments. In this clearing, our freedom is small; it comes down to recognizing that I can't change that I'm thinking or that certain thoughts will occur. What I can do is choose what to do with those thoughts. I can choose my position and therefore my actions. I can choose to whom I will lead those thoughts- Jesus, people or myself.

I think our freedom consists of choosing which conversations will govern life. I don't have to do exactly what my thoughts or feelings are telling me; I can choose a new possibility that could open the way of leading my thoughts to Jesus.

Like standing in an eddy behind a protruding rock in the ferocious flow of a mighty river, I can manage to stand in the river of preexisting conversation while not being pulled down against my will.

ALREADY KNOWING

"I already know" is like driving a car looking at the rear view mirror. It is a perspective that bases the new upon the past. *Already knowing* filters are listening by looking for what we think we already know and conforming what is being said to the paradigm of the past.

When we are filtering this way, our internal conversation asks questions such as, "What is this good for? What is its purpose? What will I get out of this?" The assessing voice of already knowing creates an illusion of comfort and control with "I already know who you are. I know what you are talking about. I know what you want."

Listening this way eliminates every other possibility existing outside our own narrow realm of experience. If we filter what we hear by listening for X's and new possibilities come along as O's, we reject the O's, or at least try to change them into X's.

We don't seek to discover what we don't know or what is possible outside our already predefined experience.

DESCRIPTION

On conscious and unconscious levels, we are immersed in strategies to keep us safe and in control. At the same time, we endorse others in doing the same. As a result we are relatively oblivious to this mutual and universal conspiracy of compromise.

The *descriptive* filter is a defensive posture that hinders us from seeing how we are showing up in life. It creates the illusion that we can control what others will think of us and that we can somehow avoid the possibility of being rejected, being taken advantage of, or betrayed.

We listen for, "Am I going to look the way I should by what is being said? Is this lining up with how I want to be viewed? Will it keep people thinking about me the way I want them to think?"

As a friend of mine has observed, "Our survival strategies are insurance policies for our egos. If something doesn't turn out the way we want, we can rationalize it, insulating ourselves from hurt, rejection, and failure."

How often have we rejected the input of others because we are afraid to see ourselves for who we really are—the good, the bad and that which could use some work? How often would we rather say nothing than risk saying something that would be considered wrong? How many minutes do we spend measuring before we speak up? In this way, how often are we inauthentic or disingenuous?

When we are listening for life to look the way it should, we avoid the pain involved in having illusory strategies interrupted. When we are committed to rejecting, ignoring or filtering out words that threaten our strategies in order to protect ourselves from possible repeats of past failures or disappointments, we eliminate interruptions that might actually free us to be in the world for others the way we most desire.

We attach ourselves to our favorite idol- how we have defined ourselves.

If I say that I am "a certain way," then I call that assessment of myself "who I am." This system of self-talk fortifies the illusion that there is some predictable, concrete, fixed self or "I."

What if there is another possibility? What if there was only a chooser and the "I" that people get to know is a culmination of conversations the observer has about itself? What if we could be "all things to all men," and the doorway to that "all things" is owning what Erasmus infers through his translation of John 1, that *we are a conversation, just like God*?

What if I am from I AM?

✡ ✡ ✡

Rocks and Quarries

✡ ✡ ✡

"Listen to me, all you who are serious about right living
and committed to seeking God.
Ponder the rock from which you were cut,
the quarry from which you were dug."
Isaiah 51:1 (The Message)

Here, Isaiah has given us one great signpost.

Isaiah is saying that if we are serious about right living and seeking God, we will examine ourselves. Although it is easy to assume that Isaiah is referring to Jesus here as "the rock," if we take a look at the Biblical symbolism that Isaiah is using, the word "rock" often refers to a "god," which literally means "idol when the 'r' is not capitalized." By using the small "r" in rock, Isaiah is exhorting us to contemplate and investigate what we adore and worship in your lives.

We can do this by examining our listening.

When we listen to others speak, what we are doing is *not* listening to what they are saying. Rather, we are listening to *what we are saying* inside our heads about their words. These internal, private conversations are conversations we have with ourselves. They are quarried from what we think will save us- ideas, assumptions, attitudes, and speculations built from what we fear, hope, or at least what we think makes us right.

If we will consider Isaiah's guidance, we will seek to stop bowing down to what automatically occurs in our internal dialogue. We will investigate how our listening is influencing our thoughts and determining our behavior, which, according to Isaiah, is merely derived from our culture and personal history, not the kingdom of God.

What might your rocks and quarries look like? Here's how you can start to find out.

Take a day and write down what your internal radar is hearing when you are conversing with other people.

1) Notice what impression forms inside your mind when someone starts to speak with you.

2) Count how many times you interrupt them.

3) Listen for questions you are asking or statements you are making inside.

4) Seek to listen as though you mean exactly what you say and people mean exactly what they say. If you are not clear what they mean, clarify until you are.

5) Notice just how much of your conversation is just automatic recitation.

As you listen, look to discover if you are asking:
Is this true for me?
Is this person honest? Or a fake?

How do I fit into what is being said?
Is this right or wrong?
What is the value here?
How can I be or get control?
Do I agree or disagree here?
What do they want from me?
What rules do I have to follow?
How should this be?
What are they not saying?
What is wrong with it? Them? Me?
What am I to do?

Investigate what meaning you are assigning to the person's words, and then ask him or her whether what you have assigned is accurate.

Look at how you react if someone asks you to do something that matters to you but sounds risky. Do you say, "I can't do that for such-and-such a reason or circumstance"? If the person counters your concerns with suggestions of how you might succeed, do you defend what you "know" based upon past experiences or other circumstances? Are you willing to consider the possibility in what they say, or do you dismiss it within seconds?

Let's see right now where the rubber meets the road.

What are you "hearing" inside? Is my probing a possibility or a threat? Are you listening for performing well? Are you finding what's wrong with what I said? Are you standing above it all? Are you confused? Anxious? Excited? Ambivalent?

Are you looking for the possibilities? Or being right?

✧ ✧ ✧

For Freedom, Christ Has

✧ ✧ ✧

*"There is no upside to freedom, not in the ordinary sense
of pleasure, fun, and benefits.*
*"Freedom introduces you to the non-natural order, the realm
of reality beyond what science can describe. The capacity*

to decide introduces you to the zone of inwardness and subjectivity. The power to choose explains to you the meaning of being a subject rather than an object, a self rather than a thing.

"Freedom explains to you the nature of ethics, ethical choices, and moral courage. Freedom explains pride and dignity, honor and glory. The self-esteem of being responsible, keeping your promises, doing your duty, and choosing accountability- in short, building civilized behavior among people would be bereft of any meaning without its foundation in free will.

"Being in charge of who we are is the essence of being human, and denying that freedom is the essence of regression to animal nature and animal behavior. To feel this, to live this, to experience its weight, and to communicate it readily- those are the inner sensations of the authentic leader.

"The great danger in being free is the temptation to use the organization not as a practice field for freedom but as the excuse for the escape from freedom- the denial of free will, choosing not to be a chooser!

"Will you cultivate the free part of you? Is your inner power inspiring? Is your energy contagious? Does claiming your freedom bring results in your organization?"[4]

Peter Koestenbaum

What do we gain from the discipline and rigor of learning how we listen? Our freedom.

In fact, I think we are always one conversation away from being free. Although freedom has many cultural definitions, it seems to me that real freedom grants us the privilege of taking personal responsibility. Through choosing who we will be, we are no longer enslaved by past circumstances.

When I consider what perfect freedom looks like, I look at Jesus. He was free to love in such a way that He didn't need to be a survivor. His level of freedom led Him willingly to the Cross, resulting in the greatest expression of liberation in the history of man.

I believe that Jesus was aware of His automatic tendencies, even to the extent that He could love those who would hate Him. He disavowed Himself of looking like any cultural image of a Messiah.

He detached Himself from any thought or feeling for revenge. He gave his betrayers the freedom to betray Him.

I believe that Jesus was so aware of His humanity that whenever His internal conversation began to engage Him, He engaged it and not vice versa. Unlike us, it never had Him.

Here and now, Jesus Christ, the Logos, has made Himself available to us. Then why are we not fully accessing His promises? Could it be because we are unwilling to first truly own what we are thinking biologically, historically, culturally? Could it be that we don't want to face our attachments?

If we will own the conversations we are having, I think we will be able to exercise the freedom Jesus purchased for us on the cross-freedom that has nothing to do with external circumstances but rather is grounded in something much greater.

Salvation: abundant (abounding) life now.

Notes:

[1] Seneca, *Hercules Oetaeus* ('Hercules on Mount Oeta').

[2] John Calvin, opening section of *Institutes of Christian Religion*, translation by Henry Beveridge, Esq. (1599).

[3] "New Listening: Key to Organizational Transformation," *When the Canary Stops Singing; Women's Perspective on Transforming Business.*

[4] Peter Koestenbaum, *Koestenbaum's Weekly Leadership Thought*: "Is There an Upside to Freedom?" June 15, 2001.

PERRRFECT

✧ ✧ ✧

The Tee-Up

✧ ✧ ✧

"Imagination is the voice of daring. If there is anything Godlike about God it is that. He dared to imagine everything."[1]
Henry Miller

One hundred and fifty pairs of eyes were watching me intently as I adjusted the microphone.

"When we make big, bold promises, committing ourselves fully to that which God has mysteriously built into our beings, then He who calls forth the dawn will also awaken in us the passions, hopes and dreams that we so fear will never be fulfilled. He who fans the flames of romance, dignity and valor will overcome us with wonder and awe."

It was the second day of our annual Association for Christian Character Development Sponsors' Conference. Gathered there were about one hundred and fifty ministry sponsors from around the globe, each one actively involved with the work of the organization. We were friends and family committed to living transformational lives throughout the world.

What I was speaking about that Saturday morning was far from what I had planned.

You see, the night before, I began to see things anew. I found myself flooded with new insight about things I had only seen at a distance, and I realized that God was wooing us individually and as a group to an impossible, unprecedented future. What we had seen together in the past was simply the appetizer. The main course was yet to be enjoyed, if we would be willing to partake. We were standing at the horizon of the *new*.

God was whispering in our ears, "Come on. Get out of the boat. Walk on water. Take the impossible as your own."

"When we make a big bold promise, we are speaking beings creating the future now, and in this way we are emulating God who speaks all things into existence. We are declaring into the void the depths of our longings believing that they will "'be,'" all the while knowing full well that we can't make them come into existence on our own. Yet we are convinced that they are possible because of that longing inside us. We are the possessors of the evidence unseen."

Halfway back in the crowd, I saw Linda Costa smiling at me.

Sitting around Linda was a clan all its own. Couples, singles, business people, ex-drug addicts, doctors, engineers. They were the Southern California contingent, the evidence now seen, people transforming purpose into character in their lives- the fruit of Linda's own big bold promise.

"When the past and present circumstances taunt, defy and mock our stand for what is said to be impossible, what are we to do? Give up? Go home? Miss the chance to walk on water?

"Or will we say "'Yes'" to the paradox of the impossible? Will we linger like the lightning rod waiting for the storm to come and, abiding in that mystical and risk-filled place, discover the footsteps of Jesus, the One who made the universe's biggest promise, the redemption of all humanity?"

I smiled back at Linda. What a self-effacing, refined lady she is-rock-solid, determined and as beatific as a lighthouse on a cliff in the midst of a winter gale.

I, for one, should know.

✡ ✡ ✡

The 125

✡ ✡ ✡

"Life is either a daring adventure or nothing. Security is mostly a superstition. It does not exist in nature."[2]
Helen Keller

"Linda, are you smoking something illegal, honey?"

"Dan, I promise that we will have 100 people."

"You have been a sponsor in Orange County now for two and a half years and you have never had trainings larger than twenty-two people. I want the first Discovery to have a minimum of one hundred."

"I know that, Dan, and I also know that the Discovery Seminar will be a life-changing experience for many people here in Southern California. I want to be the first to launch it."

"You are already $6,000 in the hole from doing the trainings. You have three kids, and your home life is going through a major storm right now. Your dad, a cop, is wondering what the heck you're doing. Linda, I love you but you are out of your mind."

"Dan, I am willing to leap. God will show up."

"*Mamma mia!* I haven't even finished writing the seminar yet. We don't even have a manual."

"Okay. When can you have it done?"

"Please understand that I want to give Discovery to you but-"

"Dan, I will make whatever shift is wanted or needed. This is what I want to do. I am committed. I am not getting off it. I promise we will have 100 people. Will you stand with me?"

"Linda, even Jesus had three loaves and a couple of fish. You already gave your lunch away."

"Dan. Do you believe in me?"

"Well, sure I do. But Linda, no one with ACCD has ever enrolled a training this large. It has not been done before. By anyone."

"Do you?"

"Oh, boy."

"Well?"

"Okay, Linda. Okay. Go. Go put a team together, and I will finish the manual in a month."

"Thank you, Dan."

"Ah, Linda. One more thing. Your dad doesn't know where I live, does he?"

It was the winter of 1997, and I was writing a new training called Discovery.

Aileen and I were living in Michigan at the time, and I had been toying with creating something new. I had been impacted by my friend, Ray, a pastor of a Vineyard church in Grand Rapids, who was wondering about the possibility of a training designed for larger groups of people in a church. He was looking for a situation where leaders and congregants alike could gain revelation about God and experience transformation in their lives.

Hearing Ray's thoughts, I crafted Discovery as a laboratory where individuals could take a fresh look at themselves and what they believed in light of what God has said through His word. The goal of Discovery was to introduce people to the possibility of transformation in their lives. Unlike the smaller venue of The Breakthrough Training, Discovery was designed for large groups numbering from 100 to 300 people.

Before I had finished writing Discovery, Linda tracked me down.

Aileen and I had known Linda for about five years at the time. Earlier in her life, Linda had gone to Bible College and had even served in the mission fields for five years.

Her evangelistic heart was always searching out the hurting, lost and needy around her. Going to something like Breakthrough was not something she would normally be inclined to do but, in 1994, Linda was among the earliest to take it.

"I had gone to so many Christian conferences in my day," Linda told me once, "that I had little interest in doing this Breakthrough thing. Wow! Was I surprised afterward! Who would have thought that those four days would have so altered the course of my life? Through Breakthrough, my vision for others got restored. I experienced healing from things that had happened in my past. *This was a great gift from God,*' I said to myself. *I'm in.*"

After Breakthrough, Linda returned home and started talking to her friends about the training. It wasn't long before she went through the process of becoming a sponsor in the Southern California region.

As a sponsor, Linda was the one who took on the visionary, logistical and financial responsibilities, risks and rewards involved with bringing ACCD trainings into her local community. Although there is always a team involved for every training, the sponsor is the one leading the charge.

Right from the start, Linda was *on it*.

As she took on the brand new Discovery Seminar, she and I were on the phone a number of times a week as I coached her. Who is she talking to? How is she in conversation with people? Is she opening up possibilities with them?

Then came the day that Linda needed to sign a contract that would lock her financially into the hotel where the training was to be held. This contract needed to be signed well before she had any guarantee that she would reach the numbers needed for the training.

"Dan, this is a stretch," she told me. "The room alone is going to cost me three times what I have spent in the past. On top of that, the hotel insists that we utilize their catering for at least one of our meals. What if I'm not doing the right thing here? What if we have to cancel the training?"

"What do you think?"

Linda paused for a moment. "I think it's an opportunity to stand for something that honors God and to put at stake what is most valuable to me."

"And, what's that?"

"Maybe the desire for security?"

"Linda, what is wanted and needed?"

"People in the training!" she replied.

"How many people are on your team?"

"Well, I have twenty-seven right now and five more who will be coming on in the next week."

"How many people did they say they would enroll?"

Linda thought about it and said, "Well, I am not clear about that yet."

"Could asking them be something that you don't want to do?

Thinking for a minute, Linda answered, "I guess I am afraid that if I ask the team for a commitment about how many people they will enroll into Discovery that they will resist and maybe even leave."

As Linda and I discussed her thoughts and fears, we talked about she often allowed these same issues of acceptance and approval stop her from asking for what she wanted or needed to have life work out.

As we worked into her life she was learning from her own revelations ways to open up the horizon for team members. Some might see her invitation to enroll others as a possibility. Others might not. Either way, having the discussion with the team about enrollment was a win-win for Linda on a personal level. Linda was seeing that by being willing to get into conversations that she dreaded, God was giving her an opportunity to trust Him in ways she had not before. And as a result she was assisting the team members to notice how scarce they often thought life was. In many ways Linda was opening the kingdom of God, abundant life for people.

"I think, Linda, if you give up to God what you are holding in your hands or hiding from Him, He will surprise you. I believe that whatever you encounter will be perfect, if you just surrender to being with it. If you will be in the problem this way, God can then open up new possibilities! The key here is to have those conversations you think are most important first."

Linda did, and God did. Whether it was hurdles of finances, pioneering something untried or opening possibility with people about the Discovery Seminar, Linda remained standing on her big, bold promise. Her promise set off a myriad of actions that would have not occurred if she had not made the promise and chose to live in alignment with it.

The most significant action was that Linda and her team reached out to others. Because of Linda's declaration, they initiated and built relationships. They became at stake for the welfare of friends and strangers alike in ways that were unprecedented for them up until that time.

Finally the day came for Discovery. Arriving at the hotel, I opened the conference room door and I saw that the room was packed.

"How many?" I asked Linda with a smile.

She was beaming. "We're at 125."

"Way to go, girl and thanks be to God!"

✧ ✧ ✧

Living as Your Word

✧ ✧ ✧

"Valor grows by daring, fear by holding back."
Publilius Syrus

The sponsors were awfully quiet as I continued what was opening up for me about the unprecedented life.

"When you make a big bold promise, there is one thing for certain. Nothing is going to turn out quite the way you expected or think it should."

I heard a loud chuckle from the crowd.

Even from way up front, I knew that snort could belong only to one person, Kris Kile. Suddenly, memories of snow banks, crude *Get Shorty* lines and freezing New England temperatures derailed me off message. I looked down at my notes, trying my best not to laugh out loud.

Kris Kile. What a man. Indefatigable. Unedited. Unflinching. He decides and does. Never down for long, Kris is a full-speed-ahead type of guy looking to see how to integrate his commitments with others to create community. And, Katie, his wife. Loyal. Strong. Kind. Straightforward.

We had been friends for about ten years now, ever since Kris and Katie took the Breakthrough Training and experienced some significant breakthroughs in their marriage and family. Soon after Breakthrough, they became ACCD sponsors in the New Hampshire/New England area.

Pushing snowy thoughts to the rear, I went on, avoiding the expression on Kris' face.

"When we live as our word, we are standing for the manifestation of promise, not the way it looks. And, in that declaration, we set up the altar upon which our natural loves and natural ways of being die, so as to be resurrected substantially new and more potent. We give ourselves completely to the process, having our promise determine who we are or are not- and how we stand in what we do.

"Making a big bold promise makes no sense to the consumer mind, but to a mind that has been transformed by Jesus the One who said, "As in heaven, here on earth." Because when you make a big, bold promise, you are doing something very few people would do. You are intentionally positioning yourself to fail. Because what you have promised, you already know you don't have the power to insure fulfilling. Circumstances and other people are not under your control, and therefore it is an act of faith.

"You are getting out of the boat, realizing that walking on water defies the natural universe and history itself.

"Your only hope is God.

"Only the paradox of believing the impossible is possible constitutes a big, bold promise. If what you are promising is something you can do by yourself, then it's not big enough. Your feet are not quite out of the boat yet. You are just feeding your family on your McDonald's Big Mac Meal and not the 5,000 with just a few loaves of bread and some fish.

"To walk on water, it means that you become like a little child again."

Glancing at Kris' wife, Katie, I remembered the day she nailed me in the kindest way. What she did reminded me of the line, "You cut me down to size and opened up my eyes" from Cold Play's song, "Swallowed in the Sea." It was during those early years of our friendship that the trainings that Kris and Katie were sponsoring were pretty low in enrollment numbers. As the trainer, I had stayed at their house a few times already when Katie spoke to me at the kitchen table.

"Dan," she said with a quiet undercurrent of sadness, "I feel like you take Kris and me for granted. I want you to hear me when I say that I love you, but it really hurts me when you act like that."

"Really?" I answered. "How do you see me taking you for granted?"

Telling me the truth in love, Katie pointed out to me a number of things that I had done, and I realized that she was completely right. I saw that my ungrateful behavior towards them could have been an outward manifestation of my complaint about the low numbers in their trainings. I saw that I had been measuring our friendship on the basis of performance.

Katie's honest love whacked me in the best way. She was after building our friendship, but not out of some kind of performance.

In so many words, Katie was saying to me at that kitchen table, "I am going to be your friend whether you accept me or not."

"You are so right, Katie. Wow. I see what you are saying." I said, "Will you please, please forgive me?"

Remembering that day, I thought about how much we had learned through living as our word. If she and Kris hadn't made that promise, I would not have had the privilege of dying to myself that day. I had been crucified, and our relationship had been resurrected from it.

Even the word *promise* is a gold mine. Basically, promise means to send forth. "It is a declaration, written or verbal, made by one person to another, which binds the person who makes it either in honor, conscience or law to do or forebear a certain act specified." As *Noah Webster's 1828 Dictionary of the American Language* distinguishes, a promise is a declaration that gives the person to whom it is made a right to expect or to claim the performance or forbearance of the act.

A promise creates an expectation in the person or persons to whom it is made; it literally transforms your personal right to yourself into a duty to others. A complete promise includes a speaker, a listener, a declaration of action, specific terms of fulfillment (what will be produced, how many) and a time agreement (by when).

In Hebrew, the word we translate as "promise" means "word." Whenever Scripture uses the phrase, "the word of the Lord," it means a promise. Similarly, we equate making a promise with "giving your word." In fact "giving your word" is close to the meaning of the Latin word *promittere* from which our word "promise" has been derived. When we make a promise, we are sending forth our word. As Jesus' was sent forth from God, the Logos made flesh, His promises entailed His whole being as the exact representation of the Father who had sent Him.

Our promises send us forth into the future worth having and create the opportunity for us to become the representation of that word and what it represents.

A primary definition of the word *"character"* is a "representation" of something. Our character is either the representation of what our word declares to others or it isn't. And when it isn't, we have the opportunity to acknowledge that and either shift how we are representing ourselves to align with our word (promise, commitment, purpose) or we can continue to act incongruently. No matter our choice, our actions in relationship to the expectation our word creates in others are what people experience as our character.

The distinction between living as your word and keeping your promise is subtle, but powerful. Although many of us equate "living as your word" to mean "keeping your promises," we can still live as our word even when we break our promises. Living as our word is to be governed by our word even in the face of a broken promise.

Let's say I invite you to meet me at the movies at 8:00 p.m. for the purpose of us getting to know one another better. If I miss that 8:00 p.m. movie, I can still live as my word if I come to you, account for my broken promise and ask you for forgiveness. If we walk out reconciliation and explore impact, consequences and what it will take to reconcile our relationship, we could become closer as friends, which was the intent of original promise even though the process looked completely upside down.

Living as your word is the context from which a broken promise is recognized and the possibility of reconciliation is opened up.

First of all, I can see that "I" am not broken; what I have done is broken my promise and have caused a break in my relationship with the one to whom I am bound by my word. I have disappointed the expectation created by my promise. Still, I can live as my word by working to reconcile and restore the peace that has been destroyed by my broken promise. The distinction here is that a broken promise means that you are out of alignment with what you have declared as your way of being *for others or the future your promise represents*. You have made a choice that is in opposition to what you have declared to the one who has accepted your word.

When I was acting in such a way that took Kris and Katie for granted, I was out of alignment with my word to love them the way I want to be loved. I was breaking my word to be their friend.

"Okay, here's the good news. With big bold promises come some big challenges. Like having all the passion and trust drained right out of a training-"

I heard another laugh. It was Kris, smiling like a Cheshire Cat.

✡ ✡ ✡

The Nor'easter

✡ ✡ ✡

"The Eskimos had fifty-two names for snow because it was important to them: there ought to be as many for love."
Margaret Atwood

"**K**ris, I think we're stuck."
          "God. This has been the training from hell."
"Hey, you were the one who just drove us into a snow bank, man."
"Like I was trying?"
"Well, there's no place like California."
"You're in New Hampshire, Dan."
"As I said. No place like California."
"Are you going to get out and push or what?"
"It's cold out there, Kris. Not to mention pitch dark."
"Dan, it is a balmy 4 degrees outside. Don't be a wimp."
"We could call AAA."
"It's 2:00 a.m. And, we're in the boonies here."
"Oh. Right."
Kris was right. The past few days of this training had been one of the most, let's say, *unusual* I had ever seen- and I had seen just about all of them. But, in some respects, that was nothing new for Kris and his New Hampshire trainings. Maybe it had something to do with that Yankee stubborn streak or perhaps a vision that overcomes. All I knew on that freezing December morning as we struggled to get our car out of the snow bank was that something had taken hold of this man and his family.
"When I took Breakthrough," Kris told me after we first met, "it brought me to deep repentance for many things, including how I had shown up with my wife and sons. Through Breakthrough, I got reconnected to them in profound ways. This has proven to be one of the most incredible experiences I have ever had with God. I am reinvigorated and my vision has been catalyzed for us being here

in New England. Katie and I are staking our roots down for the sake of the significant things that God wants to do here."

Coming out of the training, Kris and Katie immediately started sponsoring Breakthrough. The results they got would have knocked lesser people out of the ring.

Months before their first training, they worked extremely hard to enroll friends and associates to the value of what they saw possible through Breakthrough. As the training date grew close, it looked as though their first Breakthrough was going to have real impact in their community. Everything was pointing to success.

Then during the training itself, the bottom dropped out from under them. And, it was partly my fault.

I had sent them a trainer who was in some ways too inexperienced do a training on his own. The results of his behavior were devastating to the training, and many of the participants left disillusioned and offended.

Almost all of the momentum Kris and Katie had created was dissipated. Crushed but not giving up, they started over again first by reconciling the upset with graduates who were not satisfied with their experience of the training. After several months of persistently taking one step after the other, they conducted their second training with less than half the number of participants in the first training.

After working through the challenges with me, Kris and Katie made the decision to keep moving forward, doing training after training. After a number of months, they were able to recapture the momentum they had generated in the first training.

One day Kris said to me: "What we are standing for is to move culture by being in relationship. Katie and I are about being within our community and world in such a way that people see what God has said is possible for them in their lives. Yet, Dan, most days, I feel like a man who is fishing in a pond that is stagnant."

However, standing with Katie and Kris in their promise, all of us kept going. We continued to explore what was wanted and needed, seeking feedback from participants of each training and other graduates. As we did, we learned more and more about what we could provide to make the difference we were committed to deliver.

Then, came a snowstorm that threatened the training. That weekend I learned something about tenacity as well as seeing God in unexpected places.

The training was held in a small, old convent in New Hampshire. When I arrived on Wednesday night from sunny California, I was greeted by freezing cold temperatures. Once again the numbers in the training were small, with just around fourteen people, but Kris was still the optimist looking for possibility where others only saw obstacles.

"Hey, Dan, there's a woman in the training. Her name is Lata Chawla and she works at a major broadcasting corporation in Connecticut. I could really see how what you are doing could translate into the corporate arena."

"Sure. Okay," I said, remembering the conversations we had had about the value our work would have in the business community, especially with CEO's and their teams.

The first two days of the training seemed like we were hammering through concrete. There was a sense that people were not clear about what they wanted to accomplish, so we took our time discussing what those accomplishments would look like for each participant.

Then, came Saturday, the third day of the training, when I caught a weather report that broadcast a snowstorm. Sure enough, the skies were getting ominous. "A Nor'easter," the broadcast blurted.

Right on cue, the snowstorm blanketed the entire area with several feet of snow. Right in the middle of a powerful exercise dealing with forgiveness, the electricity went off. Everything came to a halt as we found ourselves in this dark convent without lights, heat or water pressure. We soon learned that the power was off not only in the convent but the entire surrounding region and, due to the extent of the outage, it was not likely to come back on for the next two or three days.

Inevitably, the question was raised. Now what? Cancel the rest of the training? One look at Kris and I knew. No way.

Instead of shutting the training down, Kris made his way through snowy roads to the local hardware store and bought a $3,000 generator out of his own pocket. He was not about to call off the training.

The generator gave us enough power for the sound system, some heat and lights. And, we charged forward, wrapped in blankets, completing the last two days a little cold but with more than a few great stories to tell.

On Sunday night, after hours of packing up the training room and putting everything into a trailer hitched to his car, Kris and I finally left the convent around 2:00 in the morning. We were bone tired and laughing as we slowly picked our way down the snow-covered roads.

Coming around a bend on a narrow country road, we saw a Canadian power truck with a crew working on the electrical lines. Unfortunately, the truck was taking up the majority of the passable road.

"Are you sure you can make it around them, Kris, with the trailer?"

"Sure."

"They're pretty far out."

"No problem, Dan. Hey, if we get stuck, those guys from the crew will help us out."

Here is, as they say, the rest of the story. Sometimes, seeing possibility can land you in a snowdrift. We got completely stuck. The power crew didn't help us out. We got covered in snow, said funny lines from the film *Get Shorty* and laughed so hard that it hurt.

Although Kris and Katie's trainings continued to be small to medium in size, the impact of their living as their word has profoundly impacted thousands of lives. God has answered their promise to move cultures.

From that snowy, no-electricity training, Lata Chawla did open up the possibility of translating our work into the corporate arena. Working as a consultant for her corporation eventually led me to Harvard Business School for additional training in negotiation. This was followed by creating a company called Culture ROI, which is now a going concern serving Disney, ESPN, Microsoft, Seagate, World Vision and other Fortune 500 companies.

Kris also connected me with Scott Larson of Straight Ahead Ministries. As we are now partnering our work with Straight Ahead, we are together moving the culture of the juvenile penal system.

Even Kris himself has gone through the process of becoming a trainer, and served as the Executive Director of ACCD for close to three years.

"You know, Dan," he said to me recently, "When I think about it, all of these great relationships and opportunities came out of some tough challenges. There were a lot of times when Katie and I wondered what to do because our immediate circumstances seemed to have absolutely no joy in them. However, I think we learned not to budge once a promise is made. We learned to be with challenges in a learning stance saying to ourselves, sometimes in complete survival, "'Huh, that's interesting. How can we navigate this?'" Instead of whining and complaining about what we say can't be done, we stay the course and always look for the gold, the presence of God, in what is possible"—even if it is in a snow bank or two!

✡ ✡ ✡

What Shows Up Is

✡ ✡ ✡

"Ring the bells that still can ring
Forget your perfect offering.
There is a crack in everything,
That's how the light gets in."[3]
~Leonard Cohen

Once again, I wished I could clone time. Jean Jobs had just given me the "time is about up" signal.

"If you had said to me when I was a teenager that having a mother who was manic depressive was perfect, I would have said that you were out of your mind. Yet, the truth is that God used my wonderful bi-polar mom to teach me what I do now. Through my childhood, I gained an innate perspective and way of being in the midst of ambiguity when things don't go the way you think they should that opens up order and direction.

"For instance, when I was growing up, we kids would never know who would be making breakfast; that person looked and sounded like our mom but that person might be a secret agent, the princess of some exotic land or even Mother Theresa herself. You just never knew.

"One morning during my early teens, I was feeling particularly stressed out because of finals week and a very big football game. On top of that, Mom was going through one of her moments. Before I got out of bed, I decided that I was going to skip school and stay home.

"However when I opened my bedroom door to go to breakfast, I saw my brother, Corey, standing at the bottom of the stairs. He was all dressed up in a black suit with a stovetop hat and black beard. He looked like Abraham Lincoln or some Pilgrim just off the Mayflower.

"'What are you doing?!'" I asked.

'Corey responded with a smirk. "'Hey, we don't know who is cooking breakfast. Why should she know who is coming?! Come on. This will really spin her. Here's a hat and beard.'"

"Cracking up, I quickly got dressed with my beard and hat and we sauntered down the stairs absolutely certain that we were going to top whatever character Mom had brewed up in her mind.

"To our shock, Mom didn't miss a beat. She kissed us on the cheeks, saying '"Good morning, boys."' She didn't acknowledge our costumes, our Pilgrim-like language or the great difficulty we were having eating with beards. Mom acted as if everything was completely normal, which it never was.

"Heading out the door still fully costumed, Corey and I were completely bummed out that our ruse had failed. In the driveway, we took off our hats and beards. Taking one look back at the house, we saw Mom standing at the huge glass windows smirking at us. She had delightfully beaten us at our own gig. She wasn't going to be hooked by our antics. And, I thought, '"That is a master in there."'

"What I learned from my mother was how to love others right through our respective problems. My mom loved us kids despite everything that was happening in her life. She fulfilled her promise to provide for us kids in the face of severe mental difficulties. She never lost her ability to love nor laugh, despite losing a normal emotional life, a husband and the way she thought life should turn out.

"What, as a child appeared to be a curse, I now see as a blessing."

Looking up, I saw Jean giving me the "Time to call it quits, I'm up next" signal. The time has come to yield the floor to the Vice President of ACCD and the best trainer with whom I have ever worked.

What makes her the best? To begin with, her uncompromising commitment to excellence in everything she does. Her willingness to have any conversation in an honest and honorable way makes her a great listener who will tell you what she really thinks. Jean is a loyal friend committed to the purpose of our ministry and relentless when it comes to standing for others. Jean is the kind of partner that any man or woman would want on their team. She lives as her word. If she ever breaks her promise, you can count on her to account and reconcile.

What makes Jean-Marie Jobs a better trainer than most is that she understands that in the training room, as in life, everything is perfect. You could say that she has a very functional relationship with breakdown!

Is life perfect? Depends on how you view it. Again, C.S. Lewis's words ring in my ears, "At the end of all things…the Blessed will say 'We have never lived anywhere but Heaven,' and the Lost, 'We were always in Hell.' And both will speak truly."

However, how we relate to life's imperfections can be perfect. We can see the possibility in everything, even the tough choices, the bad news and the discouraging ways. If I relate to life's circumstances like, "This is perfect," then I will be standing in a way that opens up the possibility for an unprecedented future.

For example, I have often walked into the first day of a training only to see monsters in the room. You can call them, "people," but when they start throwing accusations at you or accusing you of saying things you never said, you begin to wonder. Until I really practiced seeing things as perfect, I would come home complaining to God. "This is hopeless, there's no way out. Oh God, don't send me back there. I think I'll call in sick tomorrow."

By going again, standing as my promise and simply choosing to see everything as the perfect opportunity to forward my commitment, by the end of the training we would witness miraculous transformations. I would end up saying, "Wow. Look at the beauty of these people. See the amazing ways that they are being with each other."

What happened here?

When we stand as a possibility, we create a clearing for the God of "Yes and Amen" to show up in our lives and in the lives of those we love. As we open to Him, He draws out His gift in each of us, even if we don't realize that it is Him.

But it takes a willingness to see life as perfect. Such a discipline requires that we own our freedom to interpret and exercise that freedom to interpret what is happening as the seed bed for that to which we are committed.

I will never forget what Charlie Bloom, the man who trained me to be a trainer, taught me many years ago. I was still an apprentice trainer at the time. One day in the middle of a training, I was about to jump into what looked like a mess. A couple was stuck and I wanted to interject and say something to them. Right then, Charlie gently put his hand down on my knee.

"Dan, you're too quick on the draw. Stop trying to make this training turn out like you think it should. You are not a doctor commissioned to fix these folks. Your job is to discover what they are committed to and to stand with them to have it happen. It is not your job to make happen what you think should happen. If you will pause and listen, then you will discover the perfection of life, even when it looks absolutely imperfect. I want you to count to ten before you say something regarding what is happening in the training room and ask yourself what are you committed to cause when you speak. Then ask yourself, "What is it they say matters to them?"

Charlie was a wonderful teacher and to this day I am grateful for his wisdom in my life. If a trainer thinks that he or she knows what they are doing, i.e., that they have the answer, have done this training or been in this situation before, they will probably miss the boat and be of little use towards what is wanted and needed. In fact, they will most likely cause more resistance than possibility.

Said another way, when we are convinced that we have the situation nailed down, we eliminate the space for God to surprise us with His perfect way. We draw from the only space we know, which is our past. If God's present doesn't fit that past, then what we see will probably look more like a curse than a blessing.

The key is to be at peace in ambiguity and to focus on what will open up the greatest clearing for the presence of God.

By embracing the circumstances that completely assault our need for security, survival and success, we become the seed that falls into the ground so that something beautifully unprecedented can emerge. When we make a promise, it is a stand for someone else—and their future worth having.

Jean-Marie is the living expression of Charlie's coaching.

✩ ✩ ✩

Standing in the Gap

✩ ✩ ✩

"The moments of happiness we enjoy take us by surprise.
It is not that we seize them, but that they seize us."
Ashley Montagu

My phone started ringing its familiar tune. Jean-Marie was trying to track me down.

"Hey, Jean. What's up?"

"I think we need to give Monique a sabbatical from The Gap."

"Wow. Let's talk about it."

The Gap Training Services is what Jean-Marie was talking about. Monique was a promising up-and-coming trainer.

Originally an offshoot of ACCD, the GAP is a four-day experiential training program designed especially for youth. A youth pastor and someone who loves kids, Jean-Marie in 1998 took a workshop we had written and, after pooling her resources with several pastors and psychologists, tailored it specifically for youth between the ages of fourteen and eighteen years old. The Gap meets teens where they live. It addresses key character issues such as identity and purpose and opens them up to the possibility of loving God and their neighbors in authentic ways.

Throughout its development and growth, Jean-Marie's commitment has been crystal clear. She was after making a huge difference in the lives of youth throughout the world.

Through most of the years of The Gap's existence, Jean-Marie had served as the trainer for The Gap. When Jean-Marie was open and looking for another trainer who could also take that role, just at the right time a dynamic young woman crossed her path.

Monique. Real. Energetic. A thousand percent committed to youth. Who could ask for anything more? Jean-Marie and Monique hit it off instantly.

As Jean-Marie started working with Monique, training her to be a trainer, Monique threw herself into The Gap. Loving the youth she worked with, Monique fully dedicated herself to the work. She organized meetings with youth in schools and churches in all kinds of settings. She drew close to them in countless ways, counseling and supporting them in their dreams.

However as the months turned into more months, Jean-Marie began to see a longing growing in Monique's heart. She was a single woman who deeply wanted to be married. Like a wild horse roped to the stable wall, Monique was in her loyalty having a hard time forsaking the intimacy that she longed to have in her life- the kind of intimacy that comes through marriage.

Although Monique was just about to step into the role as a trainer with The Gap, Jean-Marie and I both sensed that we were missing something big. After talking together, it occurred to us that we had let Monique commit her life to The Gap in a way that was ultimately unhealthy for her and the work. We realized that the ministry had taken the place of that husband Monique so desired.

All of us had gotten out of alignment with God's ultimate best for her.

How we realized this was that Monique would have brief relationships with men that were not the best. She would meet someone and then quickly cut off the relationship. Once when I talked with her about it, I asked, "What if these relationships were not an accident? What if they were perfect? In other words, what if you are telling yourself something through repeating this same pattern?"

She looked at me like I was nuts.

I kept going. "Here's the pattern. You totally immerse your life into The Gap. Then you get lonely and start to look for companionship. You meet a guy and have a brief relationship that ends up with you doing things that you feel are compromising. You end the relationship, come back to the ministry and immerse yourself in the ministry again. Do you see the possibility that you were using the ministry to avoid dealing with what is needed to have a healthy, long-term relationship with a man?"

So, we decided to ask Monique to step out of the ministry for at least a year to give her time to get clear about what she wanted in her life and to open up serious relationships with potential husbands.

"You realize what this means, don't you?" I said to Jean-Marie, the night that we put all of the dots together. The thought that we may lose Monique was something we both dreaded, and yet we knew that somehow she was at a major juncture in her life. She needed to be let free to work this out.

"Dan, I am willing to put it all on the altar," Jean-Marie said. "This is a matter of love, not ministry business."

Although at the time, our decision did not feel like a decision of love to Monique, Jean-Marie had her ducks lined up. She was willing to let work, performance and results die for the sake of what she believed was best for her friend. Jean was willing to stand in her commitment to Monique's vision.

Love considers the wellbeing of the beloved. And, that was what Jean-Marie was doing. She was going to put what she believed was Monique's wellbeing above everything else, including the possibility of Monique's disapproval and the immediate future of the ministry.

Her stand tested the core of their friendship.

"I don't feel supported by you, Jean," Monique said, stung by our decision.

"Could it be possible," Jean-Marie answered, "that I am supporting you in ways that you don't yet see?"

None of us could have predicted what happened next. Being the woman of character that she is, Monique embraced our decision and input. She took several months to follow through on some unresolved areas in her life and got clear about what the future worth having looked like to her.

Then, one day, I got a call from a good friend. "You're not going to believe this, Dan."

"What?"

"Monique just got engaged."

"What! Who?"

"He's perfect, Dan. He's a surfer. Who loves youth and has a profound ability to make the gospel relevant to them."

"Amazing."

Today Monique and her husband have a beautiful baby boy. She is a regular contributor to the ministry in ways that support her family commitments as well. I love it when things turn out better than you expected!

✡ ✡ ✡

The Master Promise Keeper

✡ ✡ ✡

"Where nature's strength suffices there is no promise, but where human energy fails, the word of the Lord comes in."[4]
Charles Spurgeon

As I took off my microphone and the sponsors stretched, I looked around the room at all their many faces. I remembered something that Susan Scott said in her book, *Fierce Conversations*.[5] "Our conversations are our relationships," she said. "Our words together are a living expression of who we are for others."

What does this say of God, then—His words to us; our words to Him; our conversations, our relationship? Unlike you and me, I don't believe God ever fails to fulfill His "promises." What if, in the midst of our suffering and disappointment when we think all is lost, He is just beginning to fulfill His promise?

We focus on "promise" and "living as your word" throughout our ACCD trainings. There, I often ask, "Does Jesus love you? How do you know He does?" Often the answers I get range from, "The Bible tells me that He loves me," "By faith," to "I don't know." Sometimes all I get are rows of blank stares.

I think the answer to this question is straightforward. God keeps His promises.

He does what He has promised no matter what we do. It is through promises that God has chosen to reveal His love to us. It seems to me that when we live as our word, we bear that same Image of God and become expressions of the Word made flesh here and now and in this way, God transforms His purposes into our character.

How did Jesus live this out?

There are two tangible forms of Jesus' love for us. The first is that He kept all the promises He made throughout history; not only the implicit promises made in the course of being with his disciples for three years but also in the explicit promises made by the Old Testament prophets regarding the Messiah.

The second tangible way that Jesus expressed His love was that He kept His promises even when those whom He loves don't keep their promises to Him. A huge example is that Jesus did not betray His word to Judas even though Jesus was fully aware that Judas was about to betray Him resulting in His death on the cross. Jesus continued to love Judas and all the rest of the disciples even though each had or would betray Him in various ways.

Each promise kept demonstrated His love just as our kept promises demonstrate our love towards others. In fact, each time He kept a promise in the face of our broken promises, He sacrificed what He was owed from us.

The word sacrifice is very revealing in and of itself and profoundly moving in the context of relationship. The word sacrifice is defined by the dictionary this way: "the surrender or destruction of something prized or desirable for the sake of something considered as having a higher or more pressing claim."

Jesus so loves us that He is willing to surrender His expectations and His life, as well as His right to collect on His debt in exchange for the benefit of being in relationship with us for eternity. In this way we are made holy by His sacrifice because we are the object of the selfless act.

Outside of promise, you could say that every other indication of love is subjective.

Without promises, love is simply a word expressed and we are only a little better off than the young man plucking the petals off a flower alternating between, "She loves me," and "She loves me not." Our subjective feelings of love will never bridge the gap between us and another person because no one else can "feel" our feelings. No matter how strongly we feel, those feelings must be wedded to action. It is through action that we communicate to another person the measure of our true intention. Making and keeping promises authenticates and incarnates our feelings and intentions into tangible reality in the same way Jesus did for us.

The old saying, "Love is as love does," is a potent truth.

Promise is the God-ordained bond between individuals because promise is love in action. Authentic love makes itself known through our making and keeping promises to others. In a similar way, it is only through promises that we know what little we can of God's vast, infinite character and His heart of love towards us. Without promise, we have only our passing, subjective feelings to indicate whether or not there is a God who loves us.

Like the broken clock whose hands accurately tell the time twice a day, sometimes our feelings accurately reveal the love others (including God) have for us. I have heard it said, "A man's character is not validated by the quality of people whom he loves, but by the quality of people who love him." However, often our feelings mistake love for something else- anger, indifference, harshness and so on. Only through promise do we have a sure, objective basis for knowing without a doubt that God or someone else loves us.

Throughout His life, Jesus fulfilled over three hundred distinct promises that were declared about the Messiah long before His birth. A study done by a professor at MIT has calculated that the odds of fulfilling even six of those prophetic promises would be less than one in three million. Yet Jesus fulfilled them all.

Because God has made and kept His promises, He who was invisible became visible.

Similarly, our promises make our invisible desires and intentions visible to others. Until we make and keep a promise, these desires and intentions are unknown to others and are therefore of little value. A promise made and kept demonstrates in action the subjective passions and the attitude of heart from which these passions spring.

Our intentions are really irrelevant unless we put them into action. A workaholic father may have strong emotions and may claim to love his wife and children. However, if he places work over spending time with them, he has failed to make a positive difference in their lives and he has broken the inherent promises of fatherhood.

This came home to me many years ago when Elizabeth was about seven. We were picking flowers in a field when out of nowhere she exclaimed, "Daddy, I know you love me!"

"Of course I love you, sweetheart," I said, "but why did you say that?"

"Because you told me we would pick flowers and now we are-and I didn't have to remind you," she answered.

When I asked her what it would have meant to her if she had to remind me, she answered, "Then I would have known you were thinking of something else. I would have known that whatever you were thinking about was more important than me. That is how I know you love me, Daddy."

Her words knocked the wind out of me. Through the mouth of my little girl I learned that we make visible what really matters to us by the way we keep promises, not just the promises we make.

Let's take a look at what God spoke to Abraham. You might remember that Abraham left his homeland based upon God's promise to make a great nation.

After these things, the word of the Lord (the promise)
came to Abram in a vision, saying
"Do not fear, Abram, I am your shield, your exceedingly great reward."

But Abram said, "Lord God, what will You give me, seeing I go
childless and the heir of my house is Eliezer of Damascus? Then
Abram said, "Look. You have given me no offspring; indeed one born in
my house is my heir."
And, behold, the word of the Lord (the promise) came to him, saying
"This one shall not be your heir but one who will come
from your own body shall be your heir." Then He brought him outside
and said, "Look now toward heaven and count the stars if you are able
to number them." And He said to him, "So shall your
descendents be."
And he believed in the Lord and He accounted to him for righteousness.
Genesis 15:1-7

Starting with the declaration of His Nature, God made several amazing statements to Abram. Each one was a promise. From "One who will come from your own body will be your heir" to "So shall your descendents be," God's whole conversation with Abram is a series of promises. In these promises, the Lord is showing and declaring to Abram His intentions and His relationship toward him. God is revealing to Abram an unprecedented future that Abram himself would say was impossible.

Before God spoke these words, He was invisible and unseen to Abram. There were no scriptures that Abram could read, no precedent of others save the oral knowledge that had been passed down from Adam. Until God gave him His word, Abram's knowledge could only have been subjective. However when God made His promises, then Abram had physical and objective criteria that allowed him to know unequivocally the nature of God's declarations and how he would know when they were fulfilled.

Just as God's promises to Abram revealed His invisible intentions toward Abram, our promises to others reveal the intentions, hopes and aspirations we have towards others.

I came face-to-face with my own motives when I was about nine years old. I had a yo-yo toy. It was my favorite- honey-colored, smooth with shiny flecks of gold. The yo-yo was perfectly balanced and fit my hand like nothing else. With it, I could perform many tricks.

I also had a close friend named Kevin whom I loved very much. One day in order to show him just how much I cared about him, I gave Kevin my precious yo-yo. Moved by my generosity, his face lit up like a rocket. The yo-yo fit his hand perfectly, and he immediately got it to "walk the dog," go "round the world" and "rock the baby." His joy at my gift was more rewarding to me than owning the yo-yo had ever been.

One day Kevin and I got into a fight as kids often do. In the midst of our argument I demanded the yo-yo back. He refused, and my fierce love for Kevin turned to contempt. Being bigger than him, I threatened to beat Kevin up unless he gave the yo-yo back to me. At this ultimatum, Kevin started crying but managed to throw the yo-yo at me before running home.

The next day Kevin's mother called my father. After the call my father sat me down on the porch to hear my side of the story. Filled with self-righteous indignation I proceeded to put much of the blame for the argument squarely upon Kevin's shoulders.

When I finished, my father asked me to imagine what it was like for Kevin. I couldn't believe it! My father had barely acknowledged my side of the story. I felt enraged by his request. "I don't care what it was like for Kevin," I yelled as hot tears filled my eyes, "because he doesn't care about me."

My father was unmoved by my outburst. He said, "Danny, I want you to explore something with me. I don't think you would like it if

Kevin did to you what you did to him and I'm going to sit here until you tell me what it was like for Kevin."

I just sat there.

I felt like the world was pitted against me. Minutes passed and I said nothing and neither did my dad. As the silence grew, the certainty that I had been wronged slowly began to crumble. When my father didn't budge off the porch, I knew that he meant business.

When I finally retold the story from Kevin's perspective, I began to cry about what I had done and how I had treated Kevin. I wanted desperately to go to Kevin and give the yo-yo back. I wanted to right the wrong I had done, asking him to forgive me. I realized that if I were Kevin and this happened to me, I might never trust me again. I was sad about what had happen between us and I never wanted anyone to treat me the way I had treated Kevin.

Breaking my promise of friendship to Kevin showed me what I hadn't seen before. My father's persistence made it possible for me to see and address the conversation I was having about Kevin through the evidence of my broken promise. When I repented and returned the yo-yo, my actions once more showed Kevin the intention of my repentance and my commitment to our friendship.

I have chosen to believe that Jesus is the Promise of God made flesh, that He is the manifestation of God's love for me, the expression of His nature, intention and fullness. God's purpose is transformed into the character of Jesus' life.

Now it seems to me that when someone makes a promise, what comes with that promise is an invitation to the one receiving the promise to respond. Through this light in Jesus, I see God inviting us to the possibility of an intimate relationship with Himself.

Through Jesus, God is saying *"Don't be afraid to ask of Me and of people on earth until you have discovered the gift. Keep seeking until you come upon the treasure. Keep knocking until the opportunity opens wide before you."*

And He said to them, "Which of you shall have
a friend and go to him at midnight and say to him,
'Friend, lend me three loaves, for a friend of mine
has come to me on his journey and I have nothing to set before him:
and he will answer from within and say,
'Do not trouble me; the door is now shut and
my children are in bed with me; I cannot rise and give to you.'"

I say to you, though he will not rise and give to him
because he is his friend, yet because of his persistence
he will rise and give him as many as he needs."
Luke 11:5-8

In our scientific Cartesian reasoning, we can often view God's invitation to ask, seek and knock as a cause and effect process, thinking that if we sow X, then we will get X in return. I would suggest, however, that God isn't promising that we will get the result the way we think it should look by asking. However, the relationship we are seeking will be ours.

Because the kind of asking, seeking and knocking He demonstrates in this parable is relentless, unwavering commitment- the kind of commitment that views "No" as a sign to keep knocking. I believe He wants our asking, seeking and knocking to be the kind that wakes up the whole neighborhood.

Is it possible that He is asking us, "What is the promise that you are willing to stand vulnerably before the world for? How committed are you in your request?" Are you willing to see the possibility that what appears to be a 'No'" is actually My way of ordering your steps to the 'Yes'?"

I suspect that we really don't grasp how passionately confident God wants *us* to be in our asking, seeking and knocking. Asking, seeking and knocking is the commerce of the Kingdom of God. If we would realize that the basis of our asking is the assurance of His promised response (whatever that might look like), I imagine we would do a lot more of it.

The Epistle of James gives a front-row seat on asking.

If any of you lacks wisdom, let him ask of God who gives to
all liberally and without reproach and it will be given to him.
But let him ask in faith with no doubting for he who doubts is
like a wave of the sea driven and tossed by the wind. For let
not that man suppose that he will receive anything from
the Lord; he is a double-minded man
unstable in all his ways.
James 1:5-8

James continues by saying that, when our internal conversation takes us blindly along in the cultural drift, it wrecks havoc on our asking.

Where do wars and fights come from among you? Do they not come from your desires for pleasure that war in your members? You lust and do not have. You murder and covet and cannot obtain. You fight and war. You do not have because you do not ask. You ask and do not receive because you ask amiss, that you may spend it on your pleasures.

Adulterers and adulteresses! Do you not know that friendship with the world is enmity with God? Whoever therefore wants to be a friend of the world makes himself an enemy of God. Or do you think that the Scripture says in vain, "'The Spirit who dwells in us yearns jealously'"? But He gives more grace. Therefore, He says, "'God resists the proud but gives grace to the humble.'"

James 4:1-6

I think that when we ask God *and others* (seeing others as His body and as the potential avenue of His provision) and are sowing for possibility, then God brings the blessing. This blessing, however, might show up completely differently than we expect.

In Luke 6:38, Jesus tells us, "Give, and it shall be given unto you; good measure, pressed down, and shaken together, and running over, shall men give into your bosom."

When we withhold ourselves in pride by not making requests, we miss God's promised grace given to the humble. By refusing to ask, we are implying a number of things including we don't want to ask because the answer might be "no" or might not show up as we expect. Essentially, humility is the willingness to be humiliated. However, if we don't want the humiliation of hearing a "no" or the humiliation of working through circumstances, conversations, etc., to access what it is we say we long for, then we will not inherit the benefit of humility.

Sometimes we are saying that we can go it alone without Him, not really anticipating or needing any answer at all. I say, we call God a liar when we refuse to humble ourselves by asking for what we want. We are implying that He is Someone who doesn't or won't keep His promises.

The good news is that God keeps His promises, no matter what we make up about Him. Each one of them beckons us to intimacy with Him and others.

Similarly we can make and keep our promises for the sake of intimacy. Every promise we make calls us out of ourselves. Our promise is the speaking of our vision to reach someone else with the quality of relationship that meets the deepest longings of our hearts.

Yes. There is risk involved in this giving of love through promise; there is the inevitability of hurt, loss and betrayal.

However, as C.S. Lewis has captured so well, the alternative has its own great costs:

> Love anything and your heart will certainly be wrung and possibly be broken. If you want to make sure of keeping it intact, you must give your heart to no one, not even to an animal. Wrap it carefully round with hobbies and little luxuries; avoid all entanglements; lock it up safe in the casket or coffin of your selfishness. But in that casket- safe, dark, motionless, airless- it will change. It will not be broken; it will become unbreakable, impenetrable, irredeemable. The alternative to tragedy or at least to the risk of tragedy is damnation. The only place outside of Heaven where you can be perfectly safe from all the dangers and perturbations of love is Hell. I believe that the most lawless and inordinate loves are less contrary to God's will than a self-invented and self-protective lovelessness.[6]
>
> C.S. Lewis

Intimacy is built not only through the process of making and keeping promises but also in living as your word, which includes accounting for broken promises. If we are living as our word, we will account honestly for our failure in keeping promises. This accounting is an opportunity to reveal those conversations we may be hiding from ourselves and can be guided by our word toward reconciliation.

Promises are words that bind us to a future with another person. When I speak a promise to someone, I am giving that person the right to expect or claim the performance or forbearance of the act promised.

The question is when does one "claim" anything? When are we willing to ask, seek and knock when it comes to our promises with each other? How often are we willing to risk and inquire in such a way that reveals what is wanted and needed so that the possibility of the future we have declared can open up for God to meet us?

Common "cultural" sense reasons that we would claim the performance or forbearance of a promise as an action that takes place only after the promise has failed.

However, I think that this logic misses the boat.

A promise binds two people in such a way that there is an implied commitment to compel, provoke, invite and inquire into the fulfillment of the promise. It is an ongoing invitation for relationship, an active process where the person receiving the promise has equal responsibility in having the promise fulfilled as the person making it. In other words, the receiver of the promise has equal ability to respond to circumstances that may mitigate or impede the promise's fulfillment.

The act of requesting opens the possibility for a promise to be established. Once somebody has accepted a request, the promise is established and a possibility for unprecedented intimacy opens up through living as that word until it is fulfilled or, if broken, until it is reconciled.

Promises generate a powerful possibility for intimacy. When either person acts on that implied commitment for the sake of keeping the vision of the promise alive, it maintains a legacy of love, honor and respect.

We put ourselves at stake when we make a promise or receive a request. Being at stake can tempt us to be offended when someone breaks a promise to us. Depending upon what internal conversation we are heeding- whether we see ourselves as master or servant- a broken promise can be seen as a reason to be offended or as an opening to discover what is wanted and needed to open the possibility of the future that is represented by the promise.

If in a particular moment I am relating to those around me focused on myself and how others are treating me, I will be offended when someone breaks his or her promise to me. The broken promise will become an opportunity to add to my complaint and run my con or winning way. When I am focused on myself, what I will get, and how I will feel or look, then I will tend to treat all those around me as objects to serve me.

If I am detached from others having to meet my needs and if I engage the future possibilities inspiring the promise, then offense won't be the issue with me when someone breaks their promise. I will be after finding out what is wanted or needed to bring forth the future we declared. I will be open to seeing what that person is battling or struggling with so that they broke their promise. I will look to discover what is wanted and needed to have the vision that generated the promise turn out regardless of the circumstances.

Living this way sees that everyone has their own unique concerns, hopes, dreams, disappointments and failings. Being committed to the future that engendered the promise allows us to discover ways in which to fulfill our word while honoring and building faith with one another in the process.

The kind of character I am describing is extremely practical and can be seen in the life of Thomas Edison.

When Edison set out to invent the light bulb, the prospect of a small electric lamp was the holy grail of electrical research. The only electric lights at that time were huge arc lamps that put out hundreds of thousands of watts- suitable for the World's Fair and little else. Edison had a vision of replacing the ubiquitous gas lamps that lit houses and city streets with a similar network of electrical lights: small, portable lights that would be turned on and off with a flip of a switch.

He saw his vision with such confidence that he had the guts to announce his intentions to the press *before* he began. He invited reporters to visit his laboratory and told them exactly what he was going to invent.

After the fanfare of his press conference died down, Edison began his work. Soon he discovered that this was not going to be easy. He experimented with over 10,000 different materials without finding one that worked the way he had envisioned.

In that long search, Edison found himself asking, seeking and knocking in ways he had never envisioned prior to making the promise. Think of what he probably went through in the process. First, there was the thrill of the hunt. After the first several thousand experiments, avoiding humiliation might have became more important than the hunt. This was followed by boredom and the desire to move on to other projects.

By promising the entire world that he would invent the incandescent light bulb, he put himself, his reputation and his honor at risk. The stakes for failing were much higher than the cost of continuing. He had burned all bridges, and there was no turning back.

At one point a reporter had heard a certain experiment had failed for the one thousandth time. He cornered Edison in public, thinking he had Edison defeated. The reporter asked, "Mr. Edison, are you ready to concede after failing a thousand times to come up with the crucial element needed for the incandescent bulb?"

True to form, Edison replied, "Why would I quit now? I am one thousand steps closer than I was when I started."

Edison's promise carried him through years of trial and error, disappointment, ridicule and doubt. Because of his promise and commitment to that promise, the world has been forever changed.

There was something divinely human about Thomas Edison's relationship to failure. His willingness to see his circumstances as perfect allowed him to transform his purpose into the kind of character it takes to live as one's word and change the way we all live our daily lives.

Notes:
[1] Henry Miller, *Sexus*, ch. 14 (1949).
[2] Helen Keller, *Let Us Have Faith* (1940).
[3] Leonard Cohen, Anthem, from *Diamonds in the Line*.
[4] Charles Spurgeon, "Are You Now Born of the Promise or of Something Else?"
[5] Susan Scott, *Fierce Conversations* (Viking Hardcover, 2002).
[6] C.S. Lewis, *The Four Loves* (Harcourt Brace, 1960).

OUT OF THE SHADOWS

✡ ✡ ✡

Passion for Oneness

✡ ✡ ✡

Jesus spoke these words, lifted up His eyes to heaven, and said: "Father, the hour has come. Glorify Your Son, that Your Son also may glorify You, as You have given Him authority over all flesh, that He should give eternal life to as many as You have given Him. "And this is eternal life, that they may know You, the only true God, and Jesus Christ whom You have sent. I have glorified You on the earth. I have finished the work which You have given Me to do. And now, O Father, glorify Me together with Yourself, with the glory which I had with You before the world was."
John 17:1-5 (NKJV)

✡ ✡ ✡

Land of Shadows

✡ ✡ ✡

"Gonna be some changes, some changes made. Can't keep on doin' what I've been doin' these days. Better figure out something,

*things are lookin' grave, gonna be some changes,
changes made…"*
Bruce Hornsby

"**A**ileen. Hand me my crutches, would you?"

Soon I will be saying goodbye to these two skinny friends. Sure. I admit that they have been extremely supportive in a silent, ever-present way since *le grande plummet* down the mountain. Yeah. I know. Where would I be without them?

But even the best of friends have to part ways sometimes. Sometimes, you just have to *move on.*

And, that's exactly what I am going to do in T-minus two weeks and counting. Soon isn't soon enough. I am going to stuff these crutches into the back of some forgotten closet and bid them never to return, at least not on my account. So long! Farewell!

Nothing replaces the real thing.

I, for one, am ready to be finished with substitute legs and imposter realities. I am ready to walk and run once more, a changed man with metal literally in his bones. I am done with being divorced from freedom.

On a number of fronts, these ten weeks of hobbling have often seemed like one gigantic detour. That is what I *used* to think. Not now. I have come to see that this unexpected bypass is actually taking me exactly where I need to be. I discovered it in my own son's words.

"Dad, how do you attract such fantastic people into your life? I like being with your friends more than I like hanging out with my own. Tell me. How do I get friends like you have got?"

Danny and I were coming home from a three-day strategy session in Southern California for the Association for Christian Character Development, the ministry that Aileen and I started in the early 1990's, when he bowled me over with those questions.

"*Wow!*" I thought inside. "*What new thing are You doing here, God?*"

Because I had gotten sidelined through my skiing accident, I had more time to think about ACCD's future. In the process, I saw that our ministry's business model was more of a brass ceiling than a launching pad. If I wanted future generations to be able to steward this work beyond my lifetime, ACCD needed to be reinvented so that the vision and the work could be successfully transferred.

Bottom line, I needed to build now for a future that did not include me.

But how? I had some ideas but nothing solid. What I did have were willing friends who were experts in organizational structure. One of them, Jeff Serra, had been the CEO of a publicly-held company.

Just before the three-day strategic session, my son asked if he could sit in on the meeting. Although his interests had been historically skewed towards quantum physics and business, Danny had been going through some life-changing transformations since his own personal breakthrough in the Discovery Seminar. Right before my eyes, my son was becoming a man.

More than willing, I said, "Sure, Dan."

The first day of the strategic meeting felt like canoeing on some nice, calm lake. We were so steady that I started to get a little antsy over whether we were making any real progress or not. The atmosphere was so very reasoned, tranquil and pleasant.

Then, Day Two happened. Ka-boom! Right in the middle of the meeting, an explosion occurred. Forget being cool, calm and very professionally collected. We could have been auditioning for the World Wrestling Federation. One guess on who started the brawl— and the first one doesn't count.

That's right. Me.

Paddling along that morning, we had just gotten down to some brass tacks about ACCD's core operations when Jeff, the ex-CEO, made a comment about potential redundancy and micromanaging by our coaching department—a subdivision of the ministry that just happened to be run by my wife.

Well, ka-boom!

Hearing Jeff's assessment, I lost it. Like a pit bull. I got extremely defensive and instantly sure there must be a rat lurking somewhere under the table. I lashed out at Jeff saying, "You don't know what you are talking about!"

Within seconds, Jeff bit back, "What are you getting so defensive about?"

Following my assault, Aileen and Jean-Marie Jobs, the Vice President of ACCD, leaped into the ring and added their own verbal fuel to the fire. Seeing our three-against-one attack, Jeff got even more ticked off, saying, "I was just suggesting that there is a bottle-neck. But if you three are not willing to listen, then we don't need to talk about it."

In less than two minutes, all of us mature adults were acting like little children pouting on the playground.

Suddenly, my own thoughts arrested me. *"Dan, what the heck are you doing?"* they said like a slap in the face. *"What are you getting out of tearing at Jeff? What was the attack about? Why were you fending off some high ground in your head? Look at what you have done. You have caused a divorce between yourself and one of your greatest allies!"*

Shocked at myself, I immediately threw the freight train into reverse. Jeff also diffused himself, and we took a deep breath.

However despite our mutual retreat, the room was still reverber-ating with shellshock. Jeff got up and started to look down at his feet and move about in his place. Others like me silently dealt with the embers of their anger. The atmosphere was latent with unspoken conversations. We were, at that moment, a group of people together in space but divorced in reality. An uneasy but professional façade of cordiality descended upon us like a shadowy mist.

In our awkwardness, Kyle, a business process expert, took a shot at bringing the team back together. He threw out that all-too-familiar, practical recommendation, "Let's just get on with the agenda. We have a lot to accomplish here and we can get back to this topic later, if we choose."

Rather than fight him or anyone else, I shadowed myself in the mist of cordiality and said, "Okay. Fine. Sure. Let's go on."

Another moment of silence passed. Little did I realize was that, in those moments, our future was being weighed in the balance.

✧ ✧ ✧

The First Divorce

✧ ✧ ✧

"A great Sign appeared in Heaven: a Woman dressed all in sunlight, standing on the moon, and crowned with Twelve Stars. She was giving birth to a Child and cried out in the pain of childbirth.

*"And then another Sign alongside the first: a huge and fiery Dragon!
It had seven heads and ten horns, a crown on each of the seven
heads. With one flick of its tail it knocked a third of the Stars from the
sky and dumped them on earth.*

*"The Dragon crouched before the Woman in childbirth, poised to
eat up the Child when it came. The Woman gave birth to a Son who
will shepherd all nations with an iron rod. Her Son was seized and
placed safely before God on his Throne. The Woman herself escaped
to the desert to a place of safety prepared by God, all comforts
provided her for one thousand two hundred and sixty days.*

*"War broke out in Heaven. Michael and his Angels fought the Dragon.
The Dragon and his Angels fought back, but were no match for Michael.
They were cleared out of Heaven, not a sign of them left. The great
Dragon- ancient Serpent, the one called Devil and Satan, the one who
led the whole earth astray- was thrown out, and all his Angels thrown
out with him, thrown down to earth.*

*"Then I heard a strong voice out of Heaven saying, Salvation and
power are established! Kingdom of our God, authority of his
Messiah! The Accuser of our brothers and sisters thrown out, who
accused them day and night before God.*

*"They defeated him through the blood of the Lamb and the
bold word of their witness. They weren't in love with themselves;
they were willing to die for Christ. So rejoice, O Heavens, and all
who live there, but woe to earth and sea, for the Devil's come down
on you with both feet; he's had a great fall; he's wild and raging with
anger; he hasn't much time and he knows it.*

*"When the Dragon saw he'd been thrown to earth, he went
after the Woman who had given birth to the Man-Child. The
Woman was given wings of a great eagle to fly to a place in the
desert to be kept in safety and comfort for a time and times
and half a time, safe and sound from the Serpent.*

*"The Serpent vomited a river of water to swamp and drown her,
but earth came to her help, swallowing the water the Dragon
spewed from its mouth. Helpless with rage, the Dragon raged
at the Woman, then went off to make war with the rest of her
children, the children who keep God's commands and hold
firm to the witness of Jesus.*

Revelation 12 (The Message)

Once he was a beautiful creature, unlike any other. Now, we know him only in his grotesque ugliness.

Satan. The devil. The accuser. The prince of this world. Lucifer. Beelzebub. The serpent. The father of lies. A roaring lion, seeking whom he may devour. The Anti-Logos.

Beauty was Satan's beginning, not ugliness. Before time, the Scriptures depict him as a magnificent archangel, a prince of heaven, breathtakingly beautiful in every way. Covered with light-radiating jewels of sardis, topaz, diamond, beryl, onyx, jasper, sapphire, turquoise, emeralds and gold, God describes him as "the seal of perfection."

Among the millions of God's hosts, Satan was—as thought by some—heaven's highest ranking angel, second in command only to the Almighty Himself. He dwelt close to God's throne where he led all the celestial beings in worshipping the Godhead.

Like the rest of God's creation, Satan was a free being and what Satan chose to do with his freedom was to divorce God.

In heaven's name, why?

How could a perfect creature living in paradise not be satisfied with perfect Love? I don't know.

What we do know is that God's love is the constant of the universe, and in that Love, God gave Satan the freedom to reject Him. And Satan chose divorce.

In a twinkle of an "I," the archangel lost everything.

As Irwin Lutzer describes in his book, *Serpent of Paradise*,[1] "In a realm beyond our grasp, the glorious creature chose to take a cosmic gamble that would backfire. He tripped a series of dominos whose interrelationships were unknown to him. His act, once accomplished, would reverberate for all eternity. The entire universe would shudder, reeling from the shock. Even now, you and I feel the painful effects."

How could this happen? What got twisted in Satan's heart? Here are some thoughts.

Consider the possibility that before his divorce from God, Satan began to engage his own thoughts about his beauty. Musing upon his God-given radiance, Satan became more and more enamored with the thoughts he was having about himself. His great looks. His heavenly sound. His purpose in loving God. The admiration that his presence generated from others. His authority over all the rest of the angels. His proximity to God.

Satan began to believe his own press releases—*Pride*.

How you have fallen from heaven,
O star of the morning, son of the dawn
You have been cut down to the earth.
You who have weakened the nations.
*But you said in your heart, "**I will** ascend to heaven,*
***I will** raise my throne above the stars of God*
*And **I will** sit on the mount of assembly in the recesses of the north.*
***I will** ascend above the heights of the clouds;*
***I will** make myself like the Most High."*

Isaiah 14:12-13 (NASB)

With *Pride*, Satan asserted himself as separate from God.

He attributed *himself to himself* and took his greatness as independent from God, not as something that came from his maker. His relationship to his beauty and gifts became inauthentic when he asserted *himself* as their source. Satan put his own name on that part of creation, namely himself, which belonged to God. He declared his glory as "self-made," not God created.

Out of this *Pride* grew *comparison and his complaint*.

As Satan compared himself to the rest of the heavenly host, he must have thought that he looked pretty good, probably the best. When he looked at God he recognized the eternal disparity between himself and God's matchless beauty, glory and majesty.

A transformation occurred when Satan saw the difference between himself and God. Satan realized he was less. The God-created beauty and glory that had once elevated Satan and authentically distinguished him was now, in Satan's eyes, eternally wanting. Through comparing himself to God, Satan could not escape the fact of his inferiority, and he who was once God's most beautiful angel transformed into the devil.

What happened after this?

I think Satan's heart got jealous towards God. He started to want to have and be more. No longer satisfied with how God had made him, Satan began to complain. Something was missing, he reasoned. God was holding out on him somehow.

As his complaint festered, Satan started to consider ways of getting what he wanted but could not have. Namely, all that God had.

Satan's complaint matured into a rebellion. His jealousy transformed to *Envy*. Now when Satan was jealous, he desired to have what God had. With *Envy*, he was after taking what God has away from Him.

Satan did not want God to have what He had- the love, adoration and fellowship of mankind and all of creation. He believed *Envy's* delusion that if he could somehow keep God from having what Satan wanted, then Satan had a better chance of getting it for himself.

With Satan's *Envy* came the minions of gossip, slander and tale bearing.

Through the language of accusation, Satan distorted God's name to the rest of the heavenly host. He sought to separate the love of God's created beings from the Source of that love and through gossip, slander and tale bearing against God, Satan successfully enrolled one-third of the angels into divorcing God.

Their rebellion was met by the archangel Michael and other angels still loyal to God. A battle in heaven broke forth with Satan losing the fight and being cast out of heaven with the rest of the fallen angels. He and his cohorts fell to Earth, transformed from angelic beings of beauty into dark demons and evil spirits.

Satan's *Envy* made him *Greedy* for what he could not possess.

He got *Slothful* in the work he was created to do because his complaint led him to believe he deserved something more, better or different than who he was created to be with others.

Because his complaint was not satisfied, Satan's desire to be God got stronger and stronger, mutating into all-consuming *Gluttony* and *Lust*.

When his *Envy, Sloth, Gluttony, and Lust* matured to their fullest expression, Satan in his *Anger* sought to *Murder* God.

✡ ✡ ✡

Because of Envy

✡ ✡ ✡

Early in the morning the chief priests with the elders and scribes and the whole Council immediately held a consultation; and binding Jesus, they led Him away and delivered Him to Pilate. Pilate questioned Him, "Are You the King of the Jews?" And He answered him, "It is as you say." The chief priests began to accuse Him harshly. Then Pilate questioned Him again, saying, "Do You not answer? See how many charges they bring against You!" But Jesus made no further answer; so Pilate was amazed.
Now at the feast he used to release for them any one prisoner whom they requested. The man named Barabbas had been imprisoned with the insurrectionists who had committed **murder** in the insurrection. The crowd went up and began asking him to do as he had been accustomed to do for them. Pilate answered them, saying, "Do you want me to release for you the King of the Jews?" **For he was aware that the chief priests had handed Him over because of envy**. But the chief priests stirred up the crowd to ask him to release Barabbas for them instead. Answering again, Pilate said to them, "Then what shall I do with Him whom you call the King of the Jews?" They shouted back, "Crucify Him!" But Pilate said to them, "Why, what evil has He done?" But they shouted all the more, "Crucify Him!"
Wishing to satisfy the crowd, Pilate released Barabbas for them, and after having Jesus scourged, he handed Him over to be crucified.

Mark 15:1-15

✡ ✡ ✡

Cordiality Mist

✡ ✡ ✡

"Make the lie big, make it simple, keep saying it, and eventually they will believe it."
Adolf Hitler

In our moments of awkward silence, I was not sure what to do. Everyone in the planning meeting had retreated in their respective corners.

While I wanted to ask for forgiveness and explore what had happened between Jeff and me, I also did not want to resist Kyle's suggestion to move on with the agenda out of fear of my further aggravating the charged atmosphere.

Looking around the room, I said, "The agenda *is* full, and the clock *is* ticking."

More escape routes whispered in my ear. *"I imagine that we will all be okay. if we just moved on. Sure, the easiest thing to do right now is to just ignore the explosion that happened. And, besides, no one wants to challenge Jeff or you right now."*

Listening to those thoughts, I realized something horrible.

I didn't want to trust God by entering into a predictably difficult conversation about my behavior.

Just then, I heard Lawrence Edwards's steady voice. A longstanding trainer with ACCD and a man who has grown used to standing tall for the sake of others, Lawrence spoke succinctly into our predicament.

"Dan, I think *going on* is dealing with this."

"You are right, Lawrence," I said, grateful for his willingness to risk the response of others. "Everyone, can we deal with what just happened? Jeff. I was defensive and was protecting something. I know you weren't attacking me, but I felt like it. Will you forgive me?"

Jeff answered quickly, "I really am not offended Dan. It's fine."

"No. It's not. Jeff, I got hooked into my history," I answered. "Please forgive me. What I heard you say- and I know this was *not* what you were saying- was that you did not appreciate the work my wife and I have invested into building ACCD. I found myself striking back at you because I felt like I was being dominated."

Once again Jeff answered graciously, "Well, that's okay. It's all right."

As generous as Jeff was being, I knew that we weren't out of the woods yet. The cordiality mist was still gathered over us. Feeling stuck, my thoughts urged me once again to yield to the mist where there was little risk of my further exposure and hurt. The mist would hide me, Jeff and everyone else in the cold, undemanding shadows and we could get on with the job at hand. We could just "go through the motions."

As tempting as the cordiality mist appeared, my heart knew it was quicksand. What was the complaint that had inspired me to blow my stack? Why had I attacked a friend who was expressing his love for me by sacrificing his time and energy to help with what was important in our lives? What was my contempt rooted in? What was more important to me than seeking first to understand Jeff instead of making myself right?

"*God, help.*"

He did. As clear as a bell, I instantly saw what had hooked me.

I had attached my identity to the ministry. Like Satan at some level, I had co-opted the beauty of our ministry to myself- into my pride.

ACCD's success had become *my* success- and its failure was *mine* as well. Somewhere deep down inside, I had separated myself *and* the works of my hand from God as the Source. I had stolen the glory of the created thing for myself and had divorced some sliver of my being from God. *I* was jealous to be loved for what *I* had accomplished.

Because I had agreed with the conversation that the ministry was a reflection of my being, then any criticism of it meant that *I* was also being criticized. If ACCD was not perfect, then I had come up short somehow, and I was inferior to the ideal.

Anyone who wanted to change ACCD could potentially reveal my inferiority, and consequently they needed to be stopped before they could uncover my weakness. Though I wasn't consciously thinking these things when I reacted, I saw they were the deeper motivations of my heart.

"*Jeff doesn't appreciate all you have sacrificed for the ministry,*" the serpent on my shoulder whispered. "*He is not your friend. He doesn't even think you are smart enough to see what is wanted and needed to get to the next level. What he is saying right now is that you don't love the people you serve and that you get off in being in control…*"

Blah. Blah. Blah.

The more I heard the minion whining on my shoulder, the more I hated it. Somehow I knew that he drew pleasure from keeping me in his shadow. He wanted me to stay hidden in the mist of cordiality, all the while being transformed into his dark image.

✡ ✡ ✡

In the Garden

✡ ✡ ✡

"Beloved, do not believe every conversation
but test the conversations whether they are of God
because many false conversations have gone out into the world.
By this you know the Conversation of Logos: every conversation that
tells you
the Truth that Jesus Christ has purchased through His life,
death and resurrection everything you need to live in a manner
that pleases God here on earth is of God
and every conversation that seeks to nullify what Christ has done
is the lie and is not of God.
"This is the voice of the Anti-Logos,
the death-bound conversation which you heard was coming
and already resident in the world's conversation now."
John 4:1-3

After Satan fell to earth, he did to others what he had done to himself. He incited a complaint in the hearts of Adam and Eve.

In a two-minute exchange with Eve, the Anti-Logos implied that he knew something about the *Logos* that the humans, Adam and Eve, did not.

Then the serpent said to the woman,
"You will not surely die.
For God knows that in the day you eat of it
(the fruit of the tree of the knowledge of good and evil)
your eyes will be opened and you will be like God,
knowing good and evil."
Genesis 3:4-5

Personifying himself as *"ho diabolos"* or "the devil," Satan used the language of gossip, slander and tale bearing to break the bonds of relationship between Adam, Eve and God. He attributed selfishness and jealousy to the Giver of all good.

Satan insinuated that God was a liar.

Instead of challenging what the Accuser was saying, Adam and Eve engaged, believed and acted upon his conversation. They chose to be independent, separate from God's Word, the Logos. As a result, the entire human race and creation itself fell into a divorced condition to its Source.

Since that day in the Garden, all of humanity has been born into a world divorced from God.

We live in Logos where the divorcer, Satan, also exists. He is in God's skin- as we are in God's skin- and he speaks to us, seeking ever to enroll us to our deaths, just as he did with Adam and Eve.

Satan's goal is to dupe us by keeping us blind to our nature and this earthly condition of divorce. The *last* thing he wants is for us to realize that Jesus is the Being through whom we are reconciled, remarried, if you will, and made one to God. The Anti-Logos through language wants to keep us ignorant and blind to the reality of our condition and the hope inherent in Jesus Christ.

Like the delusional beings of Professor Nash in *A Beautiful Mind*, Satan works to keep us deluded about *our being in the conversation in which he and we exist*.

Said another way, Satan wants our nature to *have* us, instead of us having our nature. Through fear he urges us to complain about how our lives are turning out and how God has forsaken us. He wants us eternally divorced from God.

Why? Here's my two cents.

I think that Satan knows that if we get wise to him and the nature of our being in *Logos*, we will put our wills to the fire, admitting our wretchedness for the sake of being reconciled to God and others.

For the sake of love, we will freely die to ourselves for the possibility of becoming the substantial and glorious Imago Dei beings that God had meant for us to be. He knows that we were made to be one with God and if our eyes are opened to see Jesus, the Logos, as Satan has seen Him, we will do what Satan won't do.

We will repent.

And, in that repentance, we will be reconciled and glorified through our union with God and with one another.

I am convinced that what caused Satan's fall and essentially his damnation was that he was and is not willing to die to his own will. However, there is another possibility for us; we can be reconciled to God through Jesus.

As free *human* beings, we can say "I missed it. Forgive me."

Satan knows that once we say, "Forgive me," to God, we will be rescued, born again and permanently reunited with God. In the reconciliation, Satan will have lost his dominion over us because we will see clearly what kind of lie we have believed.

Here is how the Apostle Paul describes it:

For He (Jesus Christ) rescued us from the domain of darkness,
and transferred us to the kingdom of His beloved Son, in
whom we have redemption, the forgiveness of sins.
He is the image of the invisible God, the firstborn of all creation.
For by Him all things were created, both in the heavens
and on earth, visible and invisible, whether thrones or
dominions or rulers or authorities- all things have been created
through Him and for Him. (Even the Anti-Logos, Satan)
He is before all things, and in Him all things hold together. He is
also head of the body, the church; and He is the beginning, the
firstborn from the dead, so that He Himself will come to
have first place in everything.
For it was the Father's good pleasure for all the fullness to
dwell in Him, and through Him to reconcile all things to Himself,
having made peace through the blood of His cross; through
Him, I say, whether things on earth or things in heaven.
And although you were formerly alienated and hostile in
mind, engaged in evil deeds, yet He has now reconciled you
in His fleshly body through death, in order to present you before
Him holy and blameless and beyond reproach- if indeed you
continue in the faith firmly established and steadfast, and not
moved away from the hope of the gospel that you have
heard, which was proclaimed in all creation under heaven,
and of which I, Paul, was made a minister.
Now I rejoice in my sufferings for your sake, and in my flesh
I do my share on behalf of His body, which is the church, in filling
up what is lacking in Christ's afflictions. Of this church I was made a
minister according to the stewardship from God bestowed on me
for your benefit, so that I might fully carry out the preaching of the
word of God, that is, the mystery which has been hidden from the
past ages and generations, but has now been manifested to His
saints, to whom God willed to make known what is the riches

of the glory of this mystery among the Gentiles, which is Christ in
you, the hope of glory.

Colossians 1 (NRV)

The Enemy has some big problems on his hands. And, I'm pretty
sure he knows it.

In us lies the inevitability of his own destruction. Jesus Christ.
Christ in us, the hope of glory.

As *repented* beings in the Logos, we are now free from the dominion of Satan's voice and his complaint against God. We have the possibility now of continually recognizing his Anti-Logos conversation,
disengaging from it and opening up all the resources of possibility
that exists outside the boundaries of that complaint.

We no longer have to survive.

Rather through interdependence with God and others, we can
be transformed, made substantial and fully integrated. We can
forsake the lie of "doing it all on our own" as something worthy of
honor, glory or even time, seeing the "self-made" declaration as the
language of the Anti-Logos.

Now, all things can become new.

✠ ✠ ✠

The Edge of Substance

✠ ✠ ✠

*"Then I saw a new heaven and a new earth; for the first heaven
and the first earth passed away, and there is no longer any sea. And
I saw the holy city, new Jerusalem, coming down out of heaven from
God, made ready as a bride adorned for her husband.
"And I heard a loud voice from the throne, saying, "'Behold, the
tabernacle of God is among men, and He will dwell among them,
and they shall be His people, and God Himself will be among them,
and He will wipe away every tear from their eyes; and there will no
longer be any death; there will no longer be any mourning, or crying, or
pain; the first things have passed away.'"
"And He who sits on the throne said, "'Behold, I am
making all things new.'"*

Revelation 21 (NAS)

Jeff's eyes caught mine. He was my friend, and I had really hurt him. The rest of the world could stop turning for all I cared.

Nothing mattered more to me than to be reconciled with my friend and reestablish the peace that had been broken in the room. I did not care what it cost me. I was willing and eager to die for the sake of reconciliation. I was not about to be divorced from him or anyone else in the room.

"Jesus," I said silently. *"What I need right now is You, not some pair of crutches to limp along. Show me what is wanted and needed for oneness. Let me be a clearing for You to join us in a whole new way."*

Suddenly I heard my son's voice. "Hey, Jeff and Dad, can I give you some feedback?"

"Sure." Jeff answered well for the both of us.

"Dad, I think you really did feel what you said. Because you were feeling like you were not being appreciated, you struck out because you were afraid that someone was going to take control, *like you were the wimp on the beach and Jeff was the town bully.* I think you were acting insecure and insensitive to Jeff and the reasons why he came here to help you."

"Jeff, I don't get that you *are* all right," Danny said. "I think your feelings got hurt. I know that when my dad reacts this way to me that I get hurt. The reason that I am pretty sure that you are hurt is because up until now you were engaged in what we were doing. Now, you are pacing and have stopped making eye contact. Jeff, I just don't think you are over what happened."

With Danny's words, the flames of love burned hot.

I realized how deeply I had betrayed my friend and hurt him. As Jeff and I talked truthfully and deeply about what had happened, a greater level of intimacy opened up for us and everyone else in the room.

The cordiality mist had been replaced by the Presence of God.

Soon after the meeting, Ron, the ACCD board member who along with his wife, Alexia, has generously supported our work, called. "Dan, I would like to explore the reaction you had with Jeff. Would you mind?"

Finding that unique balance between kindness and courage, Ron and Alexia are loyal and honest individuals whom I know have been sent to me as a gift from God.

"Sure, Ron," I replied. "I'd love to."

"Dan, I have never seen you act like you did with Jeff during the planning meeting. I wondered if you realized what happened for you in the breakdown?"

I answered Ron honestly, "Ron, I feel sometimes like I am a fraud." I said, "Sometimes I get lost in seeing what I do as something separate from God, as a reflection of me, instead of something that God has His hands on. Even as I say this I am shocked, but it is true for me. Sometimes I feel that if the organization is somehow flawed, then people like you are going to wonder if I'm some kind of phony. I feel that you will see that I am not capable of doing it all and, as a result, withdraw yourself from me. I pray you can forgive me for my ego, and I promise to listen generously to you and the others as we work through this redesign regardless of the outcome."

Ron's response staggered me.

"Dan, I am so blessed by your openness. We all do things that are troubling. I feel much closer to you as a result of this conversation. Thank you for your humility and for being so open about your thoughts. You know how much we love you."

As I hung up the phone, I sat in my chair silent for a good five minutes. To me, time stopped. There was a peace that is impossible for me to put into words. It really didn't matter what happened after that, whether we did anything with the ministry or not. I could only frame what I experienced in that moment as being eternally grateful to God for being alive.

I decided to follow through on an idea that Ron had suggested. I sent out an email to everyone on the team, telling them what I had told Ron and asking the others for forgiveness. It wasn't long before I received a response from Jeff.

"Dan, I feel very unqualified to even be a part of this group of people," he said. "I take no offense to anything that you said or even how it was said. I can only think about how other relationships in my life could have been honored by this kind of authenticity and how blessed am I to be in the kind of relationship with you where a potentially negative exchange in fact created a much more intimate relationship."

The team's response reminded me of Dostoyevsky's words...

"...the wonder-working power of the Lord, who all the while has been loving you, and all the while has been mysteriously guiding you." [2]

Love wins!

What could have completely torn us apart actually brought us closer than we had been before. An incredible synergy happened, one well beyond planned human effort. We accomplished more in less time than we had in all our previous hours leading up to the point of that breakdown. And, it was rewarding, exciting and full of possibility. We got vision on how to proceed and even created a dream team to write new business plans for every segment of the organization.

Here was one more amazing part, at least to me. I was not a part of the dream team. Our future worth having was starting without me, and I praised God.

I was a free man, because I chose no longer to be hooked by the conversation that the success or failure of ACCD defined *me*. The ministry, like everything else in my life, was a gift from this wonder-working God who calls me *His* own.

✡ ✡ ✡

The Family Business

✡ ✡ ✡

"And He (Jesus) said to them,
I saw Satan fall like lightning from heaven."
Luke 10:18

We were a few hours north of Laguna Beach when Danny asked me, "Dad, how do you attract such fantastic people into your life?"

"Here is how I attract such fantastic friends, Danny," I answered. "It's what Dostoyevsky points to. I am learning not to be 'frightened at my own faintheartedness in attaining love, and meanwhile not even be very frightened by my own bad acts.' I am willing to show up and stand when needed, even at the risk of someone walking out of the relationship."

"What do you mean, Dad?"

"Well, when I blew up at Jeff, I *really* believed what I was saying, Danny," I explained. "I was giving it all I had until Jeff, Lawrence, you and others intervened in a way that I could see where I had gone off the deep end. However, in the process of the breakdown, I hurt others and was hurt myself. Although I could not force reconciliation between us, what I could do was ask Jeff for forgiveness. And, Jeff forgave me instead of walking away from the relationship. Our reconciliation created a space for a greater level of authenticity between everyone in the room. I guess what I am saying here is that fantastic people are those who choose to remain in relationship, even when it is difficult and messy. They are willing to live face to face in the ambiguity of separation without demanding their way, all the while exploring what is possible from that point on."

After a few minutes of silence, Danny replied. "Dad, what would you think about me becoming a trainer with ACCD?"

Well, I almost drove the car right off the road. "That sounds great, son!" I said with astute recovery.

But inside, I was thinking, "Of all the people on the planet, Danny is the last person I would have expected to be involved with ACCD. My son working with me! Now that's a dream come true. Whoa, what would have happened if Jeff and I never got reconciled back there? We might have cordially gotten *something done* but I would have completely missed this!"

Then I had another thought: *I am also a son. I am in my Heavenly Father's business, and His business is reconciliation.*

What if my "unexpected" blow up and subsequent reconciliation had actually been my Father's top agenda item during these last three days?

Could it be possible that our three-day meeting was *not* primarily about restructuring ACCD, in God's mind? Could it be that my Father knew about the serpents on our shoulders and wanted us to have the breakdown so that reconciliation, freedom and glory might occur between us and Him? Could it be that God was more interested in our being more substantial with Him and each other?

Wow. That's a different spin, I thought. What if ACCD was one of God's subcontractors for His business of bringing forth reconciliation among us?

As I continued to drive north, I was moved by the priority God seems to place on reconciliation. Reconciliation is not some sweet garnish to the meal; it is the main course.

Reconciliation is what God is doing on the earth.

In the New Testament, two Greek words are both translated as the English verb "to reconcile." Both words have similar meanings: "to restore a relationship of peace that has been broken" and "to set up a relationship of peace not existing before." Reconciliation does not mean to restore something to its previous state. That's not reconciliation but rehabilitation.

Reconciliation is a subjective state that means you are at peace with the other person. In the Hebrew sense, this means you have peace resulting from having your knee in your enemy's neck, knowing that you are not going to be attacked. You have dominion over what was your adversary. This metaphor is a word picture to give us an idea of what "peace" is experientially.

Here's what this metaphor is expressing about peace. Imagine being bullied by somebody so much and so often that you fear leaving your home. Then one day you have had enough. You are willing to risk great physical harm in order to stop this oppression. So you leave and take the path you know will bring you face to face with your nemesis.

Once you confronted him, you ask him to leave you alone. Instead of agreeing to your request, the bully laughs at you. So you take him on. After a long struggle, you wrestle him face down on the ground and you put your knee in his neck so he can't move. With your knee there, how do you feel? At peace.

The question to ask is who is the enemy? Well, it is not the other person.

The enemy is those thoughts, actions and circumstances that provoke us to destroy the peace. For example, let's say a boss steals an idea of an employee but afterwards asks the employee for forgiveness for what he has done. After they have worked through forgiveness, reconciliation means not allowing the offense and any further resulting thoughts, words or actions that would destroy the peace between them.

Here's another example, one from my own life.

I think women are beautiful. I always have and always will. However I don't allow myself to enter into sexual or emotional fantasies that I formerly engaged in about women other than my wife. I refuse to speak words or take actions that would break the peace of righteously relating to the countless women in my life. I have my knee in the neck of the potential desire to lust because I am keenly aware of what that enemy could produce. I don't ever want it out from under my dominion.

I think this is why Jesus exhorted his followers to "count the cost."

And whoever does not bear his cross and
come after Me cannot be My disciple.

For which of you, intending to build a tower,
does not sit down first and count the cost, whether he has
enough to finish it- lest, after he has laid the foundation, and is not
able to finish, all who see it begin to mock him, saying, '"This
man began to build and was not able to finish."' Or what king, going to
make war against another king, does not sit down first and
consider whether he is able with ten thousand to meet him
who comes against him with twenty thousand? Or else, while
the other is still a great way off, he sends a
delegation and asks conditions of peace.
So likewise, whoever of you does not forsake all that he has
cannot be My disciple. "Salt is good; but if the salt has lost its flavor,
how shall it be seasoned? It is neither fit for the land nor for the dung-
hill, but men throw it out. He who has ears to hear, let him hear!"
Luke 14:27-35 (NKJV)

I suspect that when we sin we are often not in an authentic relationship with what it is costing us. Said another way, we are not being real with the price tag of our behavior.

In my past, I used to think that I could have one-night stands with women without my behavior affecting my relationship with my wife. Obviously, at that time, the cost of my adultery wasn't very high to me.

Then I started to see how my sin was not only destroying my relationship with my wife and children, but it was also destroying the future I dreamt of with my children and their eventual families. I was degrading a sacred act of intimacy and destroying any witness I had as a man and, ultimately, for God. I was undermining everything that really mattered to me.

Counting the cost is a core discipline in our ACCD trainings.

We work with our participants by inviting them off the distortion of unhealthy shame. Such guilt often keeps people from looking squarely at what they have done. When someone is in this kind of shame, the last thing they want to do is count the cost of their actions because they are so repulsed by themselves. Avoidance becomes the winning way that he or she thinks will maintain who they *should be* instead of facing what they *have done*.

Reconciliation with God begins with our willingness to face up to what we have done in light of who we can be. It is a stand of personal responsibility where I consider how my choices impact my future worth having *and* those relationships that comprise that future. When I count the cost, I stand from the perspective of the future looking into the present and I put my foot on the necks of those enemies who want to rob me of it.

Jesus has put the burden of reconciliation on us, not the other person in the relationship. It is *not* our job to get the other person reconciled to us; that is their responsibility before God.

Jesus tells me that *I* need to be reconciled to my brother. I need to take dominion over anything within me that would destroy my peace toward him or her, including any conversation that would make the other person out as "the bad guy." I cast myself away from what would provoke me back to the offense, such as my desire for revenge or the need to look good, be in control, feel comfortable or be right.

Through choosing to rule over my thoughts, peace can be established within me. With that peace, I can listen generously and authentically to the other person and learn how I can stand *for* and not against them. I can love them- even if the other person chooses not to have peace with me- because I know *who* I am for them. I can be a free being in God's Divine process of reconciliation even when the circumstances look impossible.

My role is not to fix the problem. My job is to lead every conversation to the Light. Then, I wait on God to bring the reconciliation.

To be reconciled presupposes that you have some kind of divorce- which means that you also have conflict. If reconciliation is going to occur, you will need to step into the problem and stand for what the possibility you value.

A friend recently discovered this in a problem that looked hopeless to her. "Dan, what I saw was that God was already standing in the pile of crap. He was waiting for me to join Him in the breakdown and the mess so that together, in partnership, there could be a possibility of something glorious to happen. To really join Him, however, I had to give up my complaint about the problem existing in the first place and, even more, what the end result might look like."

I have come to realize that reconciliation has very little to do with me. In fact, the most powerful reconciliations I have experienced had practically no correlation with my actions. However what I did was to bring what was in the shadows into the light by creating a space for others to speak honestly.

I have found that once someone has felt that they have been heard, they are almost always open to hearing the other person's perspective. In the process, both parties usually discover information that gives them a bigger view of what happened even if someone has done something wrong.

Just like the Apostle Paul who was so aware of his own failings that he called himself the "chief of sinners," the more authentic I am before God about myself, the more I realize how I have been forgiven. Out of that understanding, I have the resource to forgive others for what they have done to me. To bring every conversation to the Light is to see your life, *not* yourself.

You will discover how you are showing up for others *through their eyes*. If someone said to you, "You are a dirty rotten bastard who only cares for himself," what the person is telling you is who you are for them, whether you are a dirty rotten bastard or not. They have said what is true *for them*; they are telling you who you are for them.

I started to understand this distinction when Aileen said to me once, "Dan, you are only listening to me so that you can be right about the way *you think you are*. You are not listening to me to understand *who you are to me*."

We often think the way we see things is the way it is for others. However, in order to be reconciled *to* someone else means engaging with what is *true* for them. Once we engage what is true from their perspective we can see the breakdown between the two perspectives in the relationship.

What is true for the other person might have little or nothing to do with me. Or it may have everything to do with me. Either way it is centered on how the other person has engaged and interpreted their thoughts about me. Where they are coming from is not right, wrong, good or bad. It is simply where they are standing at the moment. Recognizing that what they are saying is true for them, I stop defending myself and can begin to hear how they are seeing the relationship. I have the opportunity to understand how my words and actions contributed to their perspective towards me.

To be reconciled *with God* means that I am willing to hear from anyone how I am showing up for them. Here is another way of saying this. When I am reconciled with you, I am reconciled with God. By being reconciled to God, I am reconciled to His body. His body is men and women, flesh and blood here upon the earth.

To be reconciled means that, sometimes, individuals may choose not to be reconciled to you. They may determine not to forgive you for what you said or did- or what they interpreted your actions to mean. They may choose to carry the offense and be bitter, distrusting and angry.

Whatever their response is, you and I can still be reconciled to them. It's not easy sometimes but it is the most obvious opportunity we have to carry our "cross" in life as we are commanded to by Jesus.

Right now, in my own life, I have a dear friend whom I hurt both by my words and actions. Some of the pain I have caused him and his wife I can recognize and own. Some of it, I believe, is made up from false expectations and their own personal history.

No matter. They remain offended even though I have listened to their offense without defending my actions and asking for forgiveness. Instead, they have chosen to distance themselves from me and my family.

While it is deeply painful, I have noticed that as I think about their pain, my heart for them is still tender.

At times, I have fought angry, resentful thoughts and feelings. I have been tempted to list things they have done to me that I think, in my arrogant estimation, are equal to or worse than anything they have accused me of. Yet as I have struggled, one inevitable question keeps coming to my mind, *"If you don't care about this couple, then why do you keep dwelling on this?"*

My answer was immediate. *I love my friends passionately. I miss them. I am deeply sorry for the break in our relationship. I long for their fellowship. I miss being one with them.*

Although I didn't want to experience the pain of our separation by thinking about them, when I considered how much they meant to me, I became free from protecting myself from the suffering.

God brought a peace that rekindled my love for them even in the face of their continued rejection.

I saw that my true enemy was not my friends. My enemy was my *fear* of being destroyed, oppressed or misunderstood.

Admitting my love as well as the hurt over the loss of the friendship was paradoxically God's miraculous way of helping me get my knee onto my enemy's neck. He had enabled *me* to be reconciled to them.

He freed me to love.

There is no fear in love, but perfect love casts out fear.
For fear has to do with punishment, and he who fears is
not perfected in love.

We love, because He first loved us. If any one says, "I love God,"
and hates his brother, he is a liar; for he who does not love his
brother whom he has seen, cannot love God whom
he has not seen.

1 John 4:18-20 (RSV)

Six hours later, after more great conversation and stories of our time together, Danny and I pulled into our driveway.

I felt so full from all we had experienced during those three days in Southern California. I would not have traded one minute of what had happened for anything in the world. I felt like the luckiest person on the planet.

I was a son, happy to be in my Father's business.

Notes:

[1] Erwin W. Lutzer, *The Serpent of Paradise: The Incredible Story of How Satan's Rebellion Serves God's Purposes* (1996).
[2] Fyodor Dostoyevsky, *The Brothers Karamozov.*

INTO SUBSTANCE

✿ ✿ ✿

Becoming Substantial

✿ ✿ ✿

*I saw coming towards us a Ghost who carried something
on his shoulder.
Like all the Ghosts, he was unsubstantial, but they differed from
one another as smokes differ. Some had been whitish; this one was
dark and oily. What sat on his shoulder was a little red lizard, and it
was twitching its tail like a whip and whispering things in his ear. As we
caught sight of him he turned his head to the reptile with a snarl of
impatience. "Shut up, I tell you!" he said. It wagged its tail and
continued to whisper to him. He ceased snarling, and presently
began to smile. Then he turned and started to limp westward, away
from the mountains.
"Off so soon?" said a voice.
The speaker was more or less human in shape but larger than
a man, and so bright that I could hardly look at him. His
presence smote on my eyes and on my body, too (for there was heat
coming from him as well as light), like the morning sun at the
beginning of a tyrannous summer day.
"Yes, I am off," said the Ghost. "Thanks for all your hospitality.*

*But it's no good, you see. I told this little chap" (here he indicated
the Lizard) "that he'd have to be quiet if he came- which he insisted on
doing. Of course, his stuff won't do here; I realize that. But he won't
stop. I shall just have to go home."*
*"Would you like me to make him quiet?" said the flaming Spirit-
an angel, as I now understood.*
"Of course I would," said the Ghost.
"Then I will kill him," said the Angel, taking a step forward.
"Oh- ah- look out! You're burning me. Keep away."
said the Ghost, retreating.
"Don't you want him killed?"
*"You didn't say anything about killing him at first. I hardly
meant to bother you with anything so drastic as that."*
*"It's the only way," said the Angel, whose burning hands
were now very close to the Lizard. "Shall I kill it?"*
*"Well, that's a further question. I'm quite open to consider it,
but it's a new point, isn't it? I mean, for the moment I was only
thinking about silencing it because up here- well, it's so
damned embarrassing."*
"May I kill it?"
"Well, there's time to discuss that later."
"There is no time. May I kill it?"
*"Please, I never meant to be such a nuisance. Please- really- don't
bother. Look! It's gone to sleep of its own accord. I'm sure
it'll be all right now. Thanks ever so much."*
"May I kill it?"
*"Honestly, I don't think there's the slightest necessity for that. I'm
sure I shall be able to keep it in order now. I think the gradual
process would be far better than killing it."*
"The gradual process is of no use at all."
*"Don't you think so? Well, I'll think over what you have said very
carefully. I honestly will. In fact I'd let you kill it now, but as a
matter of fact I'm not feeling frightfully well today. It would
be most silly to do it now. Some other day, perhaps."*
"There is no other day. All days are present now."
*"Get back! You're burning me! How can I tell you to kill it? You'd
kill me if you did."*
"It is not so."
"Why, you're hurting me now."

"I never said it wouldn't hurt you. I said it wouldn't kill you."
"Oh, I know. You think I'm a coward. But it isn't that. Really it isn't. I say! Let me run back by tonight's bus and get an opinion from my own doctor. I'll come again the first moment I can."
"This moment contains all moments."
"Why are you torturing me? You are jeering at me. How can I let you tear me in pieces? If you wanted to help me, why didn't you kill the damned thing without asking me- before I knew? It would be all over by now if you had."
"I cannot kill it against your will. It is impossible. Have I your permission?"
The Angel's hands were almost closed on the Lizard, but not quite. Then the Lizard began chattering to the Ghost so loud that even I could hear what it was saying.
"Be careful," it said. "He can do what he says. He can kill me. One fatal word from you and he will! Then you'll be without me for ever and ever. It's not natural. How could you live? You'd be only a sort of ghost, not a real man as you are now. He doesn't understand. He's only a cold, bloodless abstract thing. It may be natural for him, but it isn't for us. Yes, yes. I know there are no real pleasures now, only dreams. But aren't they better than nothing? And I'll be so good. I admit I've sometimes gone too far in the past, but I promise I won't do it again. I'll give you nothing but really nice dreams—all sweet and fresh and almost innocent. You might say, quite innocent..."
"Have I your permission?" said the Angel to the Ghost.
"I know it will kill me."
"It won't. But supposing it did."
"You're right. It would be better to be dead than to live with this creature."
"Then may I?"
"Damn and blast you! Go on, can't you? Get it over. Do what you like," bellowed the Ghost: but ended, whimpering, "God help me. God help me."
Next moment, the Ghost gave a scream of agony such as I never heard on Earth. The Burning One closed his crimson grip on the reptile: twisted it, while it bit and writhed, and then flung it, broken-backed, on the turf.
"Ow! That's done for me," gasped the Ghost, reeling backwards. For a moment, I could make nothing distinctly. Then I saw, between me and the nearest bush, unmistakably solid but

growing every moment solider, the upper arm and the shoulder of a man. Then, brighter still and stronger, the legs and hands. The neck and golden head materialized while I watched, and if my attention had not wavered I should have seen the actual completing of a man- an immense man, naked, not much smaller than the Angel.

What distracted me was the fact that at the same moment something seemed to be happening to the Lizard. At first I thought the operation had failed. So far from dying, the creature was still struggling and growing bigger as it struggled. And as it grew it changed. Its hinder parts grew rounder. The tail, still flickering, became a tail of hair that flickered between huge and glossy buttocks. Suddenly I started back, rubbing my eyes. What stood before me was the greatest stallion I have ever seen, silvery white but with a mane and tail of gold. It was smooth and shining, rippled with swells of flesh and muscle, whinnying and stamping with its hoofs. At each stamp the land shook and the trees dwindled.

The new-made man turned and clapped the new horse's neck. It nosed his bright body. Horse and master breathed into the other's nostrils. The man turned from it, flung himself at the feet of the Burning One, and embraced them. When he rose I thought his face shone with tears, but it may have been only the liquid love and brightness (one cannot distinguish them in that country) which flowed from him. I had not to think about it. In joyous haste the young man leaped upon the horse's back. Turning in his seat he waved a farewell, then nudged the stallion with his heels. They were off before I knew well what was happening. There was riding if you like!

I came out as quickly as I could from among the bushes to follow them with my eyes; but already they were only like a shooting star far off on the green plain, and soon among the foothills of the mountains. Then, still like a star, I saw them winding up, scaling what seemed im-possible steeps, and quicker every moment, till near the dim brow of the landscape, so high that I must strain my neck to see then, they vanished, bright themselves, into the rose-brightness of that everlasting morning. [1]

C. S. Lewis, The Great Divorce

✡ ✡ ✡

Baseball, Greyhounds and Glory

✡ ✡ ✡

"You may be through with your past, but your past ain't through with you."
From the movie *Magnolia* (New Line Cinema, 1999)

The night was long spent when I turned off the television.
I had stayed up late to watch *The Natural*, the 1984 baseball film starring Robert Redford and Glenn Close. Although I had seen it many times before, I was drawn to watch it once again. Maybe it is because *The Natural* is about something bigger than baseball. Something eternal. To me, it is a glimpse into being reconciled with our lives as they have shown up here on earth.

The scene in the hospital between Roy Hobbs and his childhood sweetheart, Iris, is what clinches this for me. You might remember that Roy at a young age was a baseball prodigy when tragedy strikes while he is on his way to try out for a major league baseball team. Roy is shot almost to death by a beautiful woman that he met on the train.

Roy disappears into obscurity and, for all we know, that could be the end of the story. However, sixteen years later Roy steps out of the shadows back into baseball. He has been signed by a scout to the bottom-of-the-rung New York Knights. Although Roy has made it to the majors, the coach refuses to let Roy play on the team, convinced that he is way too old to be any good. Eventually Roy's perseverance, talent and circumstances work together so that he turns the coach and the team around. Through his miraculous hitting, Roy takes the Knights to the final games of World Series.

The night before the Series starts, Roy's food is poisoned by his corrupt girlfriend who is being paid off to prevent Roy from playing. When the doctors pump out his stomach, they discover the bullet that almost killed Roy sixteen years ago and they warn him that playing even one more game of baseball could cause him to bleed to death. All that Roy has worked so hard to gain seems to be up in smoke.

The night before the final game Roy is visited in the hospital by Iris who has come to New York to tell Roy that he is the father of her sixteen-year old son.

ROY: Doc says I have to quit baseball.

IRIS: Why?

ROY: Some mistakes I guess we never stop paying for. I didn't even know her.

IRIS: The girl on the train. You liked her didn't you?

ROY: Yes. But I didn't see it coming.

IRIS: How could you possibly know that she would hurt you? How could anyone?

ROY: I didn't see it coming.

IRIS: You think you should have?

ROY: Yes! But I didn't. Why didn't I?

IRIS: You were so young.

ROY: Things sure turned out different.

IRIS: In what way?

ROY: Different. For sixteen years, I lived with the idea that I could be, that I could have been the best in the game.

IRIS: You're so good now.

ROY: I could have been better. I could have broke every record in the book.

IRIS: And then?

ROY: And then. And then, when I walked down the street, people would say, "There goes Roy Hobbs, the best there ever was in this game."

IRIS: You know, I believe we have two lives.

ROY: What do you mean?

IRIS: The life we learn with. And the life we live with after that. With or without the records, they will remember you. Think of all those young boys you have influenced. There are so many of them.

Roy smiles and nods his head.

ROY: That day in Chicago, why did you stand up?

IRIS: I didn't want to see you fail.

ROY: I wish Dad could have… God, I love baseball. You going to the game tomorrow?

IRIS: Yep.

ROY: Is your son with you?

IRIS: He is. He, ah.

Just then, a nurse walks into the room and interrupts them.

IRIS: Well, I… I got to go.

I wonder about something sometimes, seeing that scene again for the millionth time. Every step of the way Roy had to choose whether to hold onto the complaint of the past or cast it off for the possibility of glory.

In the last sequence of the film, when Roy plays in a game that could kill him, I think it is ultimately out of love: love for the team, love of baseball and love of who he was meant to be. And, in those final moments, Perfect Love grants Roy a depth of glory beyond anything he could have imagined in his youth.

The lizard had been transformed into a magnificent stallion.

Aren't we a lot like Roy Hobbs?

We look back at the choices we have made and say, "I could have been the best in the game but I didn't see it coming." The whispers in our soul remind us of our many body bags filled with false starts, disappointing results and web-like entanglements. We lament what we could have been "if only," complaining even nobly sometimes, about how the train pulled out of the station without us.

Is it true? Has the train pulled out of the station? Or could it be possible that, as Roy discovers at the end of the film, God is meeting us from another train and another track?

"We're chasing a phony rabbit, Dan," a sometimes oblique friend said to me one morning over breakfast at the café.

"What? Looks like an omelet to me." I declared.

"The rabbit is not real," she said again. "It's fake but we think it's real."

"Hum," I listened, trying to put the puzzle of her thinking in place.

"I think we are longing for glory, Dan. The dazzling 'I' that God has intended all along for me. You. Everyone. All creation."

"Imago Dei."

"But what happens is that we sell out. Diminish. Fade. We end up being greyhounds, Dan."

"Greyhounds?"

"Ever been to a greyhound race, Dan?"

"Nope."

"Here you have these beautiful greyhounds- sleek, elegant champions who can run as fast as the wind. But what are they doing? They are running against each other around a filthy two-bit track chasing after a phony rabbit. It is just some fake thing on a stick that has been rigged to go faster than they can. The dogs don't get this one fact; they will never catch what they are running after."

"Duped into fake glory," I responded.

"How about the tracks we run around?" she continued. "We work, obsess and work some more. Are we any different than those in the days of Noah? I wonder. We eat, sleep, have sex, sit in commuter lines and sacrifice the people we love on the altars of 'what?'"

"Some fake rabbit."

"Dan, do you know that the life of a greyhound sucks? Dogs lucky enough to make it to the racetrack are often caged in crates for 18–20 hours per day. They are continually muzzled and are fed meat rejected by the USDA. Everything in their world has taught them to run when injured. Take a guess at what happens to a dog that's no longer bringing in the profit?"

"I can imagine."

"There is something wild that our buddy, Arthur Burk, wrote recently," my friend said taking another turn, "He said that most people reduce the call of God down to what they *think* they can handle. However what they don't realize is that when they do this God starts to oppose them Himself."

"Why?"

"I think it is because He has made each of us for glory, not ignominy. So in His perfect love He puts obstacles in our way when we are settling for anything less than-"

"The unprecedented future. The impossible."

"We think God is so thrilled if we are doing 10% of what He has designed us for in this life. Yet, the reality is that when we *are being* less than the full glorious beings we are meant to be, God Himself stands in our way. We call it tough circumstances, difficult choices or even the devil. The truth is that God opposes us because at 10% we are simply being like those ignorant greyhounds chasing after some fake rabbit in our heads. We are in a race for the eternal, Dan. Glory. That's Imago Dei."

Baseball games. Greyhound races. Glory.

As I turned out the lights, I thought about a relative whom Aileen and I had not seen for years. On a recent trip past his hometown, we took a chance at visiting him. What we experienced was like watching someone drown.

As soon as we arrived at the door, Harry's multilayered complaint greeted our eyes and our ears. The once well-cared for family home was falling apart from neglect. Harry told us that he rarely left the property, choosing instead to live hand-to-mouth. His teeth were almost completely gone because of his addiction to speed. Harry's eighteen-year-old son was nowhere in sight and just that morning, his wife had walked out on him.

Soon, Harry gave us a long list of how we had failed him. We sat there for hours, listening to what was true for him. No matter what possibilities or resources we offered, Harry refused them for one reason or another. We knew that at any moment, he could shift and forsake the complaint. We kept talking with him until Aileen and I finally decided that it was time for us to leave.

Our loved one was stuck agreeing with the lizard whispering in his ear. He was divorced. And, he was dying.

As we were getting into the car to leave, I asked Harry, "So where are you going to go from here? What is your future?"

"I don't know," Harry answered, dropping his head. "I am waiting."

"Waiting for what?" I replied back.

He had no answer until we were pulling out of the driveway. "Dan, Dan!" Harry shouted to me. "I am going to drop back and punt. Dan, I am going to drop back and punt!"

"That seems to be the strategy you have been working to get where you are now, Harry," I answered, my heart and spirit grieved.

Giving the ball away was Harry's winning way. He expected someone else to do for him what he was not willing to do for himself. As much as Aileen and I loved Harry, we could not violate his will. He was the only one who could say "Yes," to the Burning Angel's question. Until he willed, the lizard would keep on whispering.

I knew this because fifteen years ago Aileen and I had faced down that very same lizard and had made a life or death choice.

We were on the Big Island in Hawaii celebrating our 15th anniversary. Things were going great between us and the sun seemed to be shining everywhere. We were having the best time, until the morning that we decided to drive to the island's volcanoes.

As we were driving along, Aileen asked me, "Why don't you give Harry a job in the ministry?"

"How can I do that, Aileen?" I reacted with an edge. "He's not even in the ministry. What would he even do?"

Suddenly in the space of seconds, one word led to another. The conversation turned into a huge argument with both our tempers overflowing.

"Aileen," I said, "Harry is not even interested in what we are doing. I feel like you are trying to do for him what only God can do!"

"You just don't want to be bothered with him," she snapped back, "That is why you say that!"

Back and forth we went like cats in an alley until I finally took my hands off the steering wheel, grabbed her shoulders so she could hear and see me say, "Stop it!"

Feeling like an idiot, I immediately realized what I had done. Aileen was livid, telling me to stop the car so that she could get out. I refused to let her out, concerned that if she stormed off into the ancient volcanic fields where we were driving she could get injured. Aileen got even angrier but I still kept driving.

After an hour and half of driving in complete silence, we finally arrived in Hilo. Still upset, I attempted a half-hearted apology to which Aileen flipped me off with that universal hand signal. Fuming, I got out of the car, leaving the keys. I started walking and with each step, asked God to fix this mess by bailing me out.

No surprise that He didn't.

When I got back to the car, I was grateful that she hadn't driven off. However, she was still angry and refused to talk to me. On the road ahead, I saw a sign for some waterfalls. "Would you like to go to the waterfalls?" I asked like a robot.

"Yes," she answered back like a machine.

When we arrived at the turn-off for the waterfalls, I saw that it was a two-mile hike to the falls. Without a word, both Aileen and I started walking, separately. For the entire two miles, I walked about 100 yards ahead of her. When we got to the falls, I looked at them and mechanically declared, "Aren't they beautiful?" Aileen, with her arms crossed, answered in one syllable, "Yeah."

You could have made a comedy sketch out of how we were acting.

With that short exchange, we did a 180-degree turn and repeated the two miles back to the car, still walking separately. Yet with each step, my anger started to recede. *"When was the last time I felt like this?"* I asked myself. *"Why did I react this way? Why am I so insecure with Aileen?"*

Then, I remembered.

When my mom was about to disappear into one of her manic-depressive episodes, she would guilt me into taking care of my two brothers and sister. Mom would say things such as "You need to take care of Leo. He needs…" With my dad absent and my mom laying this burden on me, I would feel insecure about having the responsibility of my siblings put on my shoulders.

So when Aileen asked me to hire Harry, what flushed up inside of me was my complaint that women cannot be trusted. The lizard on my shoulder was whispering, *"Aileen wants you to take care of Harry. She's asking you to shoulder the responsibility for his life. How are you going to do it? That's a heavy, heavy load. What if you fail to solve Harry's problems, which you know you will do? Think of how much Aileen would be disappointed in you. She might even leave you."*

The lizard, using the ghosts of my past, was attempting to keep me from really hearing Aileen's request and making a contribution to her life. He was hooking me with fear that she would disappear just like my mother.

By the time Aileen reached our car, tears were also in her eyes.

"Honey," she said, "when I was growing up, Harry would come to our house with his parents and would stay for days visiting. We became great friends. Harry's dad was very abusive, even beat Harry a lot. One day when I was still little, Harry and I were riding on my bike together. I was sitting on the handle bars, and he was steering. We hit a bump, and my foot went into the spokes. When we got home, instead of being glad for the way Harry had taken care of me, his dad beat him very badly and left him bleeding in the driveway. I snuck out of the house to bring Harry some food and patch up his wounds. I made a vow to him saying, 'I will *always* take care of you, Harry.'"

"Wow. Honey, I didn't know."

"Dan, I realized now that when I asked you to give Harry a job, I was still trying to make up for the guilt I feel for Harry being beaten. Dan, please forgive me?"

As we continued to talk, we saw the complaint that had flushed up inside of Aileen. The lizard on her shoulder was whispering, *"God doesn't take care of people. So you have to take care of yourself and those you love."* We realized that she had made an illegitimate promise to Harry, and I understood the reasons behind her misguided loyalty.

As we forgave one another, what we had purposed for our lives was transforming into the character of our relationship. Despite the pain of the argument and the temptation to suppress what we were feeling, standing together in the midst of the breakdown, we gained a new level of compassion, appreciation and love for one another.

The long walk helped. We had needed time to die.

Since that day in Hawaii, our love for Harry also transformed. We love *him*, no matter what he has chosen for himself. We know that his life can change instantaneously. So we will wait, should Harry ever be willing to have the lizard die.

As Aileen and I cried, prayed and thought through what had happened at Harry's house, I returned once again to C.S. Lewis's *The Great Divorce* where I had first read the story of the lizard and the stallion.

In this allegory, the story's main character boards a bus that takes him to a land lying between Heaven and Hell. Reaching this beautiful, intermediary place where Heaven is clearly in sight, the traveler discovers that he and all the other passengers on the bus are as ghosts. They have no substance in this valley of the shadow of paradise. They are transparent phantoms.

Unlike the ghosts, there are Solid People who have come to meet the people from the bus. They are Spirits, fully fleshed human beings who radiate light. They have come down from the mountains of Heaven in hopes of convincing the ghosts to choose Heaven instead going back to hell.

All a passenger has to do to choose Heaven is give up their complaint.

In Heaven's shadow, all human natural loves, desires and reason are merely shadows of the Divine Reality. As shadows, they need to die like seeds planted in the ground so to be transformed into their eternal reality. Just as a shadow does not reveal the details of the object from which it is cast, so have the lives of these ghosts been on earth. If they will choose to stand for their transformation, they will discover that in a twinkle of an eye that they are not mere mortals but rather glorious beings.

Save one or two exceptions, the passengers chose the bus much like those greyhounds chasing that phony rabbit.

✡ ✡ ✡

The Trail Home

✡ ✡ ✡

""It may be possible for each to think too much of his own potential glory hereafter; it is hardly possible for him to think too often or too deeply about that of his neighbor. The load, or weight, or burden of my neighbor's glory should be laid daily on my back, a load so heavy that only humility can carry it, and the backs of the proud will be broken. "It is a serious thing to live in a society of possible gods and goddesses, to remember that the dullest and most uninteresting person you talk to may one day be a creature which, if you saw it now, you would be strongly tempted to worship, or else a horror and a corruption such as you now meet, if at all, in a nightmare.
"All day long we are, in some degree, helping each other to one or the other of these destinations. It is in the light of these overwhelming possibilities, it is with awe and the circumspection proper to them, that we should conduct all our dealings with one another, all friendships, all loves, all play, all politics.
"There are no ordinary people. You have never talked to a mere mortal."[2]

C.S. Lewis, *The Weight of Glory*

Imagine that you are sitting all alone at the top of a 10,000 foot high cliff, such as Half Dome in Yosemite National Park. Way down in the valley below you see a City, one that is more magnificent than anything you have witnessed here on earth.

It is the City of God.

From high up on the cliff, you see its lights shining brightly and hear the sound of music. The City's architecture is so magnificent that it takes your breath away. Every urging and longing of your heart is telling you, "Go."

From where you are sitting, high up on that cliff, the City seems so close that if you reached out your hand it seems like you could to touch it. You wish you could jump, but if you did, the fall would most assuredly kill you.

No. The only way for you to get to the City of God is to walk down the back side of the mountain. And, so you begin.

Leaving the cliff, you turn one last time to look again at the City's lights, but even though you have only gone a short distance, you can't see them anymore. With each step you take, you feel like you are getting further and further away from the City.

Soon the shadows of darkness shroud you as you stumble along in the trail and brush, you are not sure if you are even going in the right direction. As the way gets darker and more frightening, you think about turning back to the safety of the cliff.

Yet, if you turn back, you might never find your way again. Your only option is to keep going. Just as you are about to give up, you see a small but well-worn trail with a trail marker that reads "Forgiveness. Trust. Faith."

> *"Forgiveness is the name of love practiced among*
> *people who love poorly.*
> *The hard truth is that all of us love poorly.*
> *We need to forgive and be forgiven every day, every hour- unceasingly.*
> *That is the great work of love among the fellowship of the weak that is*
> *the human family."* [3]
>
> *Henri Nouwen*

When we forgive, we let it all go.

Forgiveness is a continual giving forth of oneself in relationship in spite of any injury that has been sustained. When I forgive someone, I am sending myself away from the offense that has happened to me at the hand of someone else. When I forgive someone, I am creating a clearing in the relationship that will allow for the restoration of peace and I am no longer using the offense as a justification to get even with the one who offended or hurt me.

Being reconciled, I have my knee in the neck of my enemy- which in the case of forgiveness often shows up as contempt, anger, resentment, envy and revenge. So by choosing to cast myself away from the offense and stand for reconciliation, I am preparing the way for God to enter into the situation, regardless of what the other person does.

When we refuse to forgive we are bound in ways that God doesn't intend.

Our hearts, minds and souls become attached in negative ways to the one who has hurt or betrayed us. Without forgiveness and without releasing the person from our desire for revenge, we will find ourselves in bitterness or what Francis Frangipane defines as "unfulfilled revenge." The longer that we refuse to forgive those who have hurt us, the more we are blinded by the bitterness of our conversation.

Ever wisely the Lord's Prayer leads us to "Forgive us our debts as we forgive our debtors." Among those debtors are those who have failed in their implicit or explicit promises. When we release others through forgiveness from the duty of the specific promises they have made, this release frees the other person to rededicate themselves in promise. Moreover, as we forgive, God promises to forgive us our offenses.

Most of us confuse or do not even recognize the difference between apologizing and requesting forgiveness. To forgive someone means that I do not accept someone's apology. Rather, I forgive them.

Let me explain. An apology entails the use of a "because."

I have discovered that whenever I settle for a "because," I want to be right about something, usually some romantic sensations I have about myself. And, when I want to be right, then I have become attached to my complaint, which is the explanation I use.

When we say things such as, "You see, I got angry at you because I didn't sleep well," we are justifying our behavior and making it acceptable. In fact, what I am doing is simply downloading from my complaint my own concocted logic behind my behavior and using it as the basis of my apology. Even the Greek word *"apologia"* from which we derive "apology" means "a formal defense for or justification."

Tells you something, doesn't it?

Our "because" keeps us right. It is an illusion I use to maintain being in control of my own little universe.

Our "because" is the lizard, that voice that is 100% behind us defending and justifying our actions. Through using it, we have refused to put to death all of our natural desires, thoughts or actions and have kept alive our justification for doing to others what we would never want done to ourselves.

Forgiveness is a completely different ball of wax.

When I ask or give forgiveness, I am letting it all go. No justification. No excuses. No "because."

I am saying to the other person, "Will you send yourself from the justice that you could exact against me for the wrong I did to you *or the wrong that you perceive* that I did to you?"

There have been times when I have asked forgiveness when I didn't believe I was guilty of a transgression. Although I may not see what they see in the breakdown, the fact remains that the offense is true for them. A lot of times I find myself saying, "Will you please forgive me? I can see now that I didn't see what was happening for you or how I affected you that way. Will you forgive me for that?"

When I forgive someone, then I am agreeing to no longer use that offense against the relationship.

With forgiveness, I have discovered the truth that only God can correct the past. He is the only One who can restore what has been taken from me or what was missing in the first place. I can be reconciled to others knowing that God is covering my back.

Forgiveness is the heartbeat of reconciliation.

In reconciliation, we are called to *"send ourselves from,"* to forgive the offenses, which we could use to make ourselves right about seeking revenge against the other person. However, what Jesus Christ asks us to do as free beings is to will ourselves *from* the offense towards the unprecedented future that awaits the other person.

We are to be with others as we want them to be towards us and to walk out life with God in whatever way of being demonstrates love.

✡ ✡ ✡

Trust

✡ ✡ ✡

"If we think of trust primarily in terms of vulnerability, it will seem foolish,
a weakness rather than a strength, a liability rather than an asset.
But once we think of trust as an opening,
as a foundation for new and perhaps unimagined possibilities,
then trust takes on a different appearance.
Trusting strangers becomes the very heart of wisdom,
strength rather than foolishness, a promising investment in the future
rather than a liability.
The cost of trust may on occasion be devastating
but the high cost of distrust is virtually guaranteed."[4]

Robert C. Solomon and Fernando Flores, *Building Trust*

It was the winter of 1988.

I was spending a lot of time away from home developing a ship brokering business as well as designing one of my first trainings. During these months, Aileen would often tell me how much she missed me and how she wished we could take the time to do something wonderful together. I answered her longings with assurances that this busy season would soon be over.

In the beginning of December, she began to leave the house at unusual times. I would call home looking for Aileen but would find a babysitter staying with the kids. When I asked Aileen where she had been, she said simply that she had been Christmas shopping. Although I didn't see any presents, I just shrugged off the funny feelings I was starting to have.

Then one day Aileen said she was meeting a friend for lunch at noon. A little bit after 12:00 p.m., that same friend called me looking for Aileen. "I thought she was having lunch with you," I said. There was a long silence on the other end of the phone followed by a hurried, "Oh yeah, that's right. I forgot. I better get on my way."

After that call, my funny feelings turned into suspicion. I went straight home from work to look for the mysterious Christmas presents but found nothing except a card that read "Joe's" along with a phone number written in Aileen's handwriting. Getting more and more agitated, I called the number and a man answered. I asked him his name, and he said, "Joe. Why?" I hung up quickly, not answering his question and with sweat pouring down my face.

Was Aileen having some sort of affair with Joe?

My heart and mind raced back and forth analyzing the last several months. We had been communicating so well—at least that's what I thought. Yet I had been away from home a lot. Perhaps Aileen had become so lonely in my absence that she sought out other companionship or found herself being pursued by someone.

Was our marriage on the rocks?

At that moment, I wished I were blind. I wanted all these pieces of circumstance turned evidence to go away. Although we had made vows and promises, Aileen was not a machine. She was free *not* to love me and do what she wanted, even if that meant being unfaithful.

Trying to knock some sense into my head, I decided it would be a great idea to take Aileen to the movies so that we would have time alone together. Hastily I arranged for somebody to sit with the children and called Aileen with my impromptu invitation. To my dismay, Aileen turned me down flat, saying that she was too tired and had too much to do the next morning.

I tried to reassure myself but doubt plagued me. Had someone else won Aileen's heart because I had neglected her?

The next day I asked my business partner, Mark, if he had noticed anything unusual about Aileen. He said, "No." In fact, he suggested that Aileen and I have dinner with him and his wife for the following evening. Thinking about it, I decided that after our dinner at Mark's house I would confront Aileen about my growing suspicions.

The next morning Aileen called me while I was at work.

She asked if she could meet me at Mark's house because she had errands to run before we went to dinner. Visions of a pre-dinner rendezvous with some guy named Joe grabbed me by the throat, and I became quite curt with her.

For the rest of the day I obsessed about all "the evidence." I became so moody and sullen that on the way to dinner Mark kept asking me if I were all right. I brushed him off with a smile. but I was a mess. We stopped at a grocery store. While Mark was inside, I tried to relax but to no success. All I could think about were the hours that lay ahead and what might happen.

After what seemed hours, Mark finally returned to the car, explained his delay by saying that he wasn't feeling well. I smiled but thought, "Great. This is going to be one terrific night. Aileen is probably going to be late coming from who knows where. Mark is sick, and I can't think about anything other than uncovering my wife's affair."

When we arrived at Mark's house, I dreaded seeing Aileen. What would I say? What if my worst fears were true? My heart was so heavy I was sure it was going to break when I saw her.

You can only imagine my shock when we walked inside the house and I heard a thunderous, "Surprise! Happy Birthday!" Before me stood fifty of my closest friends-many of whom I hadn't seen in years- laughing, smiling and taking pictures. Standing next to a magnificent birthday cake was Aileen with tears in her eyes and a big smile on her face.

Tears streamed down my face as I embraced my lovely wife. "You don't know how surprised I am," I managed to get out through my tears. As I admired the cake, I asked her if she had made it. "No," Aileen said, "I bought it at Joe's." Her words turned my subjective fears to ashes. Everything that had seemed so real to me moments before vanished into emptiness.

This heart-wrenching experience and others since that night have caused me to consider the nature of trust. When I asked others why they have trust in someone or something, I usually hear that the person or thing has earned that trust by doing nothing to destroy it. Yet is that answer sufficient?

… trusting is something we individually do;
it is something we make, we create, we build, we maintain,
we sustain with our promises, our commitments, our emotions
and our sense of our own integrity…
Solomon and Flores, Building Trust

I looked down at my cell phone; it was John calling me. As the Director of Talent Development at a prominent Fortune 500 company, John was a friend who had been working hard to move up in the ranks.

"I don't know if I can continue to work here, Dan," he said right off the bat. "They have hired my assistant for a position that I had been promised. I feel absolutely betrayed. After all I have given to this company, this is what they do. I don't know if I can work here ever again."

Because I have worked with many corporations, I knew that John's experience was not uncommon. My first question to him was whether he had spoken to anybody to find out why he had lost out on the promotion.

"I can't trust anyone here now," he responded emphatically. "I don't know who was in on this deal. That's why I called you, Dan. You're not on staff here at the company. I know I can trust you."

Catching his words, "You're not on staff here at the company. I know I can trust you," I saw that John was approaching me with the same kind of simple trust that he had probably given to his boss- right up to the moment he was betrayed. In order for John or the company to get anything valuable from this situation, he would need to speak wisely to those involved. Even more, he would have to initiate these conversations even while being aware that he could be betrayed again by his employers.

"What value do you see in talking to those who can do something about what happened?" I asked. "What would strengthen your ability to work with people in this company and at any future job? What could you learn about how you have trusted your boss along with how you trust me? Or yourself?"

As we worked through possible scenarios, I suspected that 99.9% of us approach trust the same way that John did.

We bestow trust simply and blindly, which keeps us from engaging problems in a way that can bring real solutions and transformation.

As delineated so well by authors Robert C. Solomon and Fernando Flores in *Building Trust in Business, Politics, Relationships and Life*, simple trust is a type of naïve optimism that takes trust for granted. It does not deliberate or anticipate the possibility of betrayal; it, like a child, assumes an overriding goodness or benevolence in others. More often than not, simple trust is the paradigm in which most of us engage the world.

Because simple trust does not see people authentically, it goes from "I can trust everybody" to "I *can't* trust anyone" when betrayed. Once betrayed, it cannot be restored. As Solomon and Flores note, "The loss of simple trust, the end of that naïve transparency, is an invitation to reflection and understanding; it is an invitation to wisdom. Simple trust is not 'true' trust anymore than a first (and equally naïve) love is 'true' love. It is wonderful if we simply find ourselves trusting in circumstances that warrant our trust, but authentic trust is that which trusts in the face of doubt and uncertainty."

Blind trust operates in denial. Like an ostrich burying its head in the sand, blind trust operates in willful self-deception. It refuses to look at evidence of betrayal or the possibilities of what might occur. Like simple trust, blind trust takes the giving and receiving of trust for granted. It no longer sees the possibility of betrayal by refusing to see evidence for distrust. Blind trust sets us up for inevitable despair because it anticipates the potential behavior of others based on history.

The impact of blind trust came home to me when one of my companies was working with an international Christian ministry that does extensive relief work in third world countries. This organization had contacted us because one of their prominent fundraisers was having a homosexual affair with one of the administrative workers in the ministry's home office.

When I interviewed Pete, the manager who had hired the man having the affair, he said, "I can't believe this is happening. I trusted Bob but he just betrayed us without any concern for who he was hurting." I asked Pete if he had done any background checks on Bob. Pete answered, "I hired Bob before I got some of the reports back, and I didn't really read them all."

When Pete and I checked the reports together, we discovered that Bob had been released from two other prominent positions for "ethical violations." I asked Pete if he had seen the comments on these reports. He responded that he vaguely remembered them, but because Bob had been doing such a great job he assumed that Bob had learned from his mistakes.

When I asked him why he had not talked to Bob about these comments on his references, the only response Pete could provide was that he didn't want to distract Bob from the great job he was doing raising money for the ministry. Unfortunately because of Pete's blind trust, any constructive possibilities for both Bob and the ministry had gone right down the tubes.

Unlike simple or blind trust, *authentic trust* recognizes the possibility of betrayal and yet still chooses to trust. It is a conscious choice to give trust out of a commitment to the possibility of a future worth having.

Authentic trust goes into any relationship or situation with its eyes wide open. As described by Solomon and Flores, "Authentic trust is both reflective and honest with itself and others. It has taken into account the arguments for distrust but has nevertheless resolved itself on the side of trust. Authentic trust is constituted as much by doubt and uncertainty as by confidence and optimism. Authentic trust, as opposed to simple and blind trust, does not exclude or deny distrust but rather accepts it and goes on to transcend it in action."

When I am trusting authentically, I diligently tend to my relationships because I realize that the trust that we have together is fragile. I honor the freedom that God has given the other person and I take into consideration what possibilities might occur. Trust is given because of what could exist relationally for a future worth having, all the while recognizing the possibility of betrayal. Authentic trust acts in the belief that benefits reaped through trusting outweigh the potential cost of betrayal.

With me and Aileen, what has sustained us through some twenty-eight years of marital highs and lows is that we continually ground our present relationship in the future worth having together. With each passing year, the greater we have made the value of that future, the harder it has become for us to betray one another's trust. However, we have never lost sight of the fact that betrayal is still always a possibility. Through recognizing that betrayal is possible, we are always vigilant to preserve our love. We are living a rewarding life together because of the freedom afforded by this kind of "eyes wide open" choice of trust.

Has it been easy? Not always. Is it fruitful? Yes.

When trust is lost in our relationships, what happens often is cordial hypocrisy. Cordial hypocrisy is pretending that trust exists when it does not. It is that polite smile, the subtle avoidance and the words of superficiality we use to hide our distrust of the other person. It is the corporate handshake. The religious nod.

I know few better killers of possibility than cordial hypocrisy. Cordial hypocrisy is being polite for the sake of false harmony.

If I have a relational breakdown with someone and don't pursue reconciliation, then the resulting cordial hypocrisy implies that the relationship is not worth having.

With cordial hypocrisy, I build a complaint filled with self-justifying rationalizations towards the other person. Something has to be wrong with me, him, her or it. Then when I see that person again, I pretend that there is trust when nothing could be further from the truth. In our interaction, I say nothing truly authentic because I have already rationalized that it is futile to try.

Like the tip of the iceberg, cordial hypocrisy is the first visible evidence of despair giving rise to moods of cynicism and suspicion that pervade our complaint. When I position myself to be right about what isn't possible in the relationship, I am shutting down the possibility of something unprecedented happening.

By being cordially hypocritical, I abandon any new possibility for the predictability of my complaint. I am choosing to be right about what is not working, all the while wondering why it seems so impossible to access the future we long to have.

When I engage cordial hypocrisy, I am running away from the problem, using the apology in my mind that goes something like, "I don't trust you enough to engage what seems unpredictable and potentially hurtful, so I will pretend I am *fine*" (*frantic, insecure, neurotic* and *emotional*).

When we are playing with cordial hypocrisy, the best thing God can do is pull our pants down and expose what we are really thinking.

Any hope for reconciliation and transformation comes through our being willing to see how inauthentic we are being—and then choosing to be with the problem even when it looks hopeless.

The paradox of God is that through imperfect vessels, He brings perfection. We live in a relationship, a partnership with the Eternal Being, who promises to bring order to chaos and release beauty if we will choose to stand and declare that future in the face of no possibility.

✡ ✡ ✡

Faith and Their Friend

✡ ✡ ✡

"Ye can know nothing of the end of all things, or nothing expressible in those terms. It may be, as the Lord said to the Lady Julian, that all will be well, and all will be well and all manner of things will be well. But it's ill talking of such questions."
"Because they are too terrible, Sir?"

"No. Because all answers deceive. If ye put the question from within Time and are asking about possibilities, the answer is certain. The choice of ways is before you. Neither is closed. Any man may choose eternal death. Those who choose it will have it.
But if ye are trying to leap on into eternity, if ye are trying to see the final state of all things as it will be (for so ye must speak) when there are no more possibilities left but only the Real, then ye ask what cannot be answered to mortal ears. Time is the very lens through which ye see- small and clear, as men see through the wrong end of a telescope- something that would otherwise be too big for ye to see at all. That thing is Freedom: the gift whereby ye most resemble your Maker and are parts of eternal reality. But ye can see it only through the lens of time, in a little clear picture, through the inverted telescope. It is a picture of moments following one another and yourself in each moment making some choice that might have been otherwise. Neither the temporal succession nor the phantom of what ye might have chosen and didn't is itself Freedom. They are a lens."
C.S. Lewis, *The Great Divorce*

I believe we have a lot more in common with Abraham than we might realize. Also, David, Daniel and Esther. Abraham Lincoln. Helen Keller and Mother Teresa.

Each of these otherwise normal people bestowed a transcendent trust, one in which they stood in faith with God for the sake of the unprecedented. I say we can also stand in a faith that transforms. We can stand with the concept that God has our back and de-signify survival conversations of life so as to live and die magnificently!

When we go into life with eyes wide open, we have the possibility of being free, going for the full potential of the time we've been given- all the while knowing that we will inevitably fail one another as human beings and life is going to look different than what we think it should. We can find the "Yes and Amen" of who we are through standing in a way that God who *is* the Logos will never break one of His promises, not one of His words to us. Even when it appears that He has betrayed every last one of them.

I haven't met someone yet who has not experienced some kind of deep sorrow, anguish, disappointment or loss. The business deal ends up in disaster. The child gets a brain tumor. Addiction is not overcome. The marriage fails. The career is a flop. A best friend lies. Life is just not what we had expected.

When something or someone we love dies right before our eyes, I know that as a human being, as someone who experiences thought and emotion, I want some answers. The knowledge of my dissatisfaction and grief demands that there must be answers somewhere. However, if I listen to the cultural and historical drift around me, the "wisdom" offered by this world ends up sounding a lot like those all too plentiful, mediocre sympathy cards with those "Thinking of You In Your Time of Loss" sentiments, offering nothing but false comfort and evident emptiness.

Our souls want to demand of God, "Where the hell were You? Why weren't You here when I needed You the most? I sent word. I pleaded for help. But You didn't come, and now it's just too late."

Two thousand years ago, Martha and Mary knew this agony. They were two single women who, along with their brother Lazarus, had opened their home and hearts to Jesus Christ.

So when Jesus Came, He found that he (Lazarus)
has been in the tomb for four days...
Then Martha, as soon as she heard that Jesus was coming,
went and met Him but Mary was sitting in the house.
Now Martha said to Jesus,
"Lord, if you had been here my brother would not have died."
John 11:17, 20-21

He was their Friend. They loved Him.

If you chronicle the journeys of Jesus, you'll see that He stayed with them in Bethany again and again. Their love mattered to Him. I imagine how much He enjoyed being there and the gifts of themselves that they gave to Him. I think of the evenings that Jesus, Martha, Mary and Lazarus must have had together, remembering the ones I have experienced with my close friends- a big meal, good conversation late into the night and plenty of laughter over the day's events and each other. I envision the atmosphere of love that must have permeated their house warmed by His presence.

They were His friends. He loved them.

Then one day when Jesus was away, a chill entered into their lives. Out of the blue, Lazarus became deadly ill, with his condition worsening with each passing hour. More than anything or anyone else, Martha and Mary needed Jesus and they needed Him now.

I suspect that it was Martha, the action-taker of the trio, who did the legwork tracking down Jesus' location in the middle of the desert and then convincing someone to run over twenty miles to get a 911 message to Him. I am sure she was thinking, "Once Jesus knows, He will come." Both she, Mary and Lazarus himself must have been certain that Jesus wouldn't let them down. He was their Friend; surely they meant more to Him than some ministry gig. He would come.

So they waited. And waited. And waited some more. Still no Jesus.

With each passing hour, like many of us who have waited in the hospital rooms or at negotiation tables or in the midst of arguing attorneys, the sisters got more and more anxious. They did everything they knew to keep Lazarus alive. They cared for his fever; they took turns staying up all night by his side. They checked the window again and again, looking for their Friend who could heal their desperate situation. But the empty night only got colder.

Right before their eyes, Lazarus died.

As they laid their brother's body in the tomb and as the mourners lamented and wailed, Mary and Martha's silence towards one another exploded with questions. *Why did Jesus not come? What did we mean to Him anyway? We know He got our message but He never came. He abandoned us. How are we going to make it now just by ourselves, two unmarried sisters absent of a brother's overseeing financial and protective care? How would we survive in this world, now that God has let us down?*

Nothing would be the same anymore. Martha and Mary were on their own, they must have thought. Perhaps, they even hoped that they would never see Christ again because the pain of seeing Him as they saw Him now would be too great. Their trust had been shattered.

Then, a shout was heard. "Jesus is coming! Jesus is coming!"

With that announcement, Martha headed out the door looking for some answers. Soon Mary follows, racing out the door with her broken heart. In their own separate ways, each sister wanted to know why He had *betrayed* them. Each told Him to His face, "Lord, if You had been here, my brother would not have died."

I wonder. How often do we say the same thing to God?

God, if You had been here, then this tragedy wouldn't have happened. God, if You had been here, then I wouldn't be facing this injustice, or prejudice, or indecision. God, if You had been here, then our government, my church, my spouse, my career, my needs would be better, happy, whole, alive. God, if You had been here, then thousands in South Africa wouldn't be dying of AIDS, there wouldn't be war, we'd have peace, I wouldn't be alone…

God, if You had been here.

How does God respond to our abandonment of trust? How does He respond to our weeping at His feet- to our frozen questions demanding to know "Why?"

Jesus weeps. Not in some helplessness or self-pity. Not in being overwhelmed by our anger. Not even being personally surprised in our loss of trust.

No. I believe He weeps because of the fallen conversation that has caused us pain and anguish. I think He weeps in groaning rage at this deceived world order of death that has mangled the hearts of those He loves, those He calls His friends.

Jesus said to her,
"I am the resurrection and the life.
He who believes in Me though he may die, he shall live."
… He cried out with a loud voice,
Lazarus, come forth!
And he who had died came out…
John 11:25, 43

Christ was and is the unprecedented Resurrection.

He didn't betray Mary and Martha's trust. They forsook and questioned Him for their disappointment. *They believed he would be "a friend" in terms of their own temporal and historical understanding.*

Despite their complaints about how Jesus "should" be a friend, He fulfilled His promise of friendship in an unprecedented way, one that they could never have imagined or understood at Lazarus' deathbed.

When we surrender our complaints and come out from behind the way life "should" be, we can move deeper and deeper into the unprecedented. We can become more and more substantial in our ability to love and influence the world. We can move out of the shadows of a history fraught with suspicion, cynicism and sarcasm and into the freedom of life eternal.

Where our faith fails, He is waiting to substantiate His promise of transforming resurrection. He asks, "Are you willing to die to yourself, come out from the way you think that life should be?"

Are you willing to be resurrected and surprised by God?

Notes:

[1] C.S. Lewis, *The Great Divorce* [1946/1973] (HarperCollins, 2001).

[2] C.S. Lewis, *The Weight of Glory and Other Addresses* [1949/1976] (HarperCollins, 1980).

[3] Henri Nouwen, *The Only Necessary Thing* (Crossroad Publishing, 1999), pp. 152–153.

[4] Robert C. Solomon and Fernando Flores, *Building Trust in Business, Politics, Relationships and Life* (Oxford University Press, 2001).

PARADISE ROAD

✿ ✿ ✿

The End of the Divorce

✿ ✿ ✿

"Breath of Heaven, lighten my darkness, pour over
me your holiness, for you are holy…"
Amy Grant

"I want to toast my good friend, Amy," my mother said, lifting her champagne glass high.

Hearing her words, everyone in the living room turned and the boisterous conversations stilled to silence. "To Amy," Mom continued on with unedited spontaneity, "Thank you for the love that you have given to me and this family. You are a dear friend!"

As Mom spoke, I heard something that I had never heard before. It was the sound of my father sobbing.

Sitting at the fireplace, surrounded by children and grandchildren, Dad was heaving with uncontrolled tears. All of us watched in silence as my seventy-two-year-old father wept from the bottom of his soul like a river set free. None of us dared to touch the holy beauty that had encompassed us. As Dad cried, I glanced at Mom and a wave of peace swept over me.

In a heartbeat, I felt the depths of what was transpiring before our eyes.

You see, when my mom and dad divorced over three decades prior, they had already been very good friends for many years. In the release of my father's tears, I caught a glimpse of the anguish and suffering he had gone through all those years because of his own failures and the weight of how he had judged himself in the tearing apart of their relationship.

After Mom and Dad divorced, my father spent about ten years in what I would call a state of confusion. He dated various women but wandered from relationship to relationship without committing himself. During that time, he floundered in his personal life and business affairs like a batter on his third strike.

As he would admit himself, Dad was a mess until the day he met Amy.

Amy is one special person. A pretty woman with brown eyes, jet black hair and olive skin, she looks like she could be my sister. In fact, her family roots go back to the same village in Italy as ours does.

Amy is clear and directed, modest and sometimes even bashful. She hates drawing attention to herself and derives great joy in being hospitable. With an impeccable eye for detail, she rarely misses anything, and, because of this ability, she is keenly aware of what is happening with others around her. Amy possesses a sharp sense of justice and is unyielding in her opinions while also able to make room for dissent.

As Amy and my father's relationship turned into marriage, Dad's life came out of confusion. With Amy's encouragement, he reached out to us kids and even towards my mom. Amy pursued and developed a deep friendship with my mother, making sure that Mom's needs were taken care of and that she was included in anything special such as Christmas holidays.

Amy and Dad continued to build the family by having their first-born, my brother Giancarlo, and a couple of years later by adopting my sister Alisa, then a young orphan girl from Russia. Their stand for family gradually took root as a legacy in all our lives.

After fifteen years of marriage, Dad did something that he previously swore he would never do. He brought my brothers into his business.

Our family, so irretrievably broken, was being pieced back together. Through small acts of kindness, honor and inclusion, the dividing lines between Amy's family and ours disappeared completely. Even better was that the family included new members, such as her mother and father, Virginia and Tony. When Tony died a few years ago, I remember being surprised at the depth of my mourning over his loss. The mourning I experienced produced a deep love and appreciation for Virginia and her children, and she became one of my favorite people in the world. Go figure. My father's mother-in-law as one of my most cherished friends. So, it was no surprise when the grieving of her passing literally threw me into days of mourning.

We were a family once again, though much bigger and different this time. Now the Tocchini family was a mixed clan of disparate people- husbands, wives, children, half-sisters, half-brothers, grandparents and parents- all reconciled under that one name. The future I had lost as a child had been resurrected into something beautifully new.

It was simply normal now to have Christmas with everyone, including Mom, at Amy and Dad's house. However, Christmas 2004 would be one that none of us would forget. Through my father's tears, in an instant, the Presence of the Holy Spirit had come and dwelt among us. With the humility of a simple toast of love and appreciation, the deep pain in my father's heart was healed and his days of mourning were transformed into tears of rejoicing. He and Mom would go to their graves as good friends and not adversaries.

As our conversation rallied once again and dessert was passed, I paused to think.

"Who is He who is this Love?" I silently wondered. "Who was this Breath of Heaven who had breathed life into us? Who is this Presence who had touched us with such eternal kindness, I asked, here in the land of shadows?"

Amid my ramblings, I watched the fire burn in the fireplace. Throwing on another log, I sat still and watched the dancing shadows cast by the flames. These shadows, although beautiful, were merely silhouettes of the real flame.

And, I wondered. Perhaps this is also the way of love here on earth.

Maybe what we know as love is still a shadow of the Real. Although we feel the undeniable reality of Love's calling upon us, yet as shadows of the flame, there is something more beyond this silhouette. As spiritual beings in this earthly experience, in our moments of silence and solitude, our gaze turns towards what we know is calling out our names.

We yearn.

It's there in the brilliant sunset. Or the heights of the great mountain peaks. We feel. Caught, snagged by it, by the delicate petals of a rose. Or the forces of a wind-swept sea. We see. The fingerprints, in the shadows something invisible, but real, present yet eternal within reach.

There is *more.*

Even if words are mute or insufficient to capture what we feel, the longing to be one with the Someone from Whom we are cast. We groan for this void of love to be satisfied.

We long to go home. To be united with Love Himself.

This night, as I watched Amy give my mom a kiss and my father laugh as he dried his eyes, I felt that yearning inside once again. Could our rejection, our aloneness, our hatred of our fallen condition of divorce, actually point us towards home?

Could Love be "the passion for oneness," as current writer Francis Frangipane and Thomas Aquinas before him have articulated?

As the fire burned bright, Aileen's hand rested upon my shoulder and my heart was turned towards this one who I love beyond what my feeble language and actions can express.

As we sat together in silence, the words of John the Apostle ran through my mind. "God is love," John said some 2,000 years ago.

God *is* love.

✡ ✡ ✡

Is This Not Love?

✡ ✡ ✡

"My beloved friends, let us continue to love each other
since love comes from God.
Everyone who loves is born of God and experiences a
relationship with God.
The person who refuses to love doesn't know the first thing about

God, because God is love -so you can't know him if you don't
love. This is how God showed his love for us:
God sent his only Son into the world so we might live through him.
This is the kind of love we are talking about-
not that we once upon a time loved God,
but that he loved us and sent his Son as a sacrifice to clear
away our sins and the damage they've done to our
relationship with God.
"My dear, dear friends, if God loved us like this,
we certainly ought to love each other."
1 John 4:5-11 (The Message).

L ove is a relationship and a Person, namely the Person of Jesus. Jesus is the substance of which our earthly love is but a shadow and a silhouette.

This is the kind of love we are talking about—not that we once upon
a time loved God, but that he loved us and sent his Son as a sacrifice
to clear away our sins and the damage they've done to our relation-
ship with God.

His entire life was completely given to reconciling us to Love. He came to end the divorce and bring us back into an eternal friendship with God.

Jesus is the Love that draws our gaze. He has drawn mine and I have received His.

Now I am no longer what I was, living out of a conversation to survive as a shadow. Now I stand in this temporal life to love as He has loved me. I willingly choose to continue His work of reconciliation.

I live and will die to end the divorce between God and all the earth.

Yet, all around me, I see that this reconciliation is not yet complete. Daily, I am bombarded with the corruption of the divorce. I have not yet witnessed pure love on the earth. Here in the shadow lands, our human, natural loves are, at best, mere silhouettes of the Divine Love.

But I am at peace, because He has come into our shadow world. Jesus has demonstrated the way home. He is the full Substance of the Father. With every breath, action and thought, Jesus Christ is Love. He was one with the Father and He chose to lay Himself down on that repulsive Roman cross for me, transforming it in his stand for Love into the glorious redemption of mankind. Love wins!

As He did, so He invites me.

Jesus whistles, inviting us, "Come on. Step out of shadows and lesser things of this temporary world." He urges us to choose life in the midst of what is horrible, hopelessly broken and destitute—all for the possibility of reconciling the divorce. In that place where tragedy seems to have no reason, He stands with me, whispering in my ears, "Look for Me, and you will find family."

As the fire burned low, I thought about who lived around the time of Abraham. The Book of Job is considered one the oldest books in existence. In it, Job is described as a man of excellence, a God-fearing individual who lived in perfect integrity. I think that Job was the kind of man you could count on. A successful father and businessman, he loved his family, community and God.

Yet despite his good heart and noble works, Job experienced an immense tragedy. In one brief turn, Job lost everything that mattered to his heart, including his children, possessions and even his health.

Seeing Job's suffering, the question seems unavoidable. "How could God do this?" We ask, "How could God, who tells us that He is love, let someone like Job suffer so greatly? How could God let bad things happen to good people?"

If we are truthful, we wonder, "Is God *really* a God of love?"

Like much of today's Christian culture, Job's friends think they have the answer to that question. They debate and reason with Job, turning the finger towards him, saying he must be at fault for what has happened. In so many words, they reprove him. "Hey, man. You reap what you sow. There must be something up here with you, Job, because God is good and what's happening here ain't."

Yet, at the end of Job's story, at the end of all things, God Himself comes to Job in the midst of his misery and does something profound.

After God had finished addressing Job, he turned to Eliphaz the Temanite and said, "I've had it with you and your two friends. I'm fed up! You haven't been honest either with me or about me— not the way my friend Job has.
So here's what you must do. Take seven bulls and seven rams, and go to my friend Job. Sacrifice a burnt offering on your own behalf.

*My friend Job will pray for you, and I will accept his prayer. He will
ask me not to treat you as you deserve for talking nonsense about me,
and for not being honest with me, as he has."
They did it. Eliphaz the Temanite, Bildad the Shuhite, and
Zophar the Naamathite did what God commanded. And God accepted
Job's prayer.*

Job 42:7-9 (The Message)

If you look at it you might say that, humanly speaking, Job's friends did not do anything wrong. They instructed Job from what was true from the Scriptures. Yet it was   Job's friends that God commanded to repent.

As I put another log on the fire, I asked myself. *What is the nature of this God? What giving of Himself was He seeking to show to Job and his friends in Job's suffering? What oneness was He opening to Job?*

What was God looking for?

✡ ✡ ✡

Getting the News

✡ ✡ ✡

*"Fear not, for I have redeemed you;
I have summoned you by name; you are mine.
When you pass through the waters,
I will be with you;
and when you pass through the rivers,
they will not sweep over you.
When you walk through the fire,
you will not be burned;
the flames will not set you ablaze."*

Isaiah 43:1-2 (NIV)

Tonight was the night. I had wanted to hear the story again. Joseph's story.

Traffic down Highway 101 towards the Edwards' home was bliss-fully light, and it wasn't long before Valerie was putting the final touches on the linguini while Lawrence and I waited at the kitchen table like a pair of hungry thieves.

Aileen and I had been friends with Lawrence and Valerie Edwards for more than ten years. The first time I met Lawrence, he was clean-ing the windows at my store in Rohnert Park. It was a small profes-sional sports memorabilia store, and Lawrence's company cleaned commercial buildings and construction sites. A mutual friend of ours, Roy Williams, managed the store, and he introduced us with, "Hey, Dan. Meet Lawrence Edwards. He is going to do the next Break-through Training." As Lawrence shot Roy "a look,'" he greeted me warmly.

After Lawrence left, I asked Roy about the "the look." Roy chuck-led. "Oh, nothing big." Roy said, "I had been talking to Lawrence about Breakthrough and before you came in, he said he wasn't inter-ested. I thought I would just give him a hard time."

Ironically, Lawrence *was* in the next training. When I saw him, I asked him about why he was there as Roy had told me that he wasn't interested in Breakthrough. Lawrence's response is how I experience him to this day.

He said with a smile, "Dan, I just came to my senses and decided to trust my friend." Lawrence is a humble man who doesn't shy away from being honest. In everything he does, there is grace, integrity, respect and loyalty. His wife, Valerie, is one of the best listeners I have ever met. Patient and kind, she is passionate about engaging life in its fullness.

Hearing "Dinner's ready," I watched Isaac, the youngest of the Edwards' clan, bound up the stairs. Following close behind was their teenage daughter, Samera, a young woman of rare elegance and radiance. After treating their dad like a long-lost teddy bear, the kids captured two plates of pasta and took off for destinations unknown. Well, at least, to me.

Watching them go, Lawrence turned to me. "It's hard to believe that it has been about ten years now."

"Has it been that long?" I said, reaching back into my memory.

"1997," Valerie said as she sat down with us. "I was forty-two years old when I got pregnant with Joseph. Samera was just turning eight years old; Isaac was about two and a half. I had always wanted to have four children and, after having complications in the past plus getting up there in years, I was so excited to find out that I was pregnant with him."

"How did you find out something wasn't quite right?" I asked.

"Well, because of my age and complications in previous pregnancies, we decided to get an amniocentesis at nineteen weeks because we didn't want any surprises," Valerie said with a laugh. "A few days after the amnio, I was at home alone when the midwife called. 'Valerie,' she said, 'the news is not good; the doctors are telling me that your baby is going to have mental and physical defects. This is all I know right now. I will call you back when I get more information.'"

I leaned back in my chair, imaging the shock that Valerie must have felt with that call.

"He had Trisomy 18." Lawrence explained, "As you know, pairs of human chromosomes are numbered from 1 through 22, with an unequal 23rd pair of X and Y chromosomes for males, and two X chromosomes for females. People with a Trisomy have an extra chromosome added to one of their normal pairs. In the case of Down Syndrome, there are three chromosomes on the 21st chromosome. Now Joseph had a third chromosome on his 18th pair. This meant that he would not only be mentally retarded but also would possibly have severe physical defects."

"From the medical perspective," Valerie joined in, "because Joseph was Trisomy 18, he would have conditions considered non-compatible with life. In so many words, the doctors were telling us that Joseph would probably not live. He could die at any point. If he made it to birth, he would most likely die shortly thereafter."

I looked at Valerie and Lawrence, wondering how they reacted to getting this news.

"At first, I didn't want to believe what I was hearing," Valerie said without me asking. "You want to believe that *something* can be done. Immediately I prayed, asking God 'What can I do, God? Is there a possibility for healing?' There had to be something, I thought."

"What did you get in prayer?"

"The only answer I could perceive to my questions and tears was 'I will be with you.'"

"That was all?"

"That must have been difficult."

"Very much so. When I got home," Lawrence said, "My response to the situation was to abort the baby. Hearing the news that the baby was Trisomy 18 was very difficult for me. I found myself resisting the whole idea of death. I didn't want to think about it, or deal with the pain and ugliness of what it would bring to my family and me. In my head, I tried to reason with the idea that maybe we weren't at the life stage yet. Underneath that bartering, there was a huge commitment on my part not to have to deal with death. I did not want to engage or entertain death, and I was looking for reasons not to have to go there.

"You see, when I was a young boy, my grandmother was a florist who spent a lot of time delivering flowers to funeral homes. As a young teenager, I would go along with her to help her with those deliveries. From those experiences, I grew up believing that the longer I did not have to engage death in any manner the better off I would be. So when I found out that the baby was in the condition that he was, my immediate thought was 'This does not have to happen. We can stop this right now.'"

"How did you as a couple decide what to do?"

Lawrence looked at Valerie. "Go ahead," she said, letting Lawrence continue.

"Things started to shift for me when we went to see a geneticist a few days after the diagnosis. The geneticist looked me in the eyes and said, 'This is not your fault, Lawrence. This is not something that came out of your genes or Valerie's. This just showed up.' I couldn't believe what she was saying. That was not the answer I wanted. No. I wanted some level of responsibility for causing this problem because then I could justify myself in being in control of fixing it. When the geneticist said, 'This just showed up,' I had a hard time accepting it. I wanted to have life framed in such a way that it made *sense*. However, the truth was that situation did not make sense. It was a random accident, for lack of a better word—a random combination of events over which we had no control. In my helplessness to make things better, I realized that I was not the core source of life. There is much more beyond what I originally ever perceived. I was just a part of something much bigger than myself."

As Lawrence spoke, I remembered when they had called Aileen and me with the news about the pregnancy.

"You probably remember, Dan, all of our friends gave us different counsel and advice."

"Yes. I do."

"You said," Valerie continued, "My prayer is that there will be redemption in this experience. I will stand with you no matter which way you choose, but either way, my prayer is that there would be redemption." Another friend, a pastor, said that he knew a couple who had gone through a similar situation and the baby lived. 'Trust God and go with it,' he said. 'You don't know what God might open up.' The final person we spoke with took Lawrence aside and said, 'Bro, if I were you, I would get rid of it now.'"

"What caused you to choose to walk out the pregnancy, especially given the prognosis?"

"Isaac and Samera," Lawrence said. "It was our kids."

"How?"

"About a week after we had gotten the news," Valerie said, "we sat down with Isaac and Samera to explain to them that there were some problems with the baby. As simply as we could, we told them that because of these complications we were not sure if the baby would live. Consequently, we were considering ending the pregnancy. Before we could say another word, Samera immediately interrupted us with 'No.'

'No, honey?' I asked. 'We can love this baby for as long as we can,' Samera repeated. 'For as long as we have him.'"

"Out of the mouth of babes."

"Hearing Samera's words helped me see what was going on inside of me," Lawrence added. "I had started to dream about having another son. How he and Isaac would room together. The three of us guys playing basketball and football. Going hunting and fishing. All those wonderful father and son things. Then we got the news, all those joys were stolen from me. Vanished in a single phone call. I had wanted to end the pregnancy because I did not want to suffer any more loss. When Samera said, 'We can love this baby for as long as we can.' I heard the solution and felt total peace inside. I would love my son for as long as he was with us, whether that ended up being a year or six minutes."

"So that meant…"

"That meant that we would continue with the pregnancy, around five months worth of time," Valerie said, "Knowing full well that the baby might die at any moment or even at birth. The only thing we knew for sure was God's word, 'I will be with you.'"

✧ ✧ ✧

God's Answer

✧ ✧ ✧

"We turn to God for help when our foundations are shaking, only to learn that it is God who is shaking them."
Charles C. West

Still sitting by the fire after Christmas dinner at my father's and Amy's house, my thoughts lingered on Job. What was God looking for?

I flipped open my Bible and, there in Job, I read through the exchanges between Job and his friends. I saw in them our own questions, opinions and complaints towards God.

"God disciplines humans through suffering." "He will never reject an innocent man but will punish the wicked." "God abuses his power in arbitrary ways." "He is an unjust Judge who is cruel and unfair to many innocent victims." "He is an angry God who is responsible for suffering and the evil things that happen in the world."

On and on and on…

In this swirl of too many human words, I was stopped by something stunningly beautiful. I saw the answer of God.

In Job's hour of greatest despair, God comes and rebukes him harshly.

Well, what does Job do? The man *rejoices*. Why? Did God give him the answers to all the questions he had asked? Did God explain why Job was suffering in the first place? Did God defend His seeming lack of intervention? Did He address Job's complaints?

No.

Then, why did Job rejoice? Because of the Presence. God's answer was His Presence. And, in that, Job rejoiced.

I think that throughout his suffering, Job had held on to a thin thread of hope. His hope was that his Friend, God, would once again be with him. Despite all the pain and confusion that Job was experiencing, he refused to let go of his relationship with God, no matter what.

Even when Job's wife mocked him with, "Do you still hold fast to your integrity? Curse God and die!" Job holds on like cement. "Divorce God," she shouted at him. Yet Job refused to let go.

Then, at the right time, God does come to Job. And, He comes in His fullness *and* with a rebuke.

I think God basically said something like this to Job:

"Who do you think you are, Job? Where were you when I cast the heavens and created all things? What makes you think that I am going to answer you? I am God; you are a mere man. I want to be clear with you, My child. I love you but you don't get to know the 'why.' The only reason you want to know 'why' is because you don't trust Me. But at least you are talking to Me and holding onto Our relationship. Your friends over there are pontificating among themselves about My word and making themselves righteous. They only date me when it is convenient for them and their philosophies. However, you are married to me. Even in the midst of mysterious tragedy, you sought the refuge of My Presence."

Do you see what I saw?

God answered *Job*, not his questions. God showed His great love for Job through showing up Himself, through His presence of "I will be with you."

What does this mean?

I think it means that having the 'right answer' means nothing to God because He *is* the Answer. The Presence is the answer. He is Love that heals even when He comes with His rebuke.

Here is another take. Believer or not, we are all aware of the corruption and decay in ourselves and in this world. We fall short with each other in countless and seemingly unending ways. Daily, there are multitudes of suffering, social injustice, inequality, hatred and evil everywhere we turn. Yet in the midst of this corruption is Love, the Presence of God.

And *that* is the paradox of life!

Dr. Peter Kreeft, Professor of Philosophy at Boston College, in his book, *The Three Philosophies of Life*, helps us understand this through the example of the love of a father towards his children. As human beings, we believe that a good father would stop his son from touching the stove by taking away his hand and saying, "Don't touch the stove, Son. It will burn you."

As God said to Adam, "Don't eat from that tree, Son. It will burn you."

Let's say that despite the father's warning, the son reaches again for the stove when his father is not looking. Just in time, the father catches his son and once again he tells him, "Don't touch the stove, Son. It will burn you."

The son, however, still tries to reach for the stove.

Eventually all of us would probably agree that a good father would allow the son to touch the stove. Why? Because until the son has burned himself- and discovers that his father is right—he will not fully trust what his father has said or that he loves him. We would see the father's actions as those of a good father teaching his son how to live safely in a dangerous world.

Now take the same principal but in a different scenario.

The father tells the son, "Do not play in the street because you could get hit by a car." Now if his son continues to play in the street and, this time, the father lets the son get killed by a car, would we say that the father is still a good father?

No. We would call him a horrible father who could have prevented the death of his child.

But not so with God! God does not prevent our deaths and yet He is good.

How can this be? Is God a bad father because He has made space in the freedom that He has given place for suffering and even death? Was God a bad father because Job suffered? I say, "No."

Why? Because we don't see. We live in the land of shadows. What we know and experience here on earth are mere silhouettes of the Real. Our Father, the Presence who is Love, is eternal. He is not in the temporal like us. He sees from the perspective of the eternal Reality. He knows what we cannot even imagine.

Another way to imagine the distance between God's ways and ours is to think of a relationship between a dog and a man. A man trains a dog to behave in such a way that it can be more loveable.

In being trained, the dog is loved and accepted by the man in very profound ways.

Does the dog understand the man's motives when he is being disciplined by his trainer? I think not. Yet even in this example, I believe that dog is far more capable of understanding his trainer's motives than we understand the actions of the Almighty.

God is the One who is Perfect Mercy.

Perfect Mercy knows suffering can lead to oneness or divorce. Suffering can produce the passion to be one or to have bitter defiance. Suffering can lead us to Love. Suffering is not from God but is a result of the choices made by the ones whom God has set free. That suffering can lead us to love and unity *is* Mercy, a Mercy that is available to those who have faith when confronted with the many faces of death.

We can question God's mercy, but I would suggest that like with Job, He will answer with His Presence and His rebuke. God has no need to defend Himself against our complaints and the reasoning that pretends to know how the Almighty *"should be."*

When He responds to us with His rebuke, we are most likely to do one of two things. We either scorn the very Presence that can resurrect and save us. Or we can surrender to who He is (not what He can do for us) and then, like Job, eternity will be ours and we will become divinely human.

Mother Teresa seemed to understand this more than most of us.

I believe that, while serving the poorest of the poor in Calcutta, all of Mother Teresa's natural, human love for others died and then was resurrected and transformed. I think that she saw the Mercy of God working in the slums *without* her. She saw that He was in the midst of the worst suffering, transforming it into a beauty that defied human reasoning. In their suffering, she saw His face, and as a result she had no contempt towards God. She knew that death was not the ultimate. Mother Teresa lived on an eternal plane while here on earth. Her being- in the best and worst of circumstances-was one with the Presence.

This, I believe, is the faith of those who answer the call of the kingdom of God. The Eternal is love; it is a Presence. God. And, here in the mere shadow of His love, faith hangs onto the possibility that what looks temporally harsh and horrible could be transformed to eternally compassionate. Hope is the possibility that Love wins!

That's what Job, the one who God called "His friend," learned.

✡ ✡ ✡

Added

✡ ✡ ✡

"Sadness opens the heart to what was meant to be and is not. Grief opens the heart to what was meant to be and is. Sorrow breaks the heart as it exposes the damage we've done to others as a result of our unwillingness to rely solely on the grace and truth of God." [2]
Dan Allender

As Lawrence poured another glass of wine, we let the moments and the memories rest upon us.

"After we made the decision to walk this pregnancy through, the unexpected happened," Valerie said.

"What was that?" I asked.

"All of our close friends vanished," she said with a laugh. "Circumstances took them right out of our lives. Some moved. Others had their marriage fall apart. The relationships at church were new because we had just joined. The support that we were counting on just disappeared. The last thing I had anticipated was walking through this experience alone. I had so many months ahead without knowing what those days would bring. I cried out to God asking, 'You said you would be here. Well, where are You?!'"

"What did you hear back?"

"He heard, 'I send My servants where I choose,'" Valerie answered. "So I had to surrender to life as it was showing up. I had to accept how God was choosing to be with me. It was tough; there's no other way to put it. I felt very isolated and alone. The pregnancy itself was getting harder and harder. Because Joseph was Trisomy 18, I had twice the normal amount of amniotic fluid. It quickly got to the point where I would wear a back brace continually. Sleeping became almost impossible. Lawrence and I were going through this together, but in some ways apart. In the midst of everything else, we had to care for Isaac and Samera."

"What shifted?"

"One day our midwife called me. She said, 'I want you to call this woman. Her name is Jennifer, and she had a baby who died.

If you can, I want you to talk with her.' Soon Jennifer and I became friends.

And I saw that God was choosing other servants to answer my loneliness. One by one, they seemed to come out of nowhere. Yet each helped us in some specific expression of love to make it through what we were facing."

I wondered out loud, "How did you and Lawrence come together during these months?"

"I think that we were together in choice," Lawrence said, "Together we had chosen this course and however it showed up, we were going to walk it out. Yet we were walking through different provisions of God, I think. Inside of me, I was thinking, 'What right do I have to say anything to Valerie? I am not going through the process of bearing this child. I should just keep my mouth shut; do the best I can. Take care of the kids.'

"For a long time, I held everything in me. Then one day a friend hired my company to clean up at his construction site. As I was working in one of the homes, he said to me, 'Man, I have never heard you this quiet. What is going on, Lawrence? What's wrong?'

"Immediately all that I had been holding inside let loose. Looking out the window, I just started crying. I spoke out everything that was going on inside of me- all the struggle, hurt, frustration and helplessness.

"When I finally turned around, I saw my friend balled up in a corner, crying. What I discovered was that the same thing had happened to him and his wife. They had lost a child between the birth of his two boys. Up until this moment, my friend had never given himself permission to cry and release the suffering inside of him.

"After that day, I saw that even in death there is a beauty. Death was not what I had been making it up to be. Although death *is* an enemy, it is not the end."

Lawrence and I turned to Valerie.

"I remember being angry at God a few times," she said. "I would ask Him, 'Why don't you heal this little guy?' He chose not to answer my 'Why, God?' So I said, 'Okay' and hung on to Samera's words. *I will love him for as long as I can.* If the only time I get is now, then I will love him now.

"What I longed for was to look at him with his eyes open. My hope throughout the months was to look into my son's eyes. To see into the windows of his heart, and show him the depths of my love. Yet as hard as the pregnancy became, that did not matter. We loved him.

"One morning, I realized that we needed to give our son a name. With all our children, their names have special meaning to us. We give them a Biblical name along with the name of someone who was particularly important to Lawrence and me.

"We named him Joseph because his name means '*Added.*'

"In the Bible, Joseph's life didn't turn out the way he thought it would. He experienced one adversity after the other. Yet in the end of his life, there was great, unimaginable redemption. With our Joseph, his life was not turning out how we thought it would but we believed that Joseph's life would *add* to our lives, even though we did not know how.

"We named him Joseph Lawrence Edwards."

✡ ✡ ✡

Accomplice

✡ ✡ ✡

"There is a way that seems right to a man, but in the end it leads to death."

Proverbs 14:12

As Aileen and I watched the logs burn in the fire, I suspected that in the midst of this Christmas celebration she was thinking about her cousin, Harry, and his absence.

Aileen's unrelenting love for Harry inspired me. In the face of his downward spiral, she saw *him*, not the Gollum creature he was becoming. Aileen refused to forget who Harry was, his presence, despite his choices, behavior and circumstances. Her love was that last thread Harry was holding onto and whether he answered that love or not, we would stay.

As Aileen spoke with experts and considered various options, I knew one thing for certain. We would not make comfortable that which was killing him. Because we loved Harry, we refused to be his accomplice.

To me, an accomplice is someone who helps you stuff your jacket with lead weights when you are about to jump overboard. An accomplice is a voluntary participant in helping you commit a crime, even those eternal ones, by encouraging or assisting you or by simply failing to prevent it when it is within their power to do so.

"Staying true to the colors" is how my prison boys would call it.

After we had enough trust built between us to speak frankly, I asked them, "How many times were you establishing your relationship based upon something criminal?" I said, "You say that a friend is someone who keeps silent about your crimes. Tell me. How many of your crew come and visits you here in prison? What happens if one of your gang refuses to participate in a crime that the rest of you are doing? What then?"

The room was dead silent. The expressions on their faces said it all. I didn't need to go any further. The results, or lack thereof, spoke loud enough.

"Seems to me that God walks a different walk," I said to them. "Look at the story of the prodigal son. The father freely let the younger son make his choice. Despite all the good ways the father has provided for him, the son walks out without so much as a 'Thanks, Dad.' Yet the father remains in relationship, ever looking for the son's return. The father refuses to forget the presence of his son. He is willing to lose the relationship completely- even possibly the son's life- for the sake of what was eternally best for the one that he loved."

I thought once again about Job.

God did not become Job's accomplice. He did not come down and answer Job's questions in an effort to defend Himself or try to convince Job of Who He is. God refused to give Job the "illusion of because," because there is no "because" with God. He is. God gave Job, and us, one answer, "I AM THAT I AM." And that is eternally sufficient.

God loves us. Why? Because He said so.

And, God lets people die. Why? Because "I AM THAT I AM."

No "because..." No "this will explain everything..." Just "I AM THAT I AM."

I wondered at the thought, knowing its truth. God is. God knows-what I don't know- from an eternal perspective. God refuses to be our accomplice; He is Someone who loves us. In love, the Presence of the Beloved is the answer to everything.

Take a look at Jesus with Peter. I know of no better distinction between a friend and an accomplice than what went down between them in Matthew 16:13-25:

Now when Jesus came into the district of Caesarea Philippi, He was asking His disciples "Who do people say that the Son of Man is?" And they said, "Some say John the Baptist; and others, Elijah; but still others, Jeremiah, or one of the prophets." He said to them, "But who do you say that I am?"
Simon Peter answered, "You are the Christ, the Son of the living God." And Jesus said to him, "Blessed are you, Simon Barjona, because flesh and blood did not reveal this to you but My Father who is in heaven. I also say to you that you are Peter, and upon this rock I will build my church and the gates of Hades will not overpower it. I will give you the keys of the kingdom of heaven; and whatever you bind on earth shall be bound in heaven and whatever you loose on earth shall have been loosed in heaven." Then He warned the disciples that they should tell no one that He was the Christ.
From that time Jesus began to show His disciples that He must go to Jerusalem, and suffer many things from the elders and chief priests and scribes, and be killed, and be raised up on the third day. Peter took Him aside and began to rebuke Him, saying, "God forbid it, Lord! This shall never happen to You!" But He turned and said to Peter, "Get behind Me, Satan! You are a stumbling block to Me; for you are not setting your mind on God's interests but man's."
Then, Jesus said to His disciples, "If anyone wishes to come after Me, he must deny himself, and take up his cross and follow Me. For whoever wishes to save his life will lose it but whoever loses his life for My sake will find it…"

What landed here?

This is what I think. When Peter answered "You are the Christ," Jesus responded with "Peter, you get it. You got the revelation from My Father." He was saying that Peter's declaration was revealed to him by God. However, Peter takes the declaration onto himself. He attaches his own identity to the revelation.

How do we know this?

Because minutes after speaking that declaration, while Jesus is telling how He must be crucified as the Lamb of God to fulfill the promises made by God in the book of Isaiah, Peter grabs Him and takes him aside, away from the rest of the disciples. Then he admonishes Jesus, saying, "You are God. This can't happen. You will not die."

And, Jesus' response?

Jesus' reaction is harsh and merciful, that same paradox Job encountered. He tells Peter, "Get behind me, Satan. You are a stumbling block. These are the concerns of men." Then Jesus turns to everyone else in the room and tells them, "If you want to follow Me, you have to pick up your cross daily. Daily you must die to this desire to save yourself."

How often do we save ourselves because we have to know "the why"?" How many times have we withheld ourselves from others because we don't know why something is the way it is? How often do we take God aside, justifying ourselves and our need to be right, before moving forward into what He has told us?

Jesus was saying to Peter and the disciples, "Take the cross and kill your need to know and predict. Then, stand and wait on God's presence."

Sonic boom. Total shift in the atmosphere of the room. Put yourself there. Jesus goes from joy to rebuke in the space of minutes. He calls his good friend, the leader of the pack, "Satan." Jesus' language is hard, even offensive.

What was Peter's crime here? His was uniquely the same as ours.

Walk the moment through from Peter's perspective. Out of his natural human love and mercy towards Jesus, Peter comes quietly but deceivingly as a friend. He pulls Jesus aside, seeking to keep his words hidden. It was unthinkable and repulsive to Peter that Jesus would ever suffer or die. Peter, in the midst of a survival conversation, was agreeing with the thought, "Life should not turn out the way I think Jesus is telling me that it will."

On some level, Peter thought that he should protect his interests in Jesus. What Peter did not see was that he was interrupting Jesus from doing that which would bring about the salvation of all mankind and the complete transformation of the world.

Can you see why Jesus so instantly reacted? Why did He call Peter a stumbling block?

If Jesus contemplated Peter's words for even a moment, I think He knew that it could cause Him to stumble in fulfilling His commitment to God and mankind. Peter's affection was a stumbling block when he sought to use it to keep Jesus from making his life more difficult or painful. Peter, in his words and actions, was Satan's accomplice in attempting to stop the reconciliation of God to man.

However, Jesus was willing to immediately interrupt His disciples, especially the ones closest to Him. The future Jesus was committed to have was greater than their approval or His own personal comfort or survival.

What was the breakdown for Peter?

Peter loved Jesus and Jesus loved him. However, also in his love for Jesus, I believe Peter had a mixed agenda. First there was his pride, the thoughts of him being elevated above the other disciples. We know from other parts of the Gospels that the disciples had debated among themselves more than once about who was the greatest among them.

Then, after Peter's declaration of "You are the Christ," Jesus affirmed him. Jesus' recognition contributed to Peter attaching his identity to the acknowledgment. In his listening, Peter heard, "Jesus is building his church on me." However, "the rock" that Jesus is referring to isn't Peter. It is the revelation of the Father that was given to Peter, namely that Jesus Christ is the Messiah.

What Peter is doing here is committing the crime of attaching himself to the glory of God and then inviting Jesus into the conspiracy. Peter's complaint was that suffering and death should never happen to the Son of God and, in the cloak of his empathy for Jesus, Peter invited Jesus Christ to join him in playing it safe, saying "For surely You shall not die!"

What happened next? Jesus refused to be Peter's accomplice.

Jesus immediately spoke to the spirit in Peter's words. He exposed that what Peter was doing had been done before time by Satan himself. He takes Peter's own identification with God's glory and completely annihilates it. Jesus separates His and God's glory from Peter- because the disciple had taken it for himself.

Jesus was saying to Peter, "Satan did this. You are doing it now. This is pride."

It's the same voice from the Garden. The same compliant, the same scam; the same spirit that originally divorced man from God. Satan goes to Adam and Eve and enrolled them by calling God a liar, saying "For surely you shall not die."

To this day, this conversation still uses our natural love and mercy to get us distracted from what is truly possible. "You should not have to suffer," this conversation tells us. "This is not the way your life should be turning out." This is an insidious, subtle and relentless complaining voice informing us of what should and should not be in our lives.

Here's the question. How many of the relationships we call friendships are really accomplices?

How many times do you and I get angry when a friend rebukes us with, "Get behind me, Satan. You are stealing the glory of God in your life. You are taking on something that you can't handle. What you are doing is ultimately going to crush you and I am not going to have any part of it. I want you to come out from behind your complaint and act on who you say you are."

What is Love? How does this hit home? Love is a passion for oneness with the Presence of God and others. Yet God can't be one with someone who is out to protect themselves at the expense of others.

At that moment, Peter did not want to be one with God. He just wanted to stay alive. He did what we have all done, and that is cloak our selfish agendas in religious clothing. Whether it is Christian, Muslim, Jewish, politically correct, environmentally correct jargon, it is all the same thing dressed in different clothing. Unlike Jesus, Who was willing to die in order to be one with those who did not understand Him or were about to betray Him, Peter would rather be isolated and alive, than one and dead.

I think that in His rebuke of Peter, Jesus was drawing Peter back to his true eternal presence, not this temporal shadow which was attempting to escape the inevitable death that leads to resurrection. Jesus, like the being of light in C.S. Lewis' *The Great Divorce*, was urging Peter not to betray the Imago Dei, the image of God, in himself. He was asking Peter for permission to kill the lizard on his shoulder that was whispering fear in his ear, inviting Peter instead into the light of heaven where he would be made substantial by allowing his purpose to be transformed into his character through the fire of circumstance.

How are you uniquely the same as Peter?

Where are you hanging onto the fear of loss? Where are you playing not to lose, what must die for the kingdom of God to be resurrected in your life? Where is love calling you to stand in the light of heaven and the fire of circumstance?

Like Mother Teresa, I believe we have the possibility now to be the eternal beings that God has spoken. I say that we can continually move forward to the City of God and, as we get closer, be transformed in an instant, bringing what was beyond the sun into this temporal realm of our lives.

We can become humanly divine, one with the Presence.

✡ ✡ ✡

For as Long as We Can

✡ ✡ ✡

"You dance over me, while I am unaware, You sing all around, But I never hear the sound. Lord, I'm amazed by you, Lord I'm amazed by you, Lord, I'm amazed by you, how you love me."[3]
Lincoln Brewster

The night with Valerie and Lawrence was beginning to run long. Dinner dishes were piled up waiting for the dishwasher, the glasses of wine were now empty, and our tears had flowed more than once.

Yet, the final chapter of Joseph's story had not yet been told.

"Thirty-nine weeks. We were almost to the end," Valerie said. "We had come so far and we were on the doorstep of seeing our son. On Tuesday of that thirty-ninth week, I went to see the midwife. We discovered that Joseph's heartbeat had become erratic. It had dropped from 120 to 90 beats. Then, two days later, on Friday, his heartbeat dropped again down to 70 beats. Sitting there in the birthing center, all I could think about was how I did not want Joseph to die in my womb. We had come so far together; I did not want to lose him now.

"The midwife said to me kindly, 'Valerie, have you had enough? Have you gone as far as you are going to go? Do you want to have this baby now?' Looking at Lawrence, I responded, 'Yes.' And we broke the water."

"What happened next?"

"After about a half an hour, I felt Joseph stop moving," Valerie said. "I felt sure that something was wrong. I asked the nurse to take a heartbeat. She could not find one. In those few short minutes, we had lost him. Joseph was gone."

"To come so far and have that happen, right when you think you have reached the finish line- it must have been very hard."

With that question, Valerie disappeared from the kitchen and within seconds returned with her hands filled with photos. There he was, their Joseph in Lawrence and Valerie's arms. With Samera and Isaac. Each picture was filled not with sorrow but the joy of his presence with them.

"He was perfect," Valerie said. "It was as though he were asleep. Yet there was no life."

"Joseph was our son." Lawrence said, "I don't know how to quite express this, but although his body was not living, his being was. He was still Joseph, and we loved him."

As I looked at the pictures, I saw one with Valerie and Lawrence walking hand-in-hand carrying a baby basket, with Isaac and Samera running alongside of them.

"We did something that, perhaps, some might think unusual," Valerie explained. "We took Joseph home with us that night. As we had said from the start, we would love him for as long as we could. This one night would be the only time this side of eternity that we would have together. So when we got home, Samera made a bed for Joseph out of her dresser drawer. Together we all held and kissed him. Throughout the night, Lawrence rocked Joseph and sang to him."

"As the night hours passed and I sang to my son," Lawrence said, "I saw how God had made each person special, regardless of their circumstances or situations. Joseph was someone special and he would always be, beyond this life and throughout eternity. I had come to accept and cherish Joseph for who he was. I had surrendered to the reality of what we had been handed and was thankful. That night, holding his tiny frame in my arms, I spoke to Joseph as his father. 'You are mine. I love you, son. This is just the situation that has happened. You will always be a part of me and I will always be a part of you.'"

"When did you take these pictures in the park?"

"The next morning," Valerie answered, "we went to the park with Joseph wrapped up in blankets and tucked in a basket. There, we enjoyed the beauty of our last moments together. Then a friend of ours, who was a funeral director, met us."

"Shortly after that morning, we had Joseph cremated," Lawrence continued. "I made a request to our friend. As Joseph's father, I wanted to be the one who took the final steps to care for my son. And, granting my request, our friend let me set the temperatures on the cremation oven and push the buttons. Then when it was over, he let me remove Joseph's ashes."

"What have you learned by having Joseph in your lives?"

"His name," Valerie said. "'He added.'" Joseph added to our lives in ways that were so unexpected. In the midst of this horrible situation that seemed to offer nothing but pain, suffering and difficulty, there was this goodness, this beauty. Love. Patience. Mercy. On his birthday, I plant a tree in his memory. To me, Joseph is like the Sequoia trees. The Sequoias are trees that grow even bigger than the redwoods. They are magnificently tall. They stand alone, bigger than what you can imagine. That's our Joseph."

"I came away with a level of understanding that comes only through personal experience," Lawrence said. "When I am with someone who is experiencing suffering, I know not to try to justify, explain or fix it. I simply am with them in it; I give room for God to do what He wants in the midst of the grief and pain. Through Joseph's life, I have lost my distain for death. I have come to see that even in death there is beauty.

"What started us on this journey was our commitment to love Joseph as long as we could. I have discovered how long that will be. It is *forever.*

"We will love him forever."

✡ ✡ ✡

Love's Last Word

✡ ✡ ✡

"Love is never abstract. It does not adhere to the universe or the planet or the nation or the institution or the profession, but to the singular sparrows of the street, the lilies of the field, 'the least of these my brethren.'"[4]
Wendell Berry

"Time to go home, honey," Aileen said quietly in my ears. The fire had burned low; the rest of the family long gone. Christmas, for this year, was over.

Driving home, I felt so full inside. We had spent an evening in the presence of love and a mere fifteen years ago, I would have not believed that such oneness would have been possible between us.

Love is the most surprising, unrelenting Presence in the universe.

Driving north on Highway 101 past one of my dad's movie theaters, I thought of Mel Gibson's *The Passion of the Christ* and the memory of one particular scene leapt out at me, like a search beam. It was the point in the film where Jesus had been beaten beyond recognition by the Romans in the public square before making Him carry His cross.

Among the crowd was his mother, Mary. Seeing the suffering of her son, the pain became too much for her to bear and she turned away from the horror of her Son's blood and broken body. Dazed by her grief, she wanders down a vacant alley, remembering a time, almost thirty years before, when Jesus fell down as a young child and how she had run and swept Him up in her mother's arms to love and nurture Him.

Just then, Mary looks up and sees Jesus carrying His cross through throngs of people down the road to Golgotha. She watches Him fall under the weight of it. As He falls, Mary races to His side. She tells Him, "I am here. I am here." Lifting her face with his blood-soaked hand, Jesus smiles and whispers to her, "See, Mother. I make all things new."

The fear that drove her from His beating was being made new by His Presence there at the cross.

Like Mary, Jesus' words stop me. "See, Dan, I make all things new, even death."

And, like her, I don't understand how or why. All I know is that He, who is the Presence, is making all things new, even our suffering.

I see that we have been given an incredible gift, all born into *Logos*. As Imago Dei, we are given the possibility to transform purpose into character. The gift of our being is the manifestation of purpose. It's not an option. There is no neutral. It simply *is* who we are.

What is this purpose? Well, I believe that there are only two possibilities, life or death—the eternal or that which is passing away.

The question is which one will we choose today?

The presence of God, Who is Life?

Or the presence of the Adversary, who is Death?

Every day we choose one or the other. In our words, actions, thoughts and decisions, we help each other towards the presence of life or the presence of death regardless of circumstance. If you are a doctor, lawyer, plumber or homeless person, your present circumstances means nothing in the eternal sense. What you are transforming into your character does.

I am convinced that the end of all things is not death. It is love and life. The Presence, Jesus—The *Logos*. May you choose Him, now and for eternity. Because in the end—Love wins!

Notes:

[1] "Breath of Heaven (Mary's song)," written by Amy Grant and Chris Eaton; copyright ©1992 Age to Age Music, Inc. (ASCAP).

[2] Dan Allender, *The Wounded Heart: Hope for Adult Victims of Childhood Sexual Abuse* (Navepress Publishing Group, 1990).

[3] http://www.lincolnbrewster.com/main.html.

[4] Wendell Berry, *What Are People For?* (North Point Press, 1990), p. 200.

INDEX